KU-482-909

Contents

For Sandra

Preface

No writer can ignore the work of other writers who have trodden the chosen path before. They may take different short-cuts, divert and digress down different alleys and topics. But they are there as surely as the mountains and the beaches, the palaces of Barcelona and the shepherd's huts in the Pyrenees. This is a book for the general reader. I have not assumed that the person with a lively interest in the affairs of Catalonia will have a knowledge of either Catalan or Spanish. Most of the books I mention are available in English. I have taken guidance from a rather large number of books in English, Spanish and Catalan, to comment on themes about which I have no special or original claim to knowledge.

The English language reader owes a special debt to Alistair Boyd, whose book *The Essence of Catalonia*, published in 1988, broke new ground in its insistence on using the correct Catalan version of place names, rather than their Castilian Spanish equivalents. This is now an established convention. Earlier writers are not to be blamed for their confusion, since the language was one of the many victims of the autocratic centralism of Francoist Spain, a regime that came to an end as recently as 1975. I have reflected on this especially in chapter 10 in the fictional accounts offered by Paul Scott and Patrice Chaplin of what Catalonia might or might not have meant to the English visitor during the Franco years. The outcome of the Spanish Civil War of 1936-1939 had not just been a question of victory by the fascist right over the liberal centre and socialist, communist and anarchist left. It had also meant the rule of Madrid over Catalans, Basques and Galicians, all of whom now enjoy their own language and institutions. The recovery of those rights was not inevitable. In the case of Catalonia, it was the massive public demonstrations of 1976 and 1977 that opened the way for a return of both a Catalan government and parliament, and the Catalan language to its rightful position as the national language of Catalonia. The use of Catalan was something claimed rather than conceded, and Spanish speakers marched shoulder-to-shoulder with Catalan speakers in demanding the Statute of Autonomy. The Catalan autonomous government has developed a policy of 'linguistic normalisation', which enjoys broad political support and considerable prestige and respect on a European level. From a cautious bilingualism, Catalonia has moved with increasing confidence to an acceptance of Catalan as the official language. These dramatic changes in the cultural and linguistic face of Catalonia are perhaps best reflected in Colm Tóibín's *Homage to Barcelona*, first published in 1990. Robert Hughes' *Barcelona*, despite its title and the author's overly modest claims to historical scholarship, is one of the most accessible accounts in English of Catalan history from the Middle Ages through to the nineteenth century.

I have followed the practice of using Catalan terms as consistently as possible, although to help the reader who may be more familiar with Spanish versions of names, I have sometimes given the Castilian form in brackets where these occur for the first time, for example Lleida (Lérida), the inland of the four Spanish provinces that make up modern Catalonia, and Empúries (Ampurias), the hauntingly beautiful Greek and Roman ruins near L'Escala (La Escala). For the country itself I have preferred the English 'Catalonia' to the Catalan form 'Catalunya', which Hughes, for example, uses. If I have occasionally used the term 'Spanish' to describe the common language of the Spanish state (and of most of South and Central America), it is for the simple reason that it is easier on the English ear than the more correct term 'Castilian' which is in general use in Catalonia, or the awkward compound 'Castilian Spanish'. As for institutions, I have tried to use English equivalents where there are English equivalents, but to keep to the original

Catalan where there is no directly comparable institution. I see little point in using the word *parlament* to describe the Catalan parliament, or *ajuntament* for 'town council'. On the other hand, the reader will find Generalitat for the autonomous Catalan government. Not least because that term connects back to mediaeval days when Catalonia was a major power in the Mediterranean world of trade and warfare.

This is also a good place to make it clear that this is a book about Catalonia, rather than the Catalan-speaking lands, which include Valencia, the Balearic Islands and the French area of Rousillon, as well as the independent principality of Andorra (where it is the official language) and the town of l'Alguer in Sardinia. The relationship between Catalonia — the four Spanish provinces governed by the Generalitat — and those other lands is controversial and is a debate which by and large belongs outside the covers of this book. The area in which Catalan is still used corresponds to the main territories of the medieval Catalan empire, often referred to collectively by Catalan nationalists as *Els Països Catalans*. Both Valencia and the Balearic Islands are separate autonomous communities within modern Spain, while Rousillon and l'Alguer are both parts of other nation states. While there is a willingness to acknowledge linguistic and cultural links with Catalonia, there is little indication of enthusiasm for the political project of a 'Greater Catalonia'.

History

The first part of this book takes a historical perspective. Writing history always entails the danger of entangling the reader in a maze of details, of dates and names, so that the wider panorama is lost. But equally there is the danger of offering up a lifeless skeleton, without the rich detail which brings the past alive and makes it real for the reader. I have compromised here. What follows is the skeletal outline. The chapters in part 1 look in more detail at key episodes in Catalan history. In chapter 1 there is the Roman and pre-Roman history which is still so evident today and which marks Catalonia out as a distinctively 'Mediterranean' land. In chapter 2 the focus will be upon the beginnings of the medieval statelets in the foothills of the Pyrenees which gradually coalesced into the fully fledged mediaeval state with its extensive Mediterranean empire which is described in chapter 3. There is then a leap forward in chapter 4 to the seventeenth century and the beginnings of the eighteenth which saw the absorption of Catalonia into Spain and its re-emergence as an Atlantic trading power and an industrial power in the nineteenth century. Finally in this section, chapter 5 recounts the cause, process and effects of the Spanish War of 1936-1939. I prefer on balance to discard the term Civil War for reasons which will become apparent in that chapter.

Catalonia's path through history has been stony and difficult. Greeks, Romans, Visigoths and Muslims all passed this way. They left their ruins. Phoenicians, Greeks and Romans successively occupied Empúries on the Costa Brava. As the name suggests, it was a coastal settlement from which they traded goods with the less sophisticated people of the interior. Its ruins are well preserved, largely because the mediaeval feudal lord chose to move his seat inland, to what is now the small market town of Castelló d'Empúries, rather than risk further raids by Muslim pirates from North Africa. There is a Roman amphitheatre in Tarragona, a Roman aqueduct nearby. There are Visigothic churches at Terrassa and elsewhere which bear witness to a heroic, proselytising church very different to the institutionalised church which followed, giving Catalonia both its characteristic forms of Romanesque and Gothic, but also tying it more closely to Christian developments in other parts of Europe. Yet Muslim craftsmen, staying on long after the political power of Muslim rulers had begun to wane, were a powerful influence on the decoration of Christian churches, especially in the area of

Lleida. The Mediterranean, which laps the shores of Catalonia from Portbou on the French frontier to the last Catalan villages of the Ebro delta, is what unites this world and gives it coherence. Like a river, it both separates those who live on its various shores, and unites them across space. It produces continuity but also shocks as more advanced technologies come into contact with those less advanced. And it links Europe with Africa.

The invasion of the Iberian peninsula by Muslims from North Africa changed radically the history of this corner of Europe. The initial impetus took Muslim armies well north into France, before they were turned back by Charlemagne at Tours in 732AD. From about 800, Christian counties began to spring up south of the Pyrenees, and in 988 the Count of Barcelona broke his ties of vassalage with the French king. Catalonia's 1,000 years of history had begun. In 1137 the crowns of Aragon and Catalonia were united and in the Middle Ages the Aragonese-Catalan Federation became the centre of a great Mediterranean empire based on sea power, trade and piracy. If its kings and queens were Aragonese, its economic power was always Catalonia and its capital, Barcelona. Then, in 1469, Ferdinand of Aragon married Isabella of Castile, thus uniting the two main states of medieval Spain. Catalonia, already in decline, became an unhappy member of this new Spanish family, more interested in European wars and American conquests than in the rights and privileges of the Catalans.

Spain turned its back on the Mediterranean world. 1492 was the year Columbus reached America. It was also the year of the expulsion from Spain of the Jews, who had made such a significant, if not always appreciated, contribution to administration, trade, crafts and medicine in medieval Catalonia. In the Middle Ages Catalonia had been an important Mediterranean power. After 1492 Catalonia became a backwater of the Spanish international empire, the axis of which was now the Atlantic and not the Mediterranean. Yet, in one of those ironies of his-

5

tory, it was the eventual involvement of Catalans in the American trade, from the mid-eighteenth century onwards, which brought Catalonia both material wealth and a new, rich source of cultural ideas which influenced the emergence of Barcelona as the great industrial and commercial centre of the Mediterranean that we know today. All over Catalonia and Barcelona are architectural signs of the colonial origins of modern Catalan wealth, while the continuing popularity of the *havanera* (literally, song from Havana in Cuba) is another reminder of this same story.

On a number of occasions between the Middle Ages and the modern period, Catalonia allied itself with the enemies of Spain (France, Austria, England, at different times). In the long war that ran from 1640-1659 they lost, but hung on to their separate identity within the Spanish state. The Catalan lands north of the Pyrenees were ceded to France at this time, and have remained part of the French state ever since. The most blatant example of the Catalan ability to back the wrong horse came in the War of the Spanish Succession which lasted from 1701 until 1714. In turn the English (perfidious Albion) and then the Austrians deserted them. The Catalans fought on rather than submit, and the date of the end of the war (11 September) is still commemorated in Catalonia as the National Day. This time there was no compromise: in 1716 the Catalans were forced to accept the *Nueva Planta* (New Deal) Acts, which abolished the institutions of Catalonia and substituted direct rule from Madrid.

New liberalised economic measures in the eighteenth century, however, opened the way for the industrialisation of Catalonia in the nineteenth century, and a strong revival of nationalism. The two were linked. This was nationalism from above rather than from below. Wealthy industrialists despised Spain not so much for nationalist or cultural reasons but because it was seen as backwards, a drag on Catalan industry, absorbing too much Catalan tax. The peasants may have spoken Catalan but they cer-

6

tainly did not read it or write it. Yet among those who could read and write, Catalan remained the chosen language for social transactions. In 1832 the Bible Society published a Catalan New Testament in London as part of its work in Spain, clear evidence of the continuing regular use of the language. It was from this bedrock of regular use that the revival of Catalan as a literary language began. With linguistic and cultural revival went the growth of a political movement, but that movement was predominantly a middle-class affair. While rich capitalists in Barcelona made money out of property development and were happy enough to flaunt their wealth with facades designed by the likes of Antoni Gaudí, the design of the traditional Catalan farm-house under whose roof employer and employee, people and animals might happily find shelter, changed very little at all. The industrial working-class was politically active but tended towards anarcho-syndicalism and various forms of socialism rather than Catalan nationalism. In any case, the Catalan working-class increasingly included many who had migrated to Barcelona from Castilian-speaking parts of Spain.

The change came in the 1920s as a direct result of the temporary military rule of Miguel Primo de Rivera. The working-class Leftists and the middle-class Catalanists had found a common enemy. The Monarchy was discredited by its acquiescence to military rule, and the Second Spanish Republic (1931–1939) was voted in. But when the Republic was declared by Francesc Macià from the balcony of what had once been the palace of the Generalitat — the mediaeval Catalan state — he declared it to be a Catalan Republic within a federal Spain. Some hard bargaining was necessary to establish the exact legal status which Catalan autonomy was to assume for the next few years. The use of the name Generalitat for the Catalan government was part of that compromise, but it is a compromise that has stood the test of time, being now used to describe the autonomous Catalan government which took power in the 1970s after the death of the dictator Franco. But this is with the benefit of hindsight. The 47 years between the Generalitat of 1931 and that of 1978 included three years of war and destruction and 36 years of dictatorship. Catalan institutions disappeared, along with the other institutions of Republican Spain. Rule from Madrid was total and arbitrary, if appallingly inefficient. Strong government was not good government.

Culture

Underlying all the material in the second part of the book is a general concern with what constitutes a national culture, how that national culture might allow for difference to thrive within it, and how it relates to wider notions of shared culture, as in European culture, or the global popular culture of films and popular music. I have attempted to deal with those aspects of culture which will be most apparent to visitors to Catalonia: what they will see in the streets, the museums and the art galleries; the music they will hear; the tourist phenomenon itself.

Chapter 6 deals with the co-existence of Christian, Jewish and Muslim cultures in mediaeval Catalonia and their subsequent replacement by a homogenised approach to culture. Chapters 7 and 8 are about the city of Barcelona. Chapter 7 looks especially at the contributions to the city of late nineteenth century and early twentieth industrialism and *Modernisme* (the eclectic Catalan version of art nouveau) in architecture and design. Chapter 8 covers the roots in the pre-war period of the more cosmopolitan city which eventually grew to host the 1992 Olympics and the 2004 Universal Forum of Cultures. Chapter 9 is about the official support given for a Catalan popular culture co-existing alongside a globalised popular culture. Mass tourism and its impact on Catalonia is the subject of chapter 10. Chapter 11 concentrates on modern visual arts and music, and the impact of a number of Catalan creative artists who obtained international status during the twentieth century. The inclusion of Picasso raises questions about exactly who counts as a 'Catalan' artist, while the story of Pau Casals is considered in some detail as an expression of the intricate connections between ideas of Catalan culture and more universal ideas of culture. I am conscious that this focus will serve as a good introduction to the more cautious approach of part 3, in which the optimism of Casals is tempered by precisely the impact of the twentieth century tragedies he lived through and which our new century seems determined to repeat.

Catalonia Today

The third part of the book discusses a number of issues which affect the present and future of Catalonia. They are part of a wider debate within Catalonia about its identity and how that should be expressed politically. There is also a recognition, however, that this debate has a more general significance, since it touches on important notions of identity in the modern world, and the relationship between localism and globalism.

Chapter 12 reviews the present state of nationalist sentiment in Europe, but places the debate in the wider context of discussions about identity and culture. It uses the 1992 Olympic Games as a case-study of how nationalism is framed by the Catalans. It also looks forward rather anxiously to the nation's political future. Chapter 13 delves into the language question and emphasises the success of the Generalitat's policy of 'linguistic normalisation' (if it moves, speak to it in Catalan). But it also queries just why a more relaxed policy of *convivència* (accommodation) between languages raises such strong emotions within Catalonia. Chapter 14 considers environmental issues, and suggests that there are problems and possibilities of life in Catalonia which transcend a nationalist approach. At the same time, the issues surrounding the use of the waters of the Ebro demonstrate how such disagreements over fundamental ecological questions become infiltrated by national and regional rivalries. Chapter 15 looks in some detail at the social reality of Catalonia today, and suggests difficult and controversial contradictions between a narrow view of 'Catalonia for the Catalans', and a broader vision of the multicultural nation of the future. This leads into the final chapter 16 which returns to the first person voice to offer a personal assessment of just where Catalonia stands in relation to the Global Age.

Acknowledgements

The cover photo is by Neus Cortés and is reproduced courtesy of the Falcons de Vilanova i la Geltrú. In addition to the many small kindnesses of complete strangers and passing acquaintances that have smoothed my way in researching this book, I would like to acknowledge the help of the many people and institutions in both England and in Catalonia who have helped me with the research for this book. They know who they are. Their advice, criticisms, friendship and support have sustained me in what has been a larger and longer task than originally contemplated. For errors of fact or analysis, I take full responsibility. Finally, this book is dedicated to my wife Sandra Payne, who has been my companion and photographer on a number of field-work visits to Catalonia.

Part 1:

Catalonia —
A Sense of History

Chapter 1

Catalonia, Antiquity and the Mediterranean

The Classical Tradition in Catalonia

The sea is a permanent part of Catalonia, whether a distant glimmer on the horizon from a peak in the Pyrenees, or a constant companion on the long shoreline that goes from the French frontier to the delta of the River Ebro. In the garden of the great Catalan musician Pau (Pablo) Casals, at Sant Salvador on the rather anonymous coastline stretching down towards Tarragona, you hear the murmuring of the Mediterranean sea on the sandy beach. It is timeless and has the ability to take on any mood that the visitor brings to it, sad and glad by turns, calm or boisterous, a good friend but a terrible enemy that has probably taken the lives of as many Catalans as all the wars in history.

El mar, la mar — the sea is very special in both Spanish and Catalan in being one of a tiny number of nouns which can be both masculine and feminine. This dual status of the word for sea does make clear the strong emotional reactions it arouses. It represents the unity of the world but also its duality. That duality is expressed not only in the masculine and feminine principles, but also in those other persistent opposites of the Mediterranean world — peace and war, love and hate.

There are two outstanding sculptures in the garden at Sant Salvador. Both are nudes. One is an Apollo by Josep Clarà (1878–1958), designed for this spot, the other a woman by Josep Llimona (1864–1934). Similar statues are found all over Catalonia, in places as public as the central Plaça de Catalunya in Barcelona, and before the Catalan parliament in the Ciutadella Park. There is even a museum in Barcelona given over to the work of Clarà. Here, as so often in Catalonia, the continuities seem so simple. It does not seem possible that two millennia of strife and upheaval separate the soothing warmth of a spring afternoon in Casals' garden from the ancient world of Phoenicians, Greeks and Romans.

Clarà was part of an artistic movement which flourished in Catalonia in the first part of the twentieth century. It was known as *Noucentisme* (the 'new-centuryism' of the 1900s) and demonstrated two rather contradictory aspects. Firstly, it laid claim to being an experience of modernity (Picasso, the true modernist, had left Barcelona in the early years of the century and was now developing Cubism, behind closed doors in a studio in Paris with Georges Braque). Like *Modernisme*, the eclectic style that prevailed in the final decades of the nineteenth century, it strove to create a modern, national culture. Secondly, and in contrast to *Modernisme*, it offered a sense of continuity with a classical, Mediterranean past. Stylistically it rejected the sentimental and the narrative, and aimed for clarity of form and content. Clutter was anathema to classicism and modernism. And yet the sculpture and painting of this school expressed an essential mystery: how to understand and express the profound sense of historical continuity that can overwhelm the visitor to the Mediterranean coast, especially outside of the tourist season, a Platonic swoon between the ever changing forms of reality and its underlying nature. This group of artists established an image of the Mediterranean world which reflected directly the material world in which they lived, and, in turn, has conditioned our minds as we look back and forth from image to reality, from painting to the sea, the vineyards, the olive groves and the pine-trees of the Catalan coast. One of the influences was certainly the major excavations taking place in Catalonia at this period, and the uncovering of art objects from ancient Greece and Rome. Yet although classicism was an important influence on their work, the painters attempted to express the essence of a Mediterranean spirit which they located in the material culture of their land as much as in the finer academic points of classical art.

One of the key artists of *Noucentisme* was not a Catalan at all, but a Uruguayan. Joaquim Torres-García (1874–1949) lived and worked in Barcelona until 1920. A typical work of his is *Orange trees facing the sea* (1920), in Barcelona's Modern Art Museum. The Mediterranean Sea provides the backdrop, the middle-ground is the Catalan landscape and the foreground contains emblematic figures, in this case two lightly clad women and a basket of oranges. The figures look out of the canvas and through the viewer, as if they are elements of a still-life composition. Torres-García could also tell a story, and he used classical myths and legends in the murals that he executed using fresco technique in public buildings in Barcelona in the second decade of the century. Those in the Saló de Sant Jordi (St George's Hall) in the Generalitat Palace in Barcelona's Old Town can still be seen and their solemnity makes a striking contrast with the orange-tree patio onto which the hall opens. The whole mural has a profound political significance in the growth of a national spirit in Catalonia. The group of young women in the centre is a symbolic representation of the broad definition of what it means to be Catalan — not just the four Spanish provinces, but also the Catalan-speaking French lands, Valencia and the Balearic Islands. The giant male nudes either side of the door symbolise the manual and intellectual work of 'building a nation'. The popular title of this mural — *The Eternal Catalonia* — makes precisely the link between history and modernity which was at the centre of this movement.

The resort of Sitges lies south of Barcelona and is protected by the rocky headland of the Garraf from the cold northerly winds which can blow for days on end during a

Catalan winter. On a winter's day, it is one of the best places to get away from the cosmopolitan excitement of Barcelona and to immerse oneself in this Mediterranean spirit. It was a Sitges artist, Joaquim Sunyer (1874–1956), who best demonstrated the influence of another great Mediterranean painter, the French Post-Impressionist Cézanne. Cézanne had reintroduced into painting the great classical theme of nudes in a landscape, and this theme of figures, clothed or unclothed, in a natural setting, is taken up by Sunyer. In a painting such as *Composition with Nudes* (c. 1916) the Cézanne influence is overwhelming, including the angled foreground trees which frame the human figures. Better known and perhaps more typical is *Cala Forn* (1917), again in Barcelona's Modern Art Museum. There is a distant view of sea and coast, but the main interest is in the foreground figures (here clothed in simple, loose-fitting garments, typical of the modern, rationalist clothes then beginning to find favour in progressive circles) and their elemental still-life possessions — a *porró* (a long-spouted drinking vessel that can be passed from person to person), a water-melon, peaches, a clay water-bottle. Where Torres-García appealed to classical stories in his murals, Sunyer created a new secular mythology which fitted in well with the spirit of resurgent nationalism in Catalonia in the early 1900s. But socially this was rather cautious, conservative nationalism, nationalism from above, one might say. A nationalism which turned its back on the noise and dirt and industrial unrest of Barcelona, in favour of the eternal values of the Mediterranean landscape.

The sculptures of Clarà are perhaps the best known and most public art produced by *Noucentisme*. As a student in Paris he had fallen under the spell of the monumental sculptures of Auguste Rodin. In 1904 he visited London and saw the Elgin Marbles in the British Museum, an experience which turned him decisively towards a classicism he was never to desert. Back in Paris, he was taken up by the fiercely nationalist ideologue and publicist of the

Noucentista movement, Eugeni d'Ors. D'Ors had a large ego — he used the pen-name *Xènius* (evocative of Genius) — but expressed his ego through patronage. He had already promoted the work of Torres-García and of Sunyer. Now it was the turn of Clarà. His *La Diosa* (The Goddess) was exhibited in a great international exhibition in Barcelona in 1911, and caused scandal only by not winning the gold medal, which went to a little-known British artist called J.J. Shannon. The cause may have been artistic, but it rapidly became political too. The Catalan establishment fell in behind their man, and at a dinner in his honour, the distinguished poet Joan Maragall proposed a poetic toast in which the sculptures of Clarà were described like this:

> They are twin sisters of those immortals,
> daughters of our sea who, now on the other side,
> have the same serenity of the antique spirit
> but with a new tenderness.
>
> (author's translation)

It is hard to write of *Noucentisme* as a movement with any kind of coherent philosophy after 1917, but it continued to influence those designers not yet moving in the direction of an all-embracing international modern style. There is little doubt that the classicism of *Noucentisme* influenced the style of the building on the Montjuïc hill above the city now known as the Olympic Stadium. This was part of an undistinguished set of buildings put up to house the International Exhibition of 1929. The outstanding exception was Mies van der Rohe's minimalist modern classic, the German Pavilion, eventually rebuilt in its original setting, and still looking just as cool and out of place as it must have done in 1929. The stadium began to acquire a certain Olympic lustre as the venue of the 'People's Olympiad' in 1936 when the official Olympic Games were to have been held in Hitler's Berlin. The boycott of the Berlin Games was supported by the Popular

Front governments in France and Spain. These plans were overtaken by the outbreak of the Spanish War in July 1936 when General Francisco Franco led an uprising against the civilian government. In 1992, the stadium, remodelled within but retaining much of its exterior form, was the main arena for the Barcelona Olympics. In one of those ironies of history which are all too frequent in Catalonia, a building erected in a style that claimed a classical lineage became the chosen venue for a modern sporting event which had little or nothing to do with the Greek tradition of sporting meetings as an alternative to war.

Perhaps the most popular expression that *Noucentisme* took was in the work of Josep Obiols (1894–1967). He continued to work in a recognisably *Noucentista* style through the 1920s and 1930s, and in a wide variety of formats: paintings, book covers and illustrations, frescoes, posters, stamps, concert programmes. In many ways, the sum total of his work represents many of the most humane aspects of Catalan life in the years immediately preceding the military rising of 1936 and the catastrophic war which followed. He was a 'public' artist, an artist at the service of his nation, leading *Noucentisme* away from its elitist path towards the democracy of the Republican period and the first great experiment in Catalan autonomy (1931–1939).This is embodied in one of his best-loved images — the 1921 poster for APEC (The Catalan Educational Association), showing a child with satchel and books striding through an idyllic, stylised landscape of birds and flowers. The cause is both democratic and Catalan: APEC was created to provide schools which would teach through the medium of the Catalan language, and to provide teaching material, books and libraries in the language too. The poster he made for the first congress of APEC in 1936 shows a more serious-faced child against a more urban setting, a flat-roofed, very modern-looking building. It is precisely the move that Catalanism made in the 1930s from a symbolic identification with the past to a movement that might begin to have meaning for the very different cultural outlook of men and women who lived in cities and worked in factories.

During the Spanish War, Obiols designed money and stamps for the Generalitat, but in the repression that followed, he retreated from public life, concentrating on painting portraits of his family and friends. His public work consisted mainly of murals at Montserrat, the mountain-top monastery near Barcelona which helped to keep Catalan culture alive during the years of the Franco dictatorship. Obiols is above all the artists of children. Children represent not only timelessness and tradition, but also the urgency of the moment, as any parent, any child, knows well. The task of a humane society is to love and care for its children, and that was an integral part of Obiols' vision. A large exhibition of his work was assembled in the Palau de la Virreina in the *Rambla* in Barcelona in 1990. This is a popular exhibition space for the Town Council, though other grander spaces have since become available, and their policy of free admission for senior citizens gave a particular atmosphere to this show. It was clear from the enthusiastic response of these older people as they went round the exhibits, that many of these people were recognising and remembering images they recalled fondly from books they had read at school, posters they had seen on the streets, coins they had jingled in their pockets. A nation needs its Obiols as well as its grander artistic figures.

Through *Noucentisme*, then, modern Catalans identified themselves with the history and values of the Mediterranean. They grew consciously into a landscape they had previously accepted unconsciously as their birthright, a rich landscape in which the human drama was played out against a backdrop of vine and olive and sea. Now it is time to look at some of the achievements of those ancient, classical civilisations in Catalonia and some of the remnants which the visitor will find still standing.

Greeks Bearing Gifts

To visit the magic of ancient Catalonia, there is only one place to go. Empúries lies on the Costa Brava, just north of the anchovy-fishing and processing town of L'Escala. The medieval rulers of Empúries gave up at some point in the later middle ages. Fed up with raids by pirates from North Africa, they moved across the salt-marshes and the water-meadows to the more sheltered settlement now known as Castelló d'Empúries. This was a sensible move, and has had the distinct advantage for visitors that the classical ruins have not been further disturbed, and that the coastal site can be excavated with no damage to later buildings or disturbance to the everyday lives of working people. The ruins have simply lain there beneath the sand-dunes waiting for their moment of revelation.

It was here at Empúries that primitive Iberia had its first contact with the classical world of Greece and Rome. That, though, is a simplification, complicated by a confusion about the term Greeks. The Rhodians, who had established a settlement at what is now Roses, across the bay to the north of Empúries, we would recognise as 'Greeks'. It is more difficult to see the Phocaeans who came to Empúries as Greeks, coming as they did from the town of Phocaea in Asia Minor (modern-day Turkey). Yet Troy itself, an archetypal Greek city, was in Asia Minor too, reminding us that the past was very different to the Europe of nation-states that we have grown up with. Phocaea itself was destroyed by the Persian King Cyrus in 540BC and it was refugees from that disaster (nothing new about refugees then) who reinforced the settlements at Alalia (Aleria in Corsica) and another trading colony called Massalia (Marseilles). Traders from Massalia had established the *paleopolis* (old town) at Empúries in about 550BC.

The Greeks settled by preference on islands and peninsulas, and their initial base was a small offshore island at the entrance to the Fluvià River, which with later silting up has become the rocky promontory on which the pretty little stone village of Sant Martí is built. The parish church is supposed to stand on the site of the original Greek temple, another example of those continuities of which the Mediterranean shores are so full. Empúries was lucky. In 535BC the Carthaginians defeated the Phocaeans off Alalia in what the Roman historian Herodotus described as the first naval battle in history, and as a result of this an earlier Phocaean settlement near present-day Málaga was also sacked. From then on, Empúries became the most important Greek settlement in Spain. As it grew, settlement extended to the mainland, where the *neapolis* or new city was established, with the port, since filled in with silt, between it and the old town on its island. This port area, now the site of fertile market gardens growing tomatoes and peppers, cucumbers and aubergines, lies inland from the narrow road that links L'Escala and Sant Martí between the sea and the ruins.

Yet such is the continuity of development and use at Empúries that although the visitor is standing in the ruins of a 'Greek' town, so much of what is to be seen is Roman. The traders of Empúries seem to have had particular skill at staying one move ahead of political change. While the Phoenicians and Carthaginians reinforced their bases in southern Spain, the Phocaeans at Massalia and Empúries allied themselves with the emerging power in the Mediterranean — Rome. A Roman expeditionary force landed at Empúries in 218BC and subsequently established headquarters at Tarraco. The Iberian tribes initially opposed Roman rule, but were overpowered by Cato following a second landing at Empúries in 195BC . It is all too easy to let the atmosphere of the place overtake you with its strong emotional appeal. The sun beats down, and a characteristic Empúries sight is a knot of visitors sheltering under a shady, fragrant pine. The pines are the natives of this coast and offer better shade than the more recently planted cypresses. The blue Mediterranean sparkles between classical columns and the bulk of the Greek and Roman breakwaters linking the outlying rocks along a stretch of beach nearly the whole way from L'Escala to Empúries. It was these breakwaters that created a safe harbour which gave access in turn to the interior and the rich agricultural lands of the Empordà. Here, then, is the proper setting for things Roman — not Hadrian's Wall or Bath or St Albans in cold, wet Britain at the outer edge of the civilised world, but Empúries and imperial Tarragona on the edge of the great tideless sea — *Mare Nostrum*, Our Sea.

In the Roman part of the town on the hilltop there is an extensive religious area which contained a series of temples to the various Roman gods, their ground-plans little different from those of primitive Romanesque churches in the Pyrenees of a millennium later. Excavation and restoration is continuing in this part of the Roman town. Another element of continuity is the forum, the place for public discussion of public affairs by those who were fortunate enough to be counted as citizens. The forum is a direct antecedent of the *plaça* of medieval Catalan towns, even to the custom of arcading the streets which lead into it. Likewise, the porticoed atrium of the larger Roman villas is a forerunner of the traditional Spanish house with its central patio. The Roman town has a spaciousness not found in the crowded streets of the neapolis, and again this contrast of busy crowded alleyways and expansive avenues and squares is a contrast not uncommon in modern Catalonia. The pedestrian precinct, a recent innovation in towns such as Barcelona, Girona and Lleida, was pioneered in the Roman forum at Empúries.

The sun starts to set early at Empúries and there are soon a few empty patches of shade on the beaches. The light is ethereal and majestic, the sea darkening to deepest ultramarine towards the horizon, shading to oranges and greens in the shallow, sandy waters by the shoreline, the sand itself the lightest beige. At its back, the dark green of pines and a sky beginning to turn pink on its western fringes. And yet this is not a peaceful land. Turbulent and violent change has been the iron law of history here as in so many other parts of Europe. Empúries itself never fully recovered from the barbarian invasions of the third century AD, and unlike Barcino (Barcelona) and Tarraco (Tarragona) was never completely rebuilt. The settlement continued to house a bishopric through the Visigothic period of Spanish history between the eventual fall of the Roman Empire and the Muslim invasions, although a seventh-century Norman invasion had probably swept away what little remained of the city some years before the Muslims arrived in or about 718. Feudal warring among the early Christian counties established by Charlemagne south of the Pyrenees as a bulwark against the possibility of further Muslim expansion into Europe, the silting up of the river, and the generally unhealthy nature of the site, all contributed to the eventual decision by the Count of Empúries to rebuild his capital at an inland site. The ruins of Empúries gradually sank beneath the sands, driven by the *Tramuntana* winds that blow fiercely down from the Pyrenees along this part of the Costa Brava. But the memory of a once great city lived on.

Roman Pleasure Grounds

The Romans ruled Spain for 600 years, and their Empire provided not just political unity but also the cultural and linguistic unity of the Latin language, and, after a few false starts including persecution and martyrdom, the Christian church. Yet the everyday Latin spoken by the peoples of the Roman Empire was never identical from one province to another, frequently acquiring features of the earlier languages of the indigenous peoples or earlier settlers like the Celtic tribes. Basque, the most ancient of Spain's languages, remained distinct, largely untouched by Latin. The various forms of everyday Latin were to give rise eventually to the emergence of Portuguese, Castilian and Catalan as separate languages.

The past in Catalonia is always present. And nowhere more so than in Tarragona. In winter especially,

Tarragona is significantly warmer and sunnier than
Barcelona, and little wonder that the Romans chose it as
their winter headquarters. On the coastal road south from
Barcelona and Sitges, the signs of the Roman presence are
very obvious. This is the great Roman Via Augusta, the
highway of imperial Roman Catalonia, which gave
Tarragona a link with Rome as strong as any twenty-first
century motorway or high-speed train. Between 200BC
and 400AD, the Romans built 13,000 miles of roads in
what is now Catalonia. To put this in perspective, by the
end of the nineteenth century Catalonia had only 15,000
miles of roads. Well before Tarragona, the Arc de Berà
looms imperiously above the olive groves and red-tiled
houses. A Roman triumphal arch, it was erected by one of
the Emperor Trajan's generals between 98AD and 117AD.
Ten metres high and five wide its giant stone blocks continued to span, until very recently, the main road from
Barcelona to Tarragona. Now the road divides into two
carriageways to pass it on both sides, and it is easy to stop
and admire the immense archway with its elegant
Corinthian columns. A little further towards Tarragona,
and again right on the main road, is the Scipios' Tower,
built of similar great blocks of local stone. The only thing
known for certain is that it has no connection with the
Scipio brothers. But such is the force of local legend that it
is unlikely that it will ever be called anything else, for it
was a Scipio whose name has come down to us through
history as the man who originally established Tarraco as a
military base in 218BC. Tarragona's early military significance was to control the troublesome tribes of the interior
who had supported the Carthaginians against the Romans
in the Punic wars. But it quickly emerged as a cultured
city for pleasure and leisure, a role which by and large it
has never since abandoned.

Approaching Tarragona from the north, past the Arc de
Berà and the Scipios' Tower, you see to the left a long view
of the beach, the ships moving in and out of the busy commercial port and on the right the heart of the

Roman-medieval city on the hill. Tarragona of the golden light on ancient golden stone, the morning sun slanting in across a glittering silver sea, touching everything, a time warp of a city. The place that most immediately puts you in touch with the life of the city, as in most Catalan towns, is the *Rambla*, the broad avenue with its central pedestrian walkway, which slopes slightly upwards towards the sea. Perhaps it is this sloping towards the sea on a due north-south axis that helps to give the *Rambla* its special quality of light, a luminosity, an absence of shadows, and yet also oblique as if caressing everything it touches. On its west side are banks and building societies, on its east side shops and cafés and a fine brick *Modernista* school built at the turn of the nineteenth and twentieth centuries. Broad and orderly, it initially seems grander than Barcelona's better-known *Rambla*, which is in reality a gorge between the high buildings of the old town, with narrow streets opening off on both sides. On the other hand, Barcelona's *Rambla* is filled with tourists, sailors, visitors from all over the world, while Tarragona's *Rambla* is more intimate, even provincial, a place where, by and large, people still know one another.

Tarragona's *Rambla* does change. The *Modernista* facades have been cleaned and restored to their 1900s glory. There are, too, newcomers, most noticeably the offices of trade unions and political parties, and a lot more bookshops. The bookshops themselves are a reflection of Tarragona's self-consciousness as an ancient city, full of esoteric monographs on the past as well as a newer generation of more popular volumes on local history. This is a city in which to pause and browse and ponder. Yet Tarragona, despite its Gothic cathedral, has never been darkly medieval, unlike the narrow alleyways of medieval Barcelona or Girona. The old nucleus of the town is surrounded and defined by the Roman walls of which more than a kilometre are clearly visible. The lower portion and the gateway surrounds are made from huge megalithic blocks, always referred to as Cyclopean, such is their size and appearance. There are sections where the walls stand solemn and imposing and alone. In other places, such as the Sant Antoni gate, Roman, medieval and modern mingle in happy abandon. The gateway itself was rebuilt in 1757, and gives access from the old city to an open play area for children, with an old people's centre on one side, the drop to the sea on another and a backdrop of houses built directly onto and above the Roman walls. A local bus squeezes through the stone arch, and the life of Tarragona's fourth millennium carries on.

The Roman amphitheatre, overlooking the sea, is first and foremost a public park. Even in April, the midday sun is hot after the cool streets of the old town. The creaking swings suggest that children have stopped off here on their way home from school. Older people are enjoying the spring sunshine — later in the year the blinding light and searing heat will make it unlikely that you will see any locals sitting in the sunshine in the middle of the day. The first bougainvillaea is coming into bloom, there is birdsong. It is hard to imagine now the wild public spectacles that took place here, including gladiators struggling with wild beasts and the occasional Christian martyrdom. No doubt there were Romans who preferred wine and good food, poetry and music, the pleasures of the public baths or the private bedroom. Perhaps the Romans too were a little ashamed of their official pleasures — the pleasures their rulers felt appropriate for the people — for the amphitheatre lies on the fringes of the Roman city. The view of the sea across the amphitheatre is unforgettable, a gentle introduction to eternity. But that can have been of little comfort to Christians being thrown to the lions.

From the amphitheatre, it is a comfortably short walk back round to the sea end of the *Rambla*, called the Balcony because of the way it dominates the railway station, the sea and the port. Modern Tarragona is an important and rather messy industrial centre, and from here the beginnings of the poorer quarters of the city are visible. The tall houses are packed tightly together, their balconies festooned with potted plants and washing. At street level cars and pedestrians act out a battle for survival. Women sit out on the pavements in rickety old chairs, babies on their laps and infants under their feet. From innumerable cheap bars come the noise of clinking glasses, juke boxes and shouted laughter, and the smell of fish and meat frying in cheap olive oil. Poverty is much the same throughout the Mediterranean. A confusion of railway sidings and cranes surround the docks and further over, on either side of the resort of Salou, is the oil terminal (which accounts for seventy-five per cent of port movements) and, farther on still, the nuclear power station. The industrial growth of Tarragona is spectacular and very recent. For the first time since Roman times, Tarragona's population has exceeded 30,000, reaching 38,000 in 1950 and well over 100,000 today. This compares with a mere 5,000 in 1600 and less than that in 1700. To put the Roman figure of 30,000 in perspective, until nearly 1800 only the two largest towns in England outside London — Norwich and Bristol — reached that figure. Such was imperial Tarragona.

To cater for the needs of such a large population on this relatively dry coast (rainfall decreases steadily to the south and west of Barcelona) large amounts of water had to be brought into the city from the hillsides inland. This produced one of the best loved and best preserved of all Roman monuments, the aqueduct six kilometres out of town in the direction of Lleida, which brought the waters of the River Francolí into the town. Two storeys of Roman arches march across the scrubby valley to create a structure 217 metres long and 27 metres high. It is possible to cross on foot, but it is not an experience to be recommended to the faint-hearted. There is no hand rail, just a low stone parapet separating you from the rocky valleyside below. The only sounds are the restless chirping of the crickets and the rustle of lizards as they twist away from human intruders through the scrub. Popularly, the aqueduct, like the restored Roman bridge at Martorell, where the Via Augusta crosses the River Llobregat, is known as the Devil's Bridge. It is a strange comment on the obscurantism and technical impoverishment of our medieval ancestors, that this custom of ascribing large civil engineering feats to the devil should be so widespread in Europe.

There are Roman remains and reminders at Barcelona too, though much less obviously so given the development of Barcelona as a major port and administrative and trading centre in the Middle Ages, and its industrial and commercial development during the last two centuries. Barcino was certainly established by the time of the reign of Augustus (29BC–14BC) and like Tarragona had aqueducts to bring water into the city. Unlike Tarragona, they have not survived. It was an important centre of exchange between sea and interior, and of land routes, including the one to the important settlement of Egara (modern Terrassa). Yet given its subsequent growth, little is left to see, except in the basement galleries of the town museum. The museum is located in a Gothic palace just a few yards from the Cathedral, in the heart of the Old Town. The palace was moved to this location from its original site in Carrer Mercaders (Merchants' Street) and in the process of putting it up on the new site, important Roman remains were found at basement level. The earliest Barcelona remains date from the first and second centuries, but Barcino at this point does not appear to have been a major settlement and was destroyed by raiders from outside the Empire in 270AD. The more important remains are those of a Roman-Christian town of the fourth and fifth centuries. This was completely surrounded by walls, fragments of which crop up like exotic blooms in the most surprising places around the Old Town. In the museum, there are excellent exhibits for those who like that sort of thing: marble and bronze statues, coins, fragments of pottery and mosaic.

A Way of Life

The pre-history of Catalonia may seem far removed from daily life in Catalonia today. Yet there is continuity. There is, for example, far from the Mediterranean itself, far from golden Tarragona or silver Empúries, the town square or *plaça* at Balaguer, in the province of Lleida, on the road to the still distant Pyrenees. Balaguer was once an important town. In the tenth century, it was the capital of the Urgell, the county that extended south from the Pyrenees and marked the southern extension of a Catalonia that was only just beginning to take shape as the various rival Christians lords squabbled among themselves and occasionally turned their attention to pushing back the frontiers of Muslim rule. There are fine houses along the river front facing modern blocks of flats set in grassland on the opposite bank. But the heart of the town is a large, arcaded square sloping gently from north to south. Here, in the shade of the thirty-eight plane trees which mark out the public space, the people of Balaguer walk and talk or sit and rest, taking the sun in winter and enjoying the shade in summer. The sandy-coloured mass of the church on the hill rises above the roofs, its clock-tower clearly visible, and next to it are the remains of a vast medieval castle, crumbling gently in order to appear more in scale with the small town it now dominates a little less every year. A solitary traffic-policeman, one of life's natural pessimists, keeps a tight hold on would-be parking offenders with his shrill whistle and admonishing index finger.

The red and green umbrellas of the café on the top side of the square extend across the roadway beneath the plane trees. People come and go, pause and linger, some to sit for hours, eating, drinking, reading the newspapers, talking of this and that which seems so important today, but will be replaced by something else equally important tomorrow. They lean towards one another as they talk, an important point emphasised by a hand gripping an elbow, disagreement marked by a wagging finger echoing that of the policeman. Interminable handshakes and kisses on both

29

cheeks are exchanged as friends and family arrive and depart. It is a scene that is repeated time and again in Catalonia, the social rituals that make society possible, but here accomplished with a style that belies the sleepy, rural atmosphere of Balaguer and speaks instead of the importance of a public open space. The *plaça* at Balaguer, then, can be taken as a symbol — a hundred and one other small Catalan towns might do as well — of one vital element of continuity in the Mediterranean world, extending far beyond the immediate proximity of the sea, and meaning far more than shards of pottery in a museum. For this is a space to be in, rather than merely to pass through. A direct descendant of the Roman forum. A way of being a citizen rather than just an inhabitant. A social work of art.

Chapter 2

Catalonia:
a Thousand Years of History?

A 'Millennial Country'? — The Romance of History
In general, the English used by the various Catalan tourist
bodies has improved markedly over the years. Gone are
the days when John Langdon-Davies (in his 1953 book
Gatherings from Catalonia) could get a rise out of the
'unspeakable white houses' at Cadaqués, or of the solemn
pronouncement that Barcelona streets are lined by
'banana trees' (both the Catalan and Castilian words for
plane-tree mean banana as well). Fortunately the oddities
of translation do not change reality. The streets of
Barcelona are still lined by elegant planes, carefully pol-
larded by the Town Council every winter, and apparently
as unaffected by atmospheric pollution as their London
cousins. The houses at Cadaqués are still blindingly white,
and it is still hard to find words to match their loveliness.
The reality, we shall discover, is rather more controversial
when it come to the description of Catalonia as a 'millennial country'. The end did not come on either 1 January
2000 or 1 January 2001, but when was the beginning? For
over twenty years, the re-established Generalitat used the
slogan to emphasise the sense of Catalonia as a historical
and well-founded nation. Similar things have no doubt
happened in other corners of Europe (Estonia, Slovenia)
where countries with ancient but controversial histories
have reappeared in recent years.

By the end of the first millennium, the Muslims (still
generally referred to in Catalonia and Spain as the Moors)

31

had been living in what we now refer to as Catalonia for nearly three centuries. They had gradually been pushed south from the Pyrenees where independent Christian Counties had been established, usually more interested in quarrelling with one another than with Muslims. But under the leadership of Al-Mansur from Cordoba, the Muslims sacked Barcelona in 985. The curious reaction of the Count of Barcelona was to break off ties of vassalage in 988 with the French King who wanted to launch a reprisal raid on the Muslims. Instead the Count opted for closer ties with his Pyrenean neighbours. From this stems 988–1988, 1000 years of Catalan history, conveniently timed to coincide with the rejuvenated Generalitat under its conservative nationalist administration.

Even archetypal conservative politicians in Catalonia are exceptional. In 1990, seated at his desk in a comfortable book-lined office high above the snarling rush-hour traffic of Barcelona, town councillor Josep Maria Ainaud de Lasarte described some of his activities during the Franco period. He had been a friend of Pau Casals, "although we didn't share the same political views", and his special task had been ferrying people across the leaky Pyrenean border — people who had their own very good reasons for not wanting to risk crossing at an official check-point. The conservatism began to cut in as the conversation developed, this silver-haired elder statesman emphasising the primacy of two things only in Catalonia's history — Christianity and democracy. He claimed that the Muslim influence in Catalonia had been insignificant, and that the influence of Judaism had always been confined to the ghetto, both of which views will be challenged later in this book. He emphasised the importance of democracy in the medieval period with the development of political institutions such as the Corts (parliament), the Generalitat (the regional government which emerged from the Corts) and the Consell de Cent (Council of One Hundred, or Barcelona Town Council). But in his view this limited democracy had also contributed to economic development through markets, guilds and the Consolat de Mar (Maritime Law Tribunal). No mention of the Jews or Muslims here. Autocratic rule was 'oriental', a view which conflicts oddly with the centuries during which Catalonia (as part of first Aragon and then Spain) was ruled by kings, queens and an unseemly assortment of military despots.

One of the most remarkable of Catalonia's own despots, a larger than life character whose biography is as miraculous, mythical and apocryphal as that of England's Arthur and Alfred, was Guifré el Pelós, which conveniently translates as Wilfred the Hairy. Robert Hughes is fascinated by him — maybe a case of auto-identification here — and waxes lyrical about the man and his legend. The most intriguing bit relates to his hairiness, or rather those bits of his body on which it is supposed to have grown (or not). Hughes recounts how the young boy, heir to the Count of Barcelona, grew up in Flanders and was only reunited with his mother after an absence of sixteen years. She recognised her hairy son by the fact that he had hair on a part of his body where it should not have been. No, we are not told the answer, by Hughes or his informant. The few facts of the matter are that this Wilfred was born in the middle of the ninth century, died in about 898 and was the leader around whom the fiefdoms lying between Barcelona and the Pyrenees coalesced. It was of course more in opposition to French rule than to Muslim rule, which persisted in the Catalan lands south of Barcelona (often referred to as New Catalonia) until the middle of the twelfth century.

It was Wilfred who founded the great monastic establishments in the foothills of the Pyrenees, especially those of the Benedictines at Ripoll and Sant Joan de les Abadesses. Oliba, the abbot of Ripoll in the early eleventh century, was also abbot of Sant Miquel de Ciuxà on the northern slopes of the Pyrenees, a fact of considerable importance because it means that this historic Catalonia identified by romantic historians comes to include those territories which since 1659 have been part of the French state. Written in this way, history either hangs together or it falls apart in a dusty pile of dates and facts and rubble. It was from a manuscript from an anonymous medieval monk of Ripoll that the touching tale of Wilfred and his mother came. Medieval monks were great scribblers and how better to pass the time than composing tales about the generous man who had set you up in the manner to which you had become accustomed and intended to continue to enjoy?

Ripoll is of special importance to Catalonia. By the end of the nineteenth century, it was a pleasant day out on the railway which goes from Barcelona to Puigcerdà via Ripoll, and then on through the Cerdanya into France, creating an unusual trans-Pyrenean route between Paris and Barcelona. Ripoll also had textile factories and iron-works, but the emotional weight of the town has always been its monastery. It has survived much, including earthquake, fire and pillage by nineteenth century anti-clerical liberals. The restoration of Santa Maria de Ripoll in the closing years of the nineteenth century, by which time Catalanism had thoroughly established itself as an industrial, cultural and political force, is now seen by many as an act of vandalism comparable with the worse excesses of the church restorers in England, against whom William Morris's Society for the Protection of Ancient Buildings raged with righteous anger. But at the time, it was viewed as an act of cultural homage: Catalonia had come home to its hairy roots, in a small railway town at the foot of the Pyrenees. Ripoll became a 'must do' on the itinerary of the Catalan *excursionistes*, who have walked and climbed their way around the sacred sites of Catalonia ever since — mountains, valleys, churches, beaches and villages. And its mid-twelfth century porch is still worth a detour. It is more a triumphal arch than a church doorway, extending the full width of the nave. Taken together, the scenes are a vivid encyclopaedia of the stories and images that proliferate in early medieval art. Here are the saints, especially the life-size figures of Peter and Paul that flank the doorway. There are scenes from the bible, including the visions of the apocalypse. There are angels of every category and, lording it over all, a Christ in Majesty. There are also carvings of the signs of the Zodiac, real and fantastic animals, scenes of daily life taken from the calendar of the seasons — ploughing, hunting, sowing and reaping. There is warfare.

Visigoths

Did nothing happen between the Romans and Hairy Wilfred? One answer is to visit Terrassa, an important textile town in the Vallès, linked to Barcelona by an attractive narrow-gauge (i.e. British gauge rather than the broad Spanish gauge) railway originating in the Plaça de Catalunya. In this rather unlikely industrial setting is one of the most remarkable groups of churches anywhere in Europe. It includes the parish church of Sant Pere, the cathedral church of Santa Maria and the baptistery of Sant Miquel. This group of churches built by the Visigoths lies directly over the Roman remains of the city of Egara. Visigoths may have been barbarians once, but in Spain they quickly acquired Christianity and sufficient culture to keep some of the achievements of Roman Spain ticking over until the invasion of the Muslims in 711 put a further spanner into the historical clockwork. The town became a bishopric in 450 and remained so for 250 years.

As at Ripoll, the restoration of these three churches was largely the work of that master of Romanesque revival — the architect, historian, rambler, skier and nationalist politician Josep Puig i Cadalfach. It is the baptistery that most perfectly conserves the primitive feel of this early stage of Christianity, as whole populations converted to the new faith. Putting an exact date on these buildings is a hard task: sixth or seventh century is the closest we can get for this remarkable building, with its Greek cross ground-plan, tiny chapels at each angle and a horseshoe-shaped east-end apse. At the centre of the church is a cupola held up by eight ancient pillars, the shafts and Corinthian capitals of which were in turn re-assembled from earlier (perhaps Roman) structures. Below this cupola is a reconstruction of the pool where these early Christians were baptised. The importance of baptism as an outward symbol of inner change is clearly stated. It was a heroic time for the faith, as it spread to become the dominant religion of Western Europe, meshing in the process with both the Roman gods and also beliefs which had persisted from the people who had lived in Iberia even before the Romans reached Catalonia. And the whole womb-like closeness of this tiny jewel of a church emphasises that sense of rebirth, the need of people to feel safe and saved, a strong psychological impulse in the success of Christianity or any other great religion.

Santa Maria, the cathedral church of the Visigoths, is more of a historical puzzle. The mosaic pavement outside is probably from the first Christian church on the site. The rectangular apse of this early church and its burial crypts have been identified from excavations beneath the later nave. For English visitors, there is particular interest in the twelfth century Romanesque paintings of St Thomas-à-Becket, found beneath later Gothic wall paintings in a transept apse. This demonstrates just how quickly the cult of Chaucer's 'holy blessed martyr' spread through Europe. The power of the church depended not least on discouraging unruly kings and politicians from assassinating archbishops, at prayer or anywhere else. To complete the circuit, the parish church of Sant Pere is clearly Visigothic at the east end, with a three-lobed apse, but the nave of the church is twelfth century Romanesque in the Lombard style, like so many other Catalan churches.

Building a Nation — Romanesque Style

The invasion of the Muslims at the beginning of the eighth century was a decisive event, exposing the internal feuding and political weakness of the Visigothic state, which disappeared from history with scarcely a backward glance. The relaunch of Christian Spain towards the end of the eighth century involved much tighter organisation in smaller units. In 785 the people of Girona, followed by those of Urgell and the Cerdanya, acknowledged allegiance to Ludovico Pio, son of Charlemagne. Allegiance was a two-way affair, and this led directly to the reconquest of Barcelona, Roman walls and all, in 801 and the establishment of a number of counties south of the Pyrenees with independent political, military and judicial control. Feudalism was out there lurking in the dark shadows of history. At the same time, the church established a network of parishes in the newly reconquered areas. Prominent among these counties were Urgell, the Cerdanya, Berga, Empúries and Besalú. 'Old' Catalonia was taking recognisable shape.

During the next two centuries, two processes were at work. Firstly, the growing importance of Barcelona. Under Hairy Wilfred the counties of Barcelona, Girona and Osona were effectively joined together, and the influence of Barcelona felt as far away as the Conflent valley, on the north-facing flank of the Pyrenees. Secondly, as we saw above, the counties south of the Pyrenees gradually asserted their independence from their Frankish overlords. But neither of these tendencies should be overestimated, as they sometimes are in the work of romantic nationalists. Contact with post-Carolingian Europe remained strong, and the independent power of the isolated Pyrenean counties lasted well into the eleventh and twelfth centuries. For the two hundred years from 800–1000, the Muslims generally had a more sophisticated culture, more advanced farming methods (especially irrigation) and more advanced systems of government than their Christian neighbours.

It was the contact, however, with the wider European world beyond the Pyrenees that opened up one of the great periods of Catalan art — the Romanesque — from about 1000. An essential feature of the Romanesque is that it was a movement which spread with great speed across Europe. Although the dream of Charlemagne to re-establish the Roman Empire was by now in tatters, there were other forces at work to bring Europe closer together. The church especially. Although Romanesque existed as a civil style (bridges, castles, houses) the impulse behind its spread was the religious reform of the Benedictines, radiating out from the Abbey of Cluny in France. The paintings and carvings in their buildings illustrated in particular bible stories and the contrasting fates of the chosen and the damned. It was a simple and effective way of bringing a certain kind of enlightenment to illiterate people — by showing them how much better off they would be if they followed the instructions of their religious leaders. The Benedictines brought order to the conduct of religious life and economic enterprise, for they were successful businessmen as well as spiritual leaders. Their monasteries became centres of material wealth and political power. They set standards in organisation and architecture which were copied in churches great and small throughout Catalonia, but especially in the well organised communities of the Pyrenean valleys. Massive masonry was used to support barrel vaults; systems of decoration, especially the blind arcades of the Lombard bands, were introduced by travelling Italian masons who spread this particular form of work from Provence through the Catalan counties.

We are lucky that, during the thousand years that have elapsed since then, not much has happened in the Pyrenees, give or take a bit of mining, a lot of reservoirs, ski-ing and the virtual extinction of the brown bears. Lucky, because the settings of so many of these churches is so striking. And since not a lot has happened, no-one has ever wanted to do very much to them. Pyrenean Catalonia, one might say, reached cruising height in the eleventh century and has remained on autopilot ever since. Most of the splendid wall paintings, altar-pieces and crosses, however, were removed long ago to the safe-keeping of the Museu d'Art de Catalunya (Catalonia Art Museum) on Montjuïc, a javelin-throw away from the Olympic Stadium. José Camilo Cela, the Spanish Nobel Prize winner and author of a fine book on the Pyrenees, was especially bitter about the removal of these treasures from the Pyrenees to Barcelona. He complained that the money spent on looking after them and paying the employees of the museum would have been better spent repairing leaky roofs and restoring the original homes of these works of art.

It is a long way from Barcelona to the Vall de Boí, and unlike Ripoll there is no railway to help. It is a trip best made in summer. This involves heading for Balaguer, where the previous chapter finished, up past the jagged, magical profile of Montserrat, and on into the dry lands around Cervera, already in the province of Lleida. Across the Urgell Canal (canal implying water for agriculture rather than transport) there is a dramatic change, for here the irrigated lands begin, with head-high maize alternating with fields of apples and pears as far as the eye can see. North from Balaguer, the road enters Aragon on the west bank of the Noguera Ribagorçana River, the frontier between Catalonia and Aragon. Eventually the road crosses back to the east side of the river and begins to climb steadily, until after Pont de Suert, a sign-post announces the only road access to the Vall de Boí. This is one of Catalonia's best-kept secrets, and even in midsummer its camp-sites, hotels and national park facilities seem almost exclusively populated by Catalans and Valencians. This is a land of rushing water, oak and pine woods, high pastures and limestone outcrops. An intimate country at least up the 2,000-metre contour in the National Park of Aigüestortes i Sant Maurici. They still make hay-stacks by the method once common to much of Europe — a central pole and the hay tossed up around it to make a conical-shaped mound. The trees in the valley are lime, ash, hazel, pine and walnut. There are midges, but the few mosquitoes seem indolent and droopy. Even in summer the nights are cold up here, and the stars sparkle crisply in the thin, mountain air.

The valley reveals itself little by little. The first village is Coll, its church set a little apart from the village among walnut-trees. The blind arcading here is not just around the apse, but continues along the nave and around the gabled west end as well. There is dressed stone inside and out, including some pretty pink granite. The roof is slate and the tower, more recent than the church, is squat and square and simple with the little slate bonnet that appears on all the churches of the valley. Inside there are some old priest seats, made of carved walnut. Anywhere else, this church would be exceptional. Here it is the norm. The municipality of Barruera which covers the whole valley and is named after the most populous and least interesting of the villages, has fifteen Romanesque churches built in the eleventh and twelfth centuries. In the Generalitat's excellent little guide to the architectural heritage of Catalonia, available in English, Santa Maria de Coll does not even merit a mention. To see why, it is necessary to go a few miles further up the valley, to the church of Santa Eulàlia at Erill-la-Vall. This is a single nave with semicircular apse and apsed side-chapels. But it is the tower that imposes itself on the visitor, slim and elegant, with five stages of paired Lombardy arches, blind arcades and dog-tooth decoration. On the north side of the church, facing the Pyrenean houses with their pretty wooden balconies and pots of geraniums, is an open porch stretching the whole length of the nave and supported by three elegant round stone columns, more Renaissance loggia than Romanesque. There is one other in the valley, at Durro, recently restored. These arcaded porches provided some sort of protection against the harsh climate of the high valley, and were probably used for meetings. No-one seems altogether sure. They are quite unusual in Catalonia, but much more common in the Castilian provinces of Ávila and Segovia, where they can be much more clearly identified with the exercise of rights and privileges given to local communities by the king.

If Erill-la-Vall is emotionally the most satisfying of the churches in the valley, it is the two churches at Taüll which are the best known, and in some ways, most bizarre. Was there some special evil present in Taüll which necessitated two churches in such a small village? Why those enormous towers to which the whole design seems subjugated? Why the consecrations so close to one another — Sant Climent on 11 December 1123 and Santa Maria the day after on 12 December 1123? At Sant Climent you can climb the tower, although it requires a good head for heights. The blind arcades are extreme in their simplicity, the paired arches occupying much of each of the six stages of the tower. Externally this gives a wonderful sense of airy lightness to the tower, but on the ascent there seems little to prevent the visitor from falling onto the Romanesque art industry below — cafes, restaurants, postcard and book shops, camp-site and apartment houses. The bells are still in place, and the largest is exquisitely carved with scenes from the life of the Virgin Mary. If Sant Climent seems given over to the tourist industry, Santa Maria, in the centre of the village, is very much still in use, with its more restrained four-stage belfry firmly locked.

What is missing from these churches only slowly becomes apparent as you travel around Catalonia. Santa Eulàlia at Erill-la-Vall, for example, is short of a twelfth century sculptural group of the Descent from the Cross, part of which is in the collection of the Museu Episcopal (Bishop's Museum) in Vic, while the other part is at the Montjuïc museum in Barcelona. A sixteenth century altarpiece has gone in a different direction altogether, to the Diocesan Museum at Seu d'Urgell. At Taüll there are reproductions to replace the missing murals and not very good ones either. At Sant Climent the artificial lighting emphasises the thinness of the colours, while at Santa Maria the great apse mural of the Three Kings is best seen on a summer's evening when the delicate, golden light is streaming through the west window all the way up the nave to the apse, softening the defects of the copy. The image fills the curved vault of the apse while below are full-length figures of the gospel writers. Of course the Catalan Art Museum at Montjuïc has made a brave effort to recreate the setting of the churches, efforts redoubled during the lengthy remodelling of the museum in the 1990s. But what can never be re-created in the heart of the city are the rocky limestone bluffs and green alpine meadows of the Vall de Boí, the distant sound of cow- and goat-bells ringing through the still, clear air. The great image at Sant Climent is that of the pancreator, Christ as omnipotent god, creator, law giver and saviour of the world, surrounded by angels, the great Christian mystery of God become human, of the union of the spiritual and the physical. At Barcelona, you see the image itself, without the setting, without the wonders of creation; at Taüll you have the wonders of creation, but a mere copy of the image. It is an unhappy divorce: God not quite at one with creation.

At another turn of the valley lies Durro, where the Generalitat has been working patiently for some years on the restoration of the church of Santa Maria. Its porch arcade is even more impressive than that that at Erill-la-Vall, with blind arcades and decorative band-work in the stone. Here the square tower is fortress-like in its imposing height and massive cross-section, and this tower and the one at Sant Joan de Boí are much more convincing than the nervous heights of Sant Climent de Taüll. On a summer's day, there are swooping swallows cavorting around the tower and a distant view of the hermitage of Sant Quirze amid the meadows, and the mountains rising bare and milky white into the blue, cloudless sky. It is a cheerful village in which holiday-makers and farmers mix happily in the local bar and the cottage gardens are full of hollyhocks and tomatoes and apple-trees.

The hermitage of Sant Quirze is a tiny nave and single apse church with magnificent views, and a distant, hidden tolling of animal-bells on the high summer pastures away across the valley. In these silent high places sound carries with absolute clarity. Yet you should not look for solitude in a place like this — for this is a popular picnic-spot and on a summer Sunday there will usually be half-a-dozen family groups at play here. The picnic is not a pilgrimage, although the distant roots of this Catalan liking for communal picnics in high places must surely go back to the tradition of the parish devotional walk to some local hilltop shrine, or even back to pre-Christian rituals. Such activities nowadays are both part of the urge of city dwellers to get away to the wide open spaces at the weekend, but also support a cultural and political identity. *Excursionisme* is a cheerful, cheap and communal activity, a way of establishing your credentials as a good Catalan. It is well organised and has a history. Puig i Cadalfach, at the end of the nineteenth century, was a keen excursionist as well as architect and nationalist politician. During the period of the Franco dictatorship, group outings to the countryside were both innocent social occasions but also building blocks in the political cause of a specifically Catalan democracy.

There is cold, crystalline fountain of drinking water at Sant Quirze, a major attraction on a hot summer's day. There is a little shade too, against the hermitage walls. This is so far from anywhere now. If places have a spirit that looks after them, then Sant Quirze de Durro will live forever. Yet this peaceful spot is represented in the Catalan Art Museum by one of the most dramatic and violent of the many works collected from Pyrenean churches. This is a painted, wooden altar-front, completed in about 1100, of the martyrdom of Santa Julita and her three-year-old son Quirze. The episodes of torture and violent death are more gruesomely portrayed than any of the battle scenes in the Bayeux tapestry, which dates from about the same time. Harold may have died from an arrow in his eye, but at least he didn't get nails hammered into his eyes, sawn in half or watch his baby boiled in a cooking-pot. It is hard to find solace in these pictures.

Pride and Humility

At the extreme eastern end of the Pyrenees lies another monastery. Again, it is a Benedictine foundation — Sant Pere de Rodes, set up in 934, some fifty years before Ripoll. When the English writer Rose Macaulay failed to visit it half-a-century ago, it was a romantic ruin. From the little holiday-resort of Port de la Selva, the ruins were clearly visible 2,000 feet above near the top of a bare mountain. That was as far as Macaulay got, and the experience stayed with her. 'The shadow of this mighty ruin haunted me and haunts me still', she wrote in *Fabled Shore*. Until 1990 it was a feeling shared by the present writer, by which time Sant Pere had finally begun to re-emerge from a slow century of patient archaeology and restoration, with additional impetus added by support from the European Union. It is a long climb up to Sant Pere, even by road. No doubt Rose Macaulay would have recognised the steep, bumpy roads, for she was forever complaining about the pot-holes and punctures which until recently were the inevitable accompaniments of a car journey around rural Catalonia. From the seaside, it is uphill all the way, unremittingly so. From the land side, the closest to the motorway, the fields and orchards of the Empordà give way more gradually to the upland landscape of vines and olives. Higher up, this in turn is replaced by the coarse, sweet-smelling scrub of the maquis, then equally sweet-smelling pine woods and eventually bare rock.

A priory church in the ninth century, the great church was consecrated in 1022 and around it flourished the many buildings of a monastic community devoted to the word of God, but also to the ownership of land, and the production of oil and wine, those staples of the Mediterranean economy. But it was the wealth of monasteries such as Sant Pere that attracted enemies. As early as the fourteenth century, the Majorcan poet Anselm Turmeda could write:

Money can cure all your woes,
So if you get it, keep it close.
Get enough, and you may become
The Pope in Rome.

For centuries, this was a sea where pirates roamed. And sometimes the pirates came ashore, doing what pirates are good at: rape, pillage and looting. Occasionally a rich man or an official would be taken away in the hope of a ransom. Fit young men would be taken for slave labour in the galleys, and fit young women would be traded in the markets of North Africa. But at least Sant Pere was safe on its mountainside, as were other settlements such as Santa Creu de Rodes. This threat of piracy did not last forever. Especially after the victory of the Spanish navy under the bastard Don Juan of Austria at Lepanto in 1571, the people moved back down to the coast, abandoning some of the more remote settlements on the Rodes mountains. Thus Sant Pere avoided the fate of other Catalan monasteries, destroyed by liberal anticlericalism in the nineteenth century. By that time it had been completely abandoned. Its rise and fall are emblematic of the rise and fall of monasticism and feudalism. The treasures of the monastery were scattered across the Western world, new as well as old. There is a bible in Paris, fragments of carved stone in Barcelona. A statue of Saint Peter himself has come to rest at the bottom of the hill, in the parish church of Port de la Selva.

Yet for all the restoration work, Sant Pere somehow manages to preserve that air of greatness come to nought: alpine plants growing in cracks in the stone, birds flitting around among the massive square columns and Corinthian capitals of the nave. And the most impressive and characteristic images of the place remain the towers, the austere fortress tower and the church tower, enormously big but light too, an effect achieved by the frequent piercings of different shapes and sizes. It was a pity that Rose Macaulay never reached Sant Pere. She was later to

45

write a novel about spiritual quest — *The Towers of Trebizond* — set in and around the distant Black Sea, but she may very well have still been haunted by the distant view and imagined grandeur of those ruined towers high above the sea.

For the energetic visitor, there is an additional climb by a tangled path through maquis and briars to the castle set on the very top of the 670-metre high hill. There is sufficient of the ruined castle left standing to provide shade, and a riot of wild flowers — pinks, thistles, succulents — and of insects — dragonflies, bluebottles, fritillary butterflies — to delight the eye. Over it all swoops a solitary swallow. The view is immense. To the south the coast towards Empúries, the ochre and green plain of the Empordà, traced by roads and speckled by villages. To the east, the road snakes down precipitously towards El Port de la Selva, with its glistening sands in front of modest houses that have so far resisted the appeal of high-rise apartment blocks. To the north lies little Llançà, where the railway from Barcelona reaches the sea, and the tiny coves up beyond Portbou into France. To the west, the mountains rise towards misty Pyrenean heights. Little wonder with these bountiful lands at their feet that the Benedictines of Sant Pere fell victims to the lure of material wealth. Or that the peasants came to hate them for it.

Foundation myths — the story of how a nation sets out on its glorious history — are all very well, but they lead down some painful paths. Perhaps it is best not to take them too seriously, to maintain the edges of the picture a little vague and out-of-focus, the story fragmentary and inconclusive. Too precise a reading of national history can lead to trouble, as the Serbs found to their cost in Kosovo. Sometimes fresh starts are called for. In any case, we have reached the sea, and it is time to focus on another chapter of Catalan history — her period as a 'great power' in the Mediterranean.

Chapter 3

The Catalan Empire

Going for Empire

The medieval Catalan empire was an extraordinary affair, and is difficult to evaluate in modern terms. Words like empire and colony send a shiver through decent people everywhere. Yet equally, we seem at times to take for granted the power and influence of multinational companies and global capital in the lives of our nations and communities. There is a benign view of the Catalan empire which emphasises its cultural merits, its literary achievements, its ability to create wealth and its respect for local rights and institutions. Then there is Robert Hughes, fresh from *The Fatal Shore*, in which he chronicled the destruction of the Aborigines in his native Australia by the convict colonies established by the British. Hughes is well liked in Barcelona, but he pulls no punches, describing what happened in Sardinia and Minorca as verging on 'cultural genocide' (*Barcelona*, p. 109). He describes how the inaptly named King Alfons II (the Liberal) invaded Minorca in 1287, slaughtered most of its male population and sold the rest as slaves. It took Minorca two hundred years to recover from this experience. Some Catalans take great pride in the fact that people in the Sardinian town of Alghero (l'Alguer in Catalan) still speaks a Catalan dialect. This is only so because Pere III executed or drove into exile the original inhabitants and replaced them with Catalan settlers.

This 'Mediterranean turn' in Catalan history was a considerable shift from the Catalonia of the Pyrenean strongholds and Romanesque churches described in the previous chapter. It is worth exploring how this change came about. The marriage of the Count of Barcelona and the Queen of Aragon in 1137 had united the two regional powers, and meant that the Catalan empire was ruled not in the name of Catalonia but of Aragon. While Saragossa remained the formal capital, Barcelona was its economic and administrative centre. This led almost directly to the conquest of the Muslim lands south and west of Barcelona, including Lleida and Tortosa, the area generally referred to as New Catalonia. The Aragonese set up *latifundis* (large estates worked by serfs) in the inland counties, while the Catalans re-populated the coastal areas with their own people. This eventually produced a complete change of direction for the Catalans. Previously the county of Barcelona had been more interested in extending Catalan influence north of the Pyrenees into the rich lands of Provence, but this ensnared the Catalans with wider European concerns, such as the rivalry between the French and English crowns for control of southern France. After the defeat of Pere I at Muret in 1213 by an army led by Simon de Montfort, this policy was reversed, and from then on the Aragonese-Catalan federation was to concentrate on spreading its power and influence southwards along the coast of Spain and eastwards through the Mediterranean islands.

Jaume I seized Mallorca (Majorca) from the Muslims in 1229 and the other Balearic Islands, Eivissa (Ibiza) and Menorca (Minorca), soon afterwards. By 1238 he had added the lands of Valencia. Later in the thirteenth century, Sardinia and Sicily fell under Catalan control. In Sicily this followed the Sicilian Vespers uprising against the French King Charles I who ruled Naples in mainland Italy. Early in the fourteenth century Catalan pirates (with official support) attacked the Byzantine Empire and for many years controlled the Duchy of Athens. As late as the middle of the fifteenth century, when Castilian influence had already become strong in a Catalonia weakened by internal division, plague and depopulation, Alfons V (the Magnanimous) conquered Naples and stayed for 25 years to rule over one of the great humanist courts of renaissance Europe. The artist Pisanello was among those who worked for him, and the portrait medal of Alfons' lieutenant Iñigo d'Avalos gives a vivid impression of the imperial ambitions of the Catalans. The reverse of the medal shows the globe, with stars, land and sea, a symbol of imperial conquest. But Barcelona was not Rome, and never had been. If Pisanello is one foot-note to Catalonia's imperial history, the other is Malmsey, the sweet wine from Sitges, in a butt of which the Duke of Clarence was supposed to have drowned. There is general agreement that the *malvasia* grape which produces the wine came from the eastern end of the Mediterranean. The details are less clear. One wine expert offers Cyprus as origin, a Spanish dictionary suggests it was brought back to Catalonia by 'crusaders'. More to the point it offers the island port of Monemvassia at the south-eastern end of the Greek Peloponnese as the origin of the word, a view with which the Oxford English Dictionary concurs but moves it back to the mainland. There is a bridge, so the gap must be small.

The political and commercial history of the medieval Catalan empire takes literary form in the chronicles of Ramon Muntaner. Born in the town of Perelada in the Empordà, he accompanied numerous Catalan expeditions, including those to Greece. He had first-hand experience of the events he described, and spent the last years of his life (he died in 1313) writing about the exploits of his companions as if they were World Cup winning sportsmen. This is not history, but hero-worship. There is no mistaking, either, the pride which Muntaner takes in his work and in the language, repeatedly telling us of far-off places where the natives speak 'the fairest Catalan in the world'. The fairest, the richest, the wisest, there is no end to Muntaner's superlatives. The truth is probably that these expeditionary heroes, the *almogàvers*, were closer to pirates and freebooters, like those of Elizabethan England, than to an imperial army. Men more inclined to pride and lust and greed than to courtly behaviour. While Muntaner does not tell his tale in these terms, he is naive enough to provide evidence for the prosecution. For example, the pirate/admiral Roger de Llúria is in port in Barcelona with fifty days to spare before attending the coronation of Alfons II in Saragossa. What to do? He begs leave of his King to go on a raiding expedition up the French coast rather than 'leaving my galley crews to get into trouble round here'. The King agrees, and off goes the hero to sack a few French towns. One particular town is sacked and burned to the ground 'except for the church, which is very pretty', a typical example of Muntaner's unintentional humour. Leaving his galleys at Tortosa in charge of his nephew Joan (the Catalan form of John), Roger suggests that he should raid 'Moorish' lands south of the Ebro in order to 'win some booty for the galleys so that the crews will be kept happy'. But first he needs to check that 'they haven't signed a peace treaty with the King'. No doubt the King was relieved to have such a considerate man in his pay.

As worrying as the dubious character and behaviour of the freebooters is a parallel strand of extremism in intellectual circles in Barcelona. Most worrying is Arnau de Vilanova (1240–1311), a complex character described by Hughes as 'a man who preached and embraced holy poverty but ... was an adviser to kings: an empirical scientist, a doctor by profession, who wrote valuable medical texts — yet embraced the most extreme forms of apocalyptic mysticism and prophesied the coming millennium and the end of the world' (<u>Barcelona</u>, pp.110/1). The Pope advised him to stick to medicine, and he became court physician to Pere II. However, in this role he exercised an enormous and generally unhealthy influence on the education of the King's sons, both of whom were to ascend the throne as Alfons II and Jaume II. He set out his millennial ideas in two books written right at the end of the thirteenth century (good timing). They included, unsurprisingly the destruction of Islam and the Jews and world dominion by the Christian king of Sicily — Pere II, of course. Hughes suggests that Vilanova's writings and personal charisma probably had as much influence on the expansionist aims of the Catalan-Aragonese monarchs as any realistic hopes of trade.

Barcelona and Trade

The Catalan empire was not just the result of Vilanova's rantings, the wealth of kings and the freebooting activities of pirates. It was also about Barcelona, where the merchants, bankers and tradespeople were the main beneficiaries of expansionist foreign policies. Trade was both a motor of conquest and its outcome. In some cases, conquest confirmed existing trading links; in others it created fresh opportunities. This trade was regulated by consulates in all the major Mediterranean towns, including in North Africa, and by the code of commercial and maritime practice consolidated in the mid-fourteenth century as the *Llibre del Consolat de Mar* (Maritime Consulate Book). It was the first book of its kind and was translated and adopted as standard practice by the other Mediterranean powers. Standing at the threshold of the capitalist age, it makes the simple, but contradictory point that markets produce the most profits when regulated, whether by the merchants of Barcelona, national governments or the unelected officials of the World Trade Organisation. By 1300 there were 126 consulates spread as far away as Flanders, Venice, Beirut and Byzantium. In these cities, Catalan traders including Catalan Jews competed with Venetians and Genoese for trade. The Catalan Jews were particularly active in the Northern African trade, exporting dried figs, rice, cheese, nuts and cloth to Africa and importing raw cotton, dyes and gold.

The Barcelona church of Santa Maria del Mar (Our Lady of the Sea) is the great public church of the Catalan Empire. It is located on the edge of the Gothic Quarter, and was once much closer to the sea than it is now. In recent years, in particular, new developments in the Old Port area have driven the sea further away still, and it takes some effort to imagine Santa Maria within spitting distance of the busy life of a medieval quayside, with stevedores, fishermen, traders, sailors and elegantly dressed merchants speaking a host of different languages and dialects. It is neatly located close to the Llotja (Stock Exchange) and at some distance from the government and administrative buildings around the Plaça Sant Jaume and the even more distant Cathedral. Barcelona's 'Gothic Quarter' surprises most visitors by its size and the way its pattern of streets and alleyways has stayed so constant over the years. Santa Maria has always been a busy church, a place for lovers' meetings, commercial plots and the blessing of expeditionary fleets, rather than for individual religious experience. It is also Catalan Gothic at its most extrovert, an exercise in pure space supported only by the internal buttresses that divide off the side-chapels, and the slim octagonal columns which crowd like forest trees around a glade at the east end. The building of Santa Maria lasted from 1329 until 1390, a period which marks the high point of Barcelona's commercial success. The three high naves divided only by the octagonal pillars make it the perfect building for civic ceremony. Unfortunately, no images have come down to us, and the only way to imagine Santa Maria is perhaps through later seventeenth century Flemish painting in which the church is represented as an integral part of commercial town life. Perhaps it was this close identification between Santa Maria and the business community which made it inevitable that, on the outbreak of the Spanish War in 1936, Santa Maria was put to the torch by the anarchists. Pews, altar-pieces and furnishings were heaped together and set alight. Until recently, the roof still bore the scars. The Cathedral was spared.

Outside, Santa Maria presents a remarkable contrast. The internal buttressing allows for sheer walls rising from the surrounding streets, but rising magically from the gloomy depths of the Argenteria (Silversmiths) street are two graceful, tapering octagonal towers, almost other-worldly in their delicacy and always catching the light that is playing up there beyond the rooftops. The silversmiths have gone, but the herbalists still ply their trade in the lit-tle shops on either side of the street. For many years a flower-seller has occupied the porch at the south-eastern corner of the church, although she no longer looks down on the bustle outside the Born market, which is being rapidly transformed into Catalonia's new National Library. The towers of Santa Maria del Mar can be picked out clearly from the heights of Montjuïc and Tibidabo. The church sits within the ancient city, which flows on around it. Santa Maria has survived, and there is very little in the acquisitive, materialistic society which Barcelona has become that can shock it. A setting for commercial trans-actions and imperial occasions, Santa Maria del Mar also represented that other world of creativity and beauty that begins where the day-to-day struggle for survival leaves off. Its grace and space were to the medieval merchant economy what *Modernisme* was to be for the Catalans of the Industrial Revolution — the beauty that was missing from their hectic everyday pursuit of wealth.

Santa Maria is not the only building in Barcelona which speaks of Catalonia's imperial, mercantile past. Not far away and within site of water — albeit a rather tame marina, rather than a serious harbour — is the Llotja. Externally it is rather disappointing, a rather fussy neo-classical building from the late eighteenth century. Yet almost miraculously, the architect took the courageous decision to preserve inside his neo-classical shell the Gothic transactions hall which dates from 1392. The orig-inal building dates from about 1360, when it was established to provide a base for Catalan traders and consuls. It is one of a number of civil, not to say civic, Gothic buildings which in some ways are more characteristic of Barcelona Gothic than the religious buildings. The view outside too is splendid, if you can forget for a moment the roar of the traffic which all the skills of modern planners and road-builders have not been able to disguise. There is the abrupt cliff face of Montjuïc, and standing out in front of it, at the foot of the *Rambla*, the statue of Columbus. He points eastwards, out to sea. To his native Genoa? Or perhaps towards the lands of Catalonia's medieval empire? Certainly not towards America. Beyond Columbus are the old royal shipyards, the Drassanes. Begun in 1275, they consisted of a series of great naves with pointed Gothic arches, which speak of sailing ships as directly as the vaults of Swindon Railway Works speak of steam engines. These buildings, where the ships that maintained Catalan supremacy in the Mediterranean for several centuries were built and repaired, have now found an appropriate modern function as Barcelona's Maritime Museum.

Barcelona: Civic Pride

The Drassanes may be the end of the story as far as the pull of the sea is concerned, but there is another tale to be told about medieval Barcelona, in many ways a more comfortable one because it is about how the chief city of the Aragonese-Catalan federation established the kinds of institutions which provided both good government for several centuries, and an example to which later Catalans could turn for inspiration.

On the left side of the *Rambla*, ascending from the port towards the Plaça de Catalunya, there is the Hospital of the Holy Cross, begun in 1403. At this period, this whole area to the left of the *Rambla*, known as the Raval, was enclosed by a wall, bringing this district of monasteries and market-gardens firmly within the jurisdiction of the city. At the same time, the *Rambla* itself was retained as an open space for processions and other city events, a role it has dutifully and dramatically fulfilled ever since. The hospital continued to be used as such right until 1911, with modifications and additions as and when required. In this same complex of buildings are the late seventeenth century Casa de Convalescència (Convalescent Home) and Acadèmia de Medicina (Medical Academy). Built during what was certainly not the 'best of times' for the Catalans, as we shall see in the next chapter, they reveal how civic pride and humanitarian ambitions can sometimes transcend the pressures of events. Throughout the twentieth century, the whole complex remained an oasis of peace in a crowded city, with its quiet sandy courtyards and ornamental orange trees belying the reputation of this side of the *Rambla* as the wild and woolly face of the city. The provincial library (now again the National Library of Catalonia) has found a pleasant home in the spacious rooms with their wide arches so characteristic of Barcelona civic Gothic. It is also home to the National Academy which promotes the sciences, and the Institute of Catalan Studies, which is the regulatory body of the Catalan language.

Outside the library is Barcelona's tribute to Sir Alexander Fleming, long a popular figure in Catalonia. He is seldom without flowers from his well-wishers, traditionally reckoned to be the prostitutes of the red light district that stretches down towards the port on this side of the *Rambla*. No doubt their customers also have reason to be thankful to the discoverer of penicillin. And if flowers are missing, his head and the bowl of the little fountain in front of him are equally popular with the local pigeons and sparrows. Writing in 1953, John Langdon-Davies also noted the reverence for Fleming in Barcelona. He told the story of the eightieth birthday celebration of the oldest flower-seller in the *Rambla*. She was able to remember occasions when royalty and aristocrats had bought bouquets and button-holes from her, but her proudest moment, the one she treasured most, had been the day when the great Sir Alexander had stopped at her stall, for his penicillin had saved the life of her dearest friend.

The civic heart of Barcelona is that part of the old town which lies to the right of the *Rambla*, and between the Cathedral and the Plaça Sant Jaume, the *Barri Gòtic*, or Gothic Quarter. Here as part of the royal palace is the Tinell Room. The aim was to impress — a place where visiting princes and ambassadors could be received, or great ceremonies take place, in a setting that spoke of the grandeur of the Aragonese-Catalan court. The room is the best and most perfect example of Barcelona civic Gothic, a vast hall thirty metres long and fifteen metres wide, with great stone diaphragm arches. This whole complex of the royal palace, including its pretty little royal chapel of Santa Àgata and the curious watchtower, is built into and above the old Roman walls on the east side of the town. They open out onto an almost enclosed open space — the Plaça del Rei (King's Square) — which despite its name, Oriol Bohigas, the influential Barcelona architect and town-planner, has called a 'republican' open space at the heart of medieval Catalan democracy. It is now a popular venue in summer for concerts and plays and the traditional open-air cultural events which Catalans appreciate as much as visitors.

The civil authorities have equally impressive buildings nearby, where the Town Hall and the Generalitat Palace face one another across the Plaça Sant Jaume. The Generalitat Palace is best seen on St George's Day (April 23) when its staircase and courtyards are decorated with red roses to commemorate the life of Catalonia's mythical patron. The orange tree courtyard with its mouldering little fountain decorated with an exquisite statue of the saint is outstanding. The two neo-classical facades on the Plaça Sant Jaume are adequate, no more. At the Town Hall, as at the Stock Exchange, neo-classicism conceals Gothic, although there is an older decorative Gothic facade down a side street — the Carrer de la Ciutat. The City Hall was the seat of the medieval *Consell de Cent* (Council of One

Hundred), a council of notables which ran the affairs of the city, just as the Generalitat ran the affairs of Catalonia. Their council chamber is another beautiful example of the broad-arched public spaces created by Catalan Gothic architects.

So much for the architecture, what about the politics? The Generalitat Palace was the homes of the Corts (parliament) which represented the bishops, nobles and rich merchants and was established in 1283. During the fourteenth century it met on a three-yearly basis, with a smaller group of twelve of its members delegated to take decisions between sessions. This is the group to which the name Generalitat properly belongs. At the Town Hall, the Consell de Cent was less strictly hierarchical than the Corts, and evolved by trial and error through the thirteenth century. From 1274 the system was as follows. A committee of five councillors, plus the mayor and chief magistrate, chose a group of one hundred leading citizens to run the affairs of the city. At the end of each year, they would elect a new committee of councillors, who would then appoint a new council. The professionals and the merchants were always in there; the controversy was always about the extent of representation of the tradespeople of Barcelona, and at a number of points down the centuries, this issue came to the fore. One way to avoid conflict was a to draw lots, a system adopted in Barcelona in 1455, by which time it was in general use throughout Catalonia. This simply moved the battle-ground to the issue of which names should go into the green bag from which the lots were drawn. The two principal rival groups were the *Biga* (beam) and the *Busca* (splinter). The *Biga* represented the aristocrats and rich merchants and was in favour of free trade; the *Busca* was the party of the weavers and the lesser merchants, the shop-keepers and the tradespeople, but they were not averse to playing the populist card when it suited them. Both groups were prepared to carry their battles to the streets of Barcelona in the shape of gang-fights. Hughes' comparison with the

57

South Bronx does seem strained, but one should not underestimate the level of violence involved in medieval democracy.

Catalans are rightly proud of their democratic traditions, limited and disputed as they may have been. They made it possible to reconcile the interests of different groups in the society, while ensuring power to two important groups, merchants and tradespeople, on whom the general prosperity of the country depended. They limited the autonomy of the king while granting him sufficient power to hold the Aragonese-Catalan federation together. The system gave the Monarchy a strong vested interest in good government, a recurring theme in the more progressive areas of Europe, especially the Italian city-states. The oath of allegiance still rings impressively in the ears of Catalans and other nations who have recent memory of dictatorship: 'We, who are as good as you, swear to you, who are no better than us, to accept you as our king and sovereign lord, provided you observe all our liberties and laws — but if not, not.' This principle of 'If not, not' still makes good sense, but even then it was not without precedent. As early as the eleventh century, under Ramon Berenguer I, the first king who could truly claim lordship over Catalonia as a whole, the *Usatges* (Customs) had been drawn up. To describe this as a 'bill of rights' is to use too modern a term, but nevertheless, it did establish the principle of negotiated settlement to disputes between citizens. The rule of law, designed initially to control the nobles, also meant that the peasants could acquire leasehold rights over land, and the stability that this gave to rural Catalonia was to serve it well down the centuries.

A Culture for a Nation
The literary output of medieval Catalonia starts rather later than the political and commercial expansion. The fanciful story of Hairy Wilfred, to which we referred in the previous chapter, would have been written down in Latin

by the monks at Ripoll. Catalan, by and large, was the language of everyday life — of trade and commerce and political argument. You argued with your spouse or neighbour, your builder or shopkeeper, in Catalan, but learned arguments were still very much conducted in Latin. The situation is complicated still further by the continuing political and cultural links with the southern French lands where Provençal was spoken. Because Provençal was the language of courtly love and of poetry and as such widely used by the fashion-conscious, twelfth and thirteenth century Catalan poets generally wrote in Provençal.

Catalan literature came of age not on the mainland but in the rich diversity of the island of Majorca. Here Christian, Jewish and Muslim ideas and influences intertwined. The philosopher and mystic Ramon Llull, who lived from about 1233 until about 1315, was a man of enormous learning and energy. Scholasticism was the characteristic medieval endeavour to square the teachings of the church with the rediscovered philosophy of ancient Greece. To scholasticism, Llull brought the additional input of a thorough knowledge of Arabic. Through Arabic he was able in turn to access Greek writers in translation and also the newer wisdom of Islam, particularly in its mystical and poetic vein. He wrote philosophy in Catalan and then translated it into Latin for the benefit of the rest of Europe. The existence of an English version of his name (Raymond Lully) says something about his widespread reputation. His *Book of the Order of Chivalry* was printed in an English translation by Caxton. His first book, written in Arabic, which was a language he knew better than Latin, was supposed to have been one million words long. If Catalan princes and merchants wanted to conquer the Mediterranean by force of arms, Llull harboured a more ambitious project: to reunite Islam and the Jews with Christianity by force of argument and logic. It was an ambition perhaps shared by the Dominican order, spiritual advisers to the Aragonese Monarchy, and an ambition which was to be promoted in harsher form within

Catalonia, as persecution of the Jews became widespread in the later Middle Ages.

Llull was a Majorcan, son of the first generation of Catalan settlers on the island, but the best-known poets writing in Catalan, Jordi de Sant Jordi and Ausiàs March, were from Valencia. Their work dates from the first half of the fifteenth century. The population and prosperity of Catalonia, together with its political and cultural hegemony, were already in decline, wasted away by plague, foreign wars and attacks on the Jews, arguably the most dynamic economic group. To the rather formalistic linking of love and death in courtly poetry, these poets brought a more vivid and immediate sense of the insubstantial nature of human affection and activity in the face of death. Death was both certain in its finality but also uncertain because it could strike without warning. Love, on the other hand, was uncertain both in its occurrence and its fickleness. The fact that the Catalan words for love and death sound identical with the addition of the definite article — *l'amor* and *la mort* — gave endless scope for word play. Love, death and mortality, then, were the themes of these poets, and with them came the influence of the first Italian Renaissance — the works of Dante and Petrarch. March's obsessively morbid reflections on the death of the beloved can at time take the identification of love and death to extremes: love is fleeting and must end in unhappiness. The law of life is solitude, deprivation, sickness and death.

If medieval writers were at times unsure of their status and language, Catalan Gothic, as both an architectural and artistic style has an extraordinary variety and beauty. The best place to obtain an overview of Catalan Gothic is, as with Romanesque, the Catalan Art Museum at Montjuïc. While religious themes predominate, there is also a rich range of subject-matter. There are a set of murals from the Aguilar Palace, which now houses the Picasso Museum in Montcada Street, depicting in rich detail the conquest of Majorca by the Catalans. This concern with details of everyday life also comes into religious pictures, in ways that can make the Romanesque seem quite restricted by contrast. A contrary view would be that the concentrated, distilled emotion of the Romanesque becomes dissipated in the fussy ornamentation of the Gothic. There are successive influences from France, from Italy (especially in the work of the Serra family) and from Flanders, culminating in the imposing works of the fifteenth century realists Lluís Dalmau and Jaume Huguet. Pere Serra was active in Barcelona in the second half of the fourteenth century. His 'Virgin, Child and angels' from the Convent of Santa Clara in Tortosa is a work of both decorative beauty and emotional purity. The Virgin's blue robe is embroidered with a repeat pattern of a golden bird, while the Christ Child holds a goldfinch in his hand. The bird symbolises the divine spirit, while the angelic musicians remind us that the purpose of art is to express that divine spark.

A bus-ride out of Barcelona city centre, up on the hills, is the Monastery of Pedralbes. Established by nuns who followed the gentle teachings of St Clare and St Francis, Pedralbes is quite different from other Catalan monasteries, established by the Benedictines and Cistercians with motives which were as much political and economic as religious. The visitor enters through the cloister and almost immediately comes to the chapel of St Michael with its murals by Ferrer Bassa. Little is known about Bassa, except that he was active between 1324 and 1348 and that he was greatly influenced by Italian painters — especially Giotto and the Lorenzetti bothers. The colours are fading, there is some chipping of the surface and the subjects (the Joys of Our Lady, Life of Christ, figures of saints) are very traditional, but the treatment is lively and at times even humorous. Like some of the early Italians, he attempted 'correct' perspective but didn't always get it right. So there is a porch above a stable door in a Birth of Christ scene which appears to be about to be blown up into the air in a howling gale of wind. On the other hand there is real human drama in the Betrayal in the Garden and formal beauty of composition in the Burial and Annunciation scenes.

As late as the 1960s and 1970s the chapel could only be visited between twelve and two on a Sunday, but the Town Hall has negotiated an agreement with the nuns which has gradually made most of the complex of older buildings open to the visitor. The nuns, meanwhile, are now living in a more modern building close by. The chapter house, the kitchens, which boast equipment from the medieval to the modern, and the hospital wing help to give an impression of the busy and essentially useful life of a small convent of this kind. The nuns have always been interested in herbalism, from the days when herbs were the only medicine available, and herbs are still grown in the cloister gardens, alongside more decorative plants.

Just as the Counts of Barcelona had used Benedictine monasticism to secure their hold on, and develop, the Pyrenean valleys, so the Aragonese-Catalan monarchs used the Cistercians to develop New Catalonia. Lands down towards the River Ebro were granted to them by Ramon Berenguer IV and this is the origin of the three vast and controversial monasteries of Poblet, Santes Creus and Vallbona de les Monges. On paper, the rule of the Cistercians placed them under an obligation to have done with corruption and the lure of worldly wealth. But like many another new broom they swept the floor clean of one set of corruption and vice only to replace it by another. The crown was not deceived, for this was just what they had in mind: religious organisations which would organise the new territories socially and economically, and create wealth in which the state could share. There are times when medieval Catalonia seems all too much like the present writ large on the pages of history.

With wealth creation in mind, the nuns at Vallbona, on the edge of the plains of Lleida, drained the marshy valley and set up farms and villages. The approach to Poblet on the Francolí River is an unforgettable sight even today —

wide open views of rich, fertile country with vines, corn and fruit trees in abundance. The monks of Santes Creus extended their feudal powers across the rich olive and vine-growing country of the Penedès and the lowlands inland from Tarragona. At its peak, Poblet had jurisdiction over seven baronies, owned sixty villages and appointed the mayors of ten towns. A French visitor in 1316 reported that the monastery owned 53 mules, 40 horses, 1,100 calves, 1,215 sheep, 1,500 goats and 162 pigs. The monks who now live at Poblet are friendly and well informed about both the history of which they are custodians and also events outside their walls. This has never been a place shut off from the world. Poblet and Santes Creus were the preferred places of burial for the Aragonese-Catalan kings, and there are elaborate monuments to various Catalan monarchs. There is always an airy lightness to this New Catalonia Gothic, a celebration of life rather than a meditation on death, a sensuality which matches the pleasure-loving nature of Mediterranean culture and seems to mark a decisive break with the harsher world of the Pyrenees.

On a hill overlooking the Ebro, Tortosa Cathedral is the apotheosis of the new attitude to Gothic. The town itself promises very little. There are dull suburbs out along the road to Tarragona, dusty in summer, mired and puddled in winter. It owes its existence to the fact that for centuries it commanded the lowest crossing of the Ebro, one of the mightiest rivers in all Spain. But since the beginning of the last century, the main road and railway have crossed the river down at Amposta on the edge of the delta with a more recent motorway crossing nearby. The fate of Tortosa has been that of so many estuarial towns: trade ground to a halt back in the eighteenth century as the delta began to silt up to form the extensive rice paddies of today. Tortosa has acquired a shabby, old-fashioned air unlike that of any other Catalan town. But once through the suburbs, Tortosa begins to shyly show off its charms: art nouveau first and then penetrating back through the centuries, Renaissance and Gothic. The heights of Tortosa are occupied by the castle, now a state-run hotel or *parador*. There can be few hotels with a site as splendid, high above the city and the green Ebro snaking off inland between bare, cruel mountains — the badlands of Catalonia. The site has been successively Iberian and Roman settlements, Muslim fort and Catalan royal palace. But from here you look straight down upon the Cathedral and its network of flying buttresses and pinnacles which are as unique in Catalonia as Tortosa's first impressions of shabby decline. It reveals its structure at once, a nave with two aisles and a double ambulatory. From here there is an easy climb down between little houses and big cactuses to enter eventually through an archway into the cloister and then into the main church.

Inside the Cathedral is one outstanding work of art — the retable of the main altar, painted wood in an Italianate style, telling the life history of the Virgin Mary. The Virgin and Child are the centrepiece of the altar but the story flows on around this central image. In a series of panels and scenes, the altar tells of the annunciation and the birth with all those precious details which even the least religious will remember from school carol services — the shepherds in the fields, the child and his parents in the stable with the farm animals and the angels, who seem just as real as any of the other lifelike figures in the scene. From the ambulatory it is also possible to inspect the reverse of the retable. If the scenes that face the congregation are the light and optimistic view of life, here all is darkness and pessimism: Jesus betrayed by a kiss, a symbol of affection turned into a symbol of betrayal, then the agony of the crucifixion and the mystery of the empty tomb.

The Long Decline Begins

At Tortosa, we have returned to the Mediterranean, the focus of Catalonia's medieval adventures. Long gone are the ships of war or even the small trading vessels that once plied up and down the coast, across to Italy and North Africa and into the eastern reaches of the Mediterranean. Super-tankers, container vessels and, occasionally, USA aircraft carriers now rule the waves, as only Barcelona and Tarragona have facilities sufficiently big to give harbour to them. But what does remain is the fishing industry, in several dozen small harbours from the Ebro to the French border. The tuna and the coral have gone, but there is still a ready supply of food within easy reach of the shore (some would say too easy, fearing over-fishing). The sea is part of the Catalan consciousness, as it is for the English. As with English, the language betrays the importance of the sea to the Catalans. So *aferrar-se com un pop* (to cling on like an octopus) comes to mean taking up a strong doctrinal or political position. Hughes points to both the absolutism of the sea — the power and responsibility of the captain — but also its democracy, with the sharing of catch and profits. He quotes an old popular refrain that goes:

A la mar	At sea
no hi ha teu	There is no yours
ni meu.	Or mine.
A la mar	At sea
tot es teu	All is yours
i tot es meu.	And all is mine.

But the sea was not able to compensate for ever for the problems on dry land. Neither prayer nor medicine seemed able to avoid repeated visitations of the plague. The population of Catalonia is reckoned to have halved between 1350 and 1500, to a figure of some 300,000. There was social conflict too, particularly between the great landlords and the peasants. The Aragonese-Catalan kings seemed to have lost the touch which in conditions of economic growth balanced the competing interest of town and country, rich and poor, merchants and craftspeople. Alfons IV earned the title of the Magnanimous for favouring the peasants, but having abolished the hated *remences* (taxes on peasants) in 1455, he was forced by the rich to reinstate them the following year. The peasant agitators took the name *remences* from the taxes for which they were liable. War broke out in 1462 between king and nobles with peasant uprisings as a backdrop. In the towns artisans fought merchants; in the countryside peasants fought landowners, especially in the foothills of the Pyrenees beyond Girona. Joan II appeared to have won but it was a hollow victory. In order to secure support from Castile, which was being courted by the Catalan nobles, he married his son Ferran in 1469 to the Castilian princess Isabel. As Ferdinand and Isabella, they ruled as the 'Catholic Monarchs' and set Spain off in a new direction which had nothing to do with the Mediterranean and from which Catalans were to be firmly excluded. Aragon was bound into Castile, with Catalonia thrown in for good measure. Castile was much bigger than Catalonia and, in contrast to the present day position, more densely populated. There was trouble ahead.

Chapter 4

Backing the Wrong Horse

Living on the Edge

The Pyrenees are shared territory, and not just between France and Spain. There are Basques at the Atlantic end, Catalans at the Mediterranean end, both nations sprawling down the mountain sides north and south. And somewhere in the middle is Andorra, a tax haven still searching for a democratic future: the joint titular rulers are the President of France and the Bishop of Seu d'Urgell in the Segre valley on the 'Spanish' side. The Segre rises in France and flows across the bucolic plain of the Cerdanya into Spain. To the north are the high Pyrenees bordering Andorra, to the south the jagged peaks of the Cadí. Facing due north their steep slopes see the sun only in summer. In winter ominous black walls of bare rock stand out against snow-filled gulleys and snow-capped tops. But access to the Cerdanya from Barcelona is now simple: in addition to the train service, there is a fine road tunnel opened in the 1980s and a good connecting road (at least in stretches) down the Llobregat valley towards Barcelona and its network of coastal motorways. Part at least of the funding has come from the European Union. The new road has been of great assistance to the tourist and second homes industries, but not everyone approves. The Cerdanya has lost that special sense of an isolated paradise it once had.

Despite its new-found popularity, it is easy to leave the cars behind in the Cerdanya. Less easy to leave behind are people, given the Catalan love for not only the high places of their country, but also for sharing them with others. One particularly attractive ascent begins from a fork in the Bellver-Puigcerdà road at Ger (these odd, monosyllabic place-names are typical of the Cerdanya). From Meranges, which lives from farming and tourism, a mountain track climbs precipitously upwards through a wilderness of pine forests, wild raspberries and a profusion of pinks, thyme, heather, thistles, camomile and harebells, for this is the sunny, south-facing side of the valley. At the top of this track is the Refugi de Malniu, half mountain refuge and half snack-bar. From here it is a short, stiff walk to the lake of Malniu, an impressive landscape of giant boulders, rhododendrons and juniper. There are wild horses too, not the stunted ponies one might expect at over 2000 metres, but large, sleek beasts ambling about their business by the lake-side. There is swimming in the black, silent waters, in the foot or so of sun-drenched water that sits uneasily above the cold, mysterious depths. Across in France there are hot springs where nudity is the order of the day, both summer and winter, but in these high, cold tarns the swimmer must take care.

If Puigcerdà, with its railway station, frontier post, filling stations, shops and restaurants, is the largest town in the Cerdanya, there is little doubt that Bellver is the prettiest. At the Font de Talló, a little spring just outside the village, there is a tiny chapel and shrine, a picnic table and wood and stone benches, and on Easter Monday the local children come to sell sweet wine and *coca* (an almond-flavoured pastry) to visitors. The water gurgles gently from the earth, the crickets sing, the wind sighs in the willow trees, sounds as typical of the Cerdanya as the bells of the mixed herds of goat and sheep which in winter are taken out to the local pastures, and in summer up to the high alpine pastures above. Nearby is Bellver's own volcano, its crater marked by a shallow depression some six metres across, with butterflies dancing among the thyme and the sweet scent of pine permeating the air.

Bellver has changed little over the years, give or take some holiday homes on the fringes, although its characteristic capped church tower at the highest point of the town has been joined by a television transmission mast. Like most towns and villages in Catalonia, Bellver celebrates its *festa major* (main festival) in August. It sums up so well the charm of the Cerdanya, where people still live relatively close to the natural order of things. There is an open-air market in the main square, an irregular arcaded space fashioned out of bare stone at the top of the hill, a market cluttered with stalls selling honey, goat cheeses, pickled cheeses, herbs, sausages, dried flowers and the many varieties of mushrooms collected locally, dried and much used in local cooking. Exactly the kind of market which the English have tried to re-invent with their Farmers' Markets. The children sell great bunches of herbs which they have been up the mountains to collect.

Contact across the border, legal and illegal, is a constant of both Basque and Catalan life. Laurie Lee, in *As I Walked Out One Midsummer Morning*, recounts an alarming crossing into Spain in the early months of the Spanish War. Following his guide in the darkness across the mountains, his only hope of survival was to keep up with the shadowy figure hurrying on ahead of him. But as ever the only true drama of a Laurie Lee story is Laurie Lee. We can never know how much of the tale is truth and how much fiction. Cela, in his travel book on the Lleida Pyrenees, also tells a story of an 'unofficial' crossing to see a relation on the French side, walking across a remote bit of border in the Vall d'Aran. Even before the European Union abolished border controls, there were numerous points where it could be crossed unofficially with some ease, at least one of them along a paved road. This relates to the town of Llívia, the little enclave of the Spanish state a few miles beyond the official border at Puigcerdà. The Editorial Alpina map and guidebook of the Cerdanya treat the valley, French and Spanish, as a whole. Use of this map makes the following diversion possible: from the

French Conflent valley and Sallagossa (Saillagouse), turn aside from the international road which carefully skirts Llívia, turn right by the station along the road through Ro and drive straight into the town. Llívia is a relaxed kind of place — even before the Euro was introduced in 2002 it accepted payment in pesetas or francs, a model of the new Europe where money-making can take place regardless of international frontiers and national governments. It also has some historical interest, with what claims to be the oldest pharmacy in Europe, and an ancient stone tower used as a prison on the ground-floor and with a chamber above where the Town Council, chosen by lot, used to meet. How Llívia came to be an anomaly in the otherwise clear division of the Cerdanya between France and Spain we shall now reveal.

The Lucky Escape

The Revolt of the Catalans in 1640 is one of the few episodes in Catalan history (apart from the Spanish War of 1936-39) which is well covered in English, thanks to the monumental work of Sir John Elliott. As we saw in the last chapter, Catalonia's economic decline was followed by its absorption into a Spanish federation with Castile, but it remained a recognisable political entity with its own rights and privileges and its own institutions. Elliott's book spans 42 years in 600 pages. It is certainly exhaustive. Drawing on many unpublished, original sources, Elliott gives a brilliantly detailed account of Catalan society at a critical moment in its history, in transition from the late medieval to the early modern. The character, policies and influence of the Count Duke of Olivares, the key Castilian politician of his age, are analysed, and Elliott pays particular attention to his desire that Catalonia should contribute financially towards Spain's dream of European hegemony. When Olivares wrote in 1640, 'Really, the Catalans ought to see more of the world than Catalonia', he was arguably firing the first broadside of globalisation. In 1516 the Hapsburg Charles (First of Spain, Fifth of the Empire) had come to the Spanish throne, but each Hapsburg emperor-king swore to uphold and observe Catalan laws. Beyond that they had little interest in Catalonia. Barcelona was still a rich city, but its growth was slow, and it was Seville and Cádiz in the far south-west of Spain which enjoyed the royal monopoly on trade with the colonies in America.

Catalonia did not take part in the political agitations in other parts of Spain as the Hapsburgs tightened their grasp on political power. There was conflict between the emperor-kings and the great cities of Castile with their jealously guarded municipal rights. The *germanies* (guilds of merchants and artisans) rose in Valencia and Majorca. Philip II altered some of the traditional freedoms of Aragon. In each case, the Catalans remained silent. 'If not, not' — the principle that had regulated relations between monarch and subjects in medieval Catalonia — was something to keep quiet about. Rights had been replaced by royal prerogative. There was an uneasy peace between Catalonia and her new relations. The inevitable quarrel was precipitated by the Count Duke of Olivares, the chief minister of Philip IV. His ambition was no less than to establish a uniform set of laws, levies and taxes across Spain, whatever its peoples with their separate local traditions might think. Spain needed the money, not for Spain, but to finance wider Hapsburg interests in Europe. Olivares wanted money and he wanted men for the Army, for the Thirty Years War was in full swing from 1618 onwards. Under the Union of Arms, Catalonia was required to raise 16,000 men. In 1622, and again in 1635, there was war with France. Catalan towns and villages objected both to having to feed and quarter foreign troops stationed on their land, and to being conscripted into Hapsburg armies. In 1640 the authorities imprisoned several members of the Barcelona Council of One Hundred, and Pau Claris, priest and President of the Generalitat. In response 1,500 peasants entered Barcelona and freed the prisoners.

This was the beginning of a major war that was to rumble on from 1640 to 1652 and in the nineteenth century was to give Catalonia its national song *Els Segadors* (The Reapers) for it had been peasants preparing for the harvest who had initiated the revolt in the summer of 1640. Just as Catalonia had not come to the assistance of Valencia and Majorca, so now the Majorcans and Valencians in turn stood to one side. There was only one place to look for support and that was to France. It was a serious error of judgement. Under Pau Claris, the Generalitat pronounced Louis XIII king of Catalonia, and a French army marched in and defeated the Hapsburg army at Montjuïc. But most of the French army departed in 1648, leaving the Catalans alone. After a year's siege, Barcelona surrendered in 1652. Apart from the disgrace of Olivares, little had been won, and territory lost. Under the terms of the Treaty of the Pyrenees in 1659, the French took the Catalan counties of Roselló (Rousillon), Conflent, Vallespir and the upper half of the Cerdanya. This redrawing of the map reduced the population of Catalonia by one fifth. But someone in a palace somewhere did not get it quite right. And the town of Llívia remains to this day stranded among the green fields of France.

In 1659 no-one believed that the Treaty of the Pyrenees had settled the border for all time. The keenness of the French to hang on to their new possessions is apparent from the money they spent to employ Vauban and his colleagues to fortify the village of Mont Lluís (Mont Louis) at the head of the Conflent valley and the town of Vilafranca de Conflent (Villefranche-du-Conflent) further down the valley towards Perpinyà (Perpignan). Mont Lluís in particular was a brand new fortress controlling the entrance to the Conflent valley from the Cerdanya, although Vilafranca had been fortified since the Middle Ages. Nowadays, Vilafranca is predominantly a tourist town, its narrow streets packed with restaurants and craft shops full of leather, wool, dried flowers, honey and jam, herbs and spices. People seem busier and quicker here than in the small towns across the frontier. There are 'We speak Catalan' signs in shops and even 'We are Catalan' slogans at the roadside. But the Catalan names of villages are reluctantly posted below the French ones, and the Catalan effort seems both less natural, and to have gained less official recognition, than is the case over the border. The centralised French state appears to have been extremely successful in eliminating indigenous language and culture.

The Unlucky Trap

Rather to their own surprise, the Catalans were permitted to keep many of their separate institutions after 1659. They had certainly backed the wrong horse in the 1640s and 1650s. In 1701 they seemed to have backed a racing certainty, in the shape of the Archduke Charles of Austria. The details are complex, and beside the point, but the last Spanish Hapsburg Emperor-King, Carlos II, had died without an heir. All Europe had an interest in the outcome. The man who ascended the Spanish throne was the French Philip of Anjou, the first Spanish Bourbon, who ruled as Felipe V. This virtual union of two of the great powers of Europe was unacceptable to England, to Austria and to Holland. The Catalans, who had been betrayed by their French allies fifty years before and had been treated rather better than they deserved by the Hapsburgs, supported the Austrian candidate. How could they lose?

In 1702, an anxious Felipe V visited Barcelona with wild promises to the Corts. In view of his later reputation as Spain's centralising king *par excellence*, we can be confident of their insincerity. Certainly there were assurances of Barcelona's status as a free port with some participation in the American trade, and Philip made the right sort of noises about Catalan traditions and autonomy. There was even mention of Roselló, Valencia and the Balearics ... The Catalans refused to believe him, but at least acted with some caution. In 1703, Charles was crowned in Vienna as Charles III of Castile, but also of Aragon and

Catalonia. In 1705, with the war going well, Catalonia declared publicly for Charles. Charles invaded Spain, but did not receive the support he had been promised by the English fleet. Perfidious Albion was playing her usual tricks. By 1711, Charles was retreating north out of Catalonia and the Catalans were left to discover at their leisure that there is no such thing as a racing certainty.

In 1713 England made its separate peace. In 1714 Charles became, rather to his own surprise, Charles VI of the Holy Roman Empire, a job he clearly found more appealing than Charles III of the unruly Iberians. The English and the Dutch, as alarmed by too close an alliance between Austria and Spain as they had been by too close an alliance between France and Spain, were now quite sure that Charles must be kept permanently out of Spain. The Catalans were left on their own, and had only their own heroism by which to remember a disastrous war. It was an advance instalment of 1936, with every male over the age of fourteen issued with a gun. The Bourbons laid siege to Barcelona, led by an unlikely general — the Duke of Berwick, bastard son of the deposed James II of England. People starved, religious fanaticism ruled, and Barcelona, led by its Council of One Hundred, did not surrender. On 11 September 1714, the Bourbons entered Barcelona, and two centuries later 11 September became the national day of Catalonia. The Bourbons clearly thought that such a rash, intemperate people needed to be saved from themselves, or at least from their leaders. All things must change.

* * *

On the main road from Barcelona to Lleida is the attractive little town of Cervera. This is a pleasant, if unspectacular, part of Catalonia, outside the irrigated plain of Lleida but surrounded by olive-groves, almond trees and (in spring) green fields. For nearly three centuries in the early Middle Ages, this was a war zone and the villages tend to huddle together on hilltops. Besides, water is usually in short supply and this again explains the small number of settlements. The main road plunges into a tunnel through the hill on which Cervera is set. For many motorists, a glimpse of the late medieval walls or a church-tower in the rear-view mirror is all they ever see of Cervera. On the Barcelona side of Cervera, the restoration of the old city walls shows that the town always had a certain status. But there is nothing to prepare you for the monstrous grandeur of the university buildings which dominate the centre of town. The University was erected between 1718 and 1740 in the grand classical manner, its massive buildings arranged around two courtyards. Cervera has worked hard over the years to find a use for its university: a school occupies part of it, the Institut Français has passed this way, there is a study centre for UNED, Spain's Open University. Catalonia, one senses, is partly ashamed of Cervera, partly baffled at the level of ambition and vision needed to find a new use for such a white elephant in a small, provincial town.

Cervera is no stranger to Catalan history. Three times it has played its part in the history of its country. It was here in 1359, in a house in the Carrer Major (high street) that the Corts decided to institute the Generalitat, a civil power to balance royal power. Then in 1469, the marriage contract was signed here between Isabella of Castile and Ferdinand of Aragon which was to draw to a close the power of Catalonia as an independent state. Act 3 in Cervera was to be the aftermath of 11 September 1714. By 1716, Felipe had fixed the new rules (the *Nova Planta*) under which Catalonia was to be integrated into the rest of his Spanish state. The institutions of both Barcelona and Catalonia, built up and carefully protected over the centuries, were swept away: Corts, Generalitat and Council of One Hundred. The Catalan language was banned from official use. Military rule was imposed on Barcelona, and a whole swathe of the city demolished to build the fortress of the Ciutadella (now park, zoo and unlikely home of the Catalan parliament). The Catalan universities of Lleida and Barcelona were abolished. And this is where Cervera comes in, a quiet provincial spot where a university could grow free from the political passions of the great cities. From 1726 to 1842 it was Catalonia's only university. The Bourbons may have been autocratic but they were not stupid. Later in the eighteenth century they were to produce a state-sponsored Enlightenment to equal those of France or Russia. But Cervera itself was never especially enlightened. In an address to Ferdinand VII, the arch-conservative king who restored 'order' after the Napoleonic Wars, the university stated: 'Far be from us the dangerous novelty of thinking' (Brenan, The Spanish Labyrinth, p. 50). The university is above all a monument, a symbol, of a certain ideal of centralised, monolithic, orderly society which appeared all-powerful in its day, but which held the seeds of its own destruction. If society was an organism to be understood and controlled by the same scientific methods that were beginning to be applied to the physical world, then who was to say what constituted a good society, and who was to write its rules?

New forces were already stirring in Europe which were to overwhelm the absolutist regimes of the eighteenth century, impaled upon the contradictions between autocracy and science. If France was never the same after 1789, then neither was Spain. It was in Cádiz in Spain that the first liberal constitution in Europe was agreed, in 1812. Nineteenth century Spain swayed between Monarchy and Republic, church and secular interests, conservatives and liberals, but everywhere the authority of the state was challenged. By 1842, Barcelona again had its university, and the movement known as the *Renaixença* (Renaissance) of Catalan language and literature had begun. Such a long-term outcome would have been far from the minds of those who watched the Bourbon troops enter Barcelona on 11 September 1714.

The Catalan Phoenix

Victor Alba, a veteran of the Spanish war of 1936-39 who spent six years in Franco's prisons before eventually creating a new life for himself as a writer and North American university professor, emphasises the economic changes which lay behind Catalonia's startling recovery from the defeat of 1714. The eighteenth century saw the emergence in Catalonia of a new middle-class, whose industry and trade were much more closely integrated into the rest of Spain, and even with the Spanish Empire, than had been the case in earlier centuries. For Alba, Catalonia 'came out of the back room' of history (Catalonia: a Profile, p. 39). Together with the Basque Country, it became the main social and economic force for change in Spain. Catalan businessmen supported the changes instituted by the enlightened monarchs of the second half of the eighteenth century — measures such as the decision in 1778 to open trade with America to all Spaniards and end the Seville/Cádiz monopoly, the removal of laws which prevented women and children from working, and tariff protection. These measures favoured the growth of new industries. The Jesuits were expelled in 1778 for their opposition to change. The Royal Commercial Junta, established in Barcelona in 1758, presided over a textile industry of two thousand factories by the end of the century. In other parts of Spain, economic modernisation from the top down foundered in the years of the Napoleonic Wars and the loss of most of the American empire at the beginning of the nineteenth century. But in Barcelona, it began a process of economic growth which continued almost without interruption until the outbreak of the Spanish War in 1936.

By 1800, Barcelona was a city of nearly 100,000 people, tightly constrained within the city walls. There were villages on the narrow plain between sea and mountains, many of them preserved as at least names of modern suburbs — Horta, Sant Gervasi, Gràcia, Sarrià — but only one zone of settlement outside the wall could be called part of the city. This was the still surviving district of the Barceloneta (little Barcelona) which was home to many of the city's fishing families. It had been built to replace the district destroyed by the Bourbons in order to build the Ciutadella fortress. Through the nineteenth century, Barcelona's population rose steadily, reaching 184,000 by 1857, 337,000 in 1877 and half a million by the century's end, by which time the walls were a distant and fading memory. There was steady movement from country to city, and a progressive transformation from a traditional society of aristocrats and peasants to one of an urban working class exploited by an industrial and commercial bourgeoisie. In most of the rest of Spain, life went on much as it had done before, rooted in the problems and perspectives of the past. For all its lack of national institutions, Catalonia had again acquired a distinct identity within the Spanish state.

More than anything, the forces that drove this bounding expansion of Barcelona, and to a lesser extent of the whole country, were part and parcel of the very reforms brought in by the Bourbons. If much of the rest of Spain was indifferent to tariff reform or the relaxation of the laws which stood in the way of the full exploitation of labour, Catalan industrialists knew very well how to use these changes. Above all, the new rules which permitted Catalan participation in the American trade were a motor of economic development. By the middle of the nineteenth century, strange new buildings had started to appear along the coasts of Catalonia. These buildings reflected not just the wealth of their owners as buildings have always done, but new and exotic tastes in design and decoration. These were the houses of a group referred to variously as *indianos* (Indians) or *americanos* (Americans), Catalans who had made their fortunes in America, and especially in Cuba and Puerto Rico, the two Caribbean colonies that remained after the collapse of the Spanish empire at the beginning of the nineteenth century.

These processes can be seen at work not just in Barcelona, but also in smaller towns along the Catalan coast. Why, for example, does the small industrial, fishing and seaside town of Vilanova i la Geltrú, south of Sitges, have a railway station that looks more like a colonial palace than a station? The answer is that it was paid for by Francesc Gumà i Ferran, a local boy who had gone out to Cuba at the age of seventeen in 1850. He was by no means alone. Vilanova historians have calculated that 1,200 local people went to Cuba to make their fortunes in the first sixty years of the nineteenth century. Between 1803 and 1817, 24% of all the Catalans who arrived in Cuba came from this one town. Gumà i Ferran worked as a merchant and financier in Cuba. On his return to Vilanova, his range of activities reflected the varying ways in which returning migrants impacted on the growth of the town. He was instrumental in establishing the Banc de Vilanova, which in turn provided finance for the Italian firm Pirelli to build a factory there in 1902. First as a manufacturer of tyres, and later of fibre optics, Pirelli has been a mainstay of the local economy ever since. Gumà i Ferran, apart from his railway interests, set up the publishing house of the local newspaper in 1879, now published in Catalan as the *Diari de Vilanova*. He was also responsible for a local park and for the heavy new facade of the church of Saint Anthony. In similar fashion, the public water supply, schools and hospitals also benefited from the new wealth. There was property speculation, especially along the *Rambla*, the main street of the town leading down from the old town centre towards the sea. And that meant more work for architects and designers.

In Barcelona itself, the richest symbol of Catalonia's new wealth is the rather run down porticoed neo-classical block called the *Porxos d'en Xifré* opposite the Stock Exchange, remarkable at first sight only for the well-known Set Portes (Seven Doors) restaurant on the ground floor. Josep Xifré had made his fortune exporting sugar grown on slave estates in Cuba to the United States of

America. Returning to Barcelona in 1831 he rapidly diversified into banking and property, and became the largest property owner in town. The arcades are decorated with reliefs which depict the 'heroes' who had opened up America to contact with Europe — Columbus, Magellan, Cortés, Pizarro — and the sources of the wealth of the Caribbean: slaves, bananas and coffee especially. Amid the noise and fumes of this part of town, it is all too easy to miss the symbolism. Xifré was not the only Catalan bourgeois to use wealth acquired in America to build more wealth at home. Miquel Biada traded guns in Venezuela where they were used to exterminate troublesome Indian tribes, set up the first steam-driven cloth mill in his home town of Mataró, and built Spain's first railway — from Mataró to Barcelona, opened in 1848. The textile empire of the Güell family was based on America too. Joan Güell, father of Gaudí's patron Eusebi Güell, began his working life in a textile factory in Havana, Cuba. And after various travels and adventures, including losing an uninsured vessel piled high (too high?) with goods for Cuba, Güell established a cloth factory in the Barcelona suburb of Sants — now home to Barcelona's main railway station. Little wonder that the adjacent park is called the Park of Industrial Spain.

The Powder Keg of Nineteenth Century Catalonia

From unlikely beginnings in the *Nova Planta*, designed by the Bourbons to put an end to Catalan rights, a new and powerful industrial force had appeared. But political problems remained, exacerbated by the growing disparity between industrial, modernising Catalonia and the generally reactionary society, its economy still linked to agriculture, of the rest of Spain. The drama of modern Catalonia had begun.

First among these problems was the church. The Jesuits had been expelled from all of Spain in the eighteenth century, and there was growing opposition to the role of the church in the social and economic life of the country. The church also actively intervened in political struggles between liberals and conservatives which dominated much of the first half of the nineteenth century in Catalonia. At times this erupted in open warfare, for example in the 1827 *Guerra dels Agraviats* (War of the Malcontents) or later in the three Carlist Wars. Ultra conservative supporters of absolute monarchy and the church set fire to farms and shops owned by suspected liberals. Outside Barcelona, factories were burned, their very existence identified as a threat to traditional values. In 1833, on the death of Ferdinand VII, this rural agitation was transformed into the first of the Carlist wars, with the traditionalists backing Carlos, the brother of the autocratic dead king Ferdinand VII, against the liberal supporters of the three-year old queen who reigned as Isabel II. The Carlists claimed that a woman could not inherit the throne of Spain. At one level, Carlism was supported by rural Catalonia, but at another it contributed to the growth of Barcelona, with large numbers of peasants fleeing the countryside to find work in its factories. And in almost contrary manner to the expected conservatism of rural Catalonia, anti-clericalism erupted in 1835. The traditionalists might burn the factories, but the liberals would burn the monasteries. This began in Reus, south of Tarragona, in revenge for attacks on local liberals. It led to the burning of the Cistercian monastery at Poblet, the Carthusian convents at Scala Dei and Montalegre, and the Benedictine monastery at Sant Cugat del Vallès. In Barcelona it led to the Burning of the Convents, the worst violence of a violent century, which began with the throwing of benches and rubbish into the bullring at a bullfight supposed to celebrate the infant queen's birthday. Nowadays Catalans seldom attend bullfights, but still throw cushions down from the upper tiers of the stands to express their discontent on a bad night at the Camp Nou football ground. From the bullring to the convent of the Capuchins in the *Rambla* was a small step. This was not about religion, or rather not about religious belief, but about the centuries long support given by the church as an institution to absolute monarchy. When anarchists burned the churches in Catalonia in 1936, they received the same popular acclaim as their liberal counterparts a century earlier.

Little link then with English liberalism? After all, English liberals did not go around burning churches. But there was a link, in the person of Juan Álvarez Mendizábal, who chose 1835 to return to Spain from exile in England. Isabel II's regent welcomed him into the liberal government as Minister of Finance. He had learned a lot in England. In particular he had become convinced of the virtues of the free market, as laid down in the doctrines of Adam Smith. We do not know if he had also studied the dissolution of the monasteries as practised by Henry VIII. For Mendizábal, there was one easy solution to the power of the church — to abolish it. Or rather to pass a law declaring that most church land was now state land. It could now be sold at auction, thus benefiting state coffers but also bringing a new dynamism to the economy. It was much the same trick that Henry VIII had pulled. Soon four fifths of church land in Barcelona had been sold off. Three quarters of the church lands in Catalonia in both town and country were sold between 1837 and 1845, and everywhere it was the urban bourgeoisie who were the winners.

The second problem was this: Catalonia was growing in power, but what was Catalonia? A region of Spain was the official answer, carefully divided into provinces for strictly administrative purposes along French lines by the liberals who had come to power with the infant queen in 1833. In the traditions of the French Jacobins, they were centralists by nature. But even during the French revolutionary period, and again at the meeting in Cádiz in 1812 which had drawn up Europe's first liberal constitution, the question of Catalan rights had been raised. In 1794 the Jacobins had even offered to buy off the Catalans by creating an independent Catalan Republic. Slowly the Catalans reinvented their own traditions, reinvented a time when they had been powerful, when Catalan rather than Spanish had been the language of literature, business and the state. From the 1830s, poetry began to be written in Catalan, which had remained the daily language of the street in both town and village. In 1859 the medieval *jocs florals* (Floral Games) were revived with competitions for music and literature. Romanticism revered the past, and the past was Catalan. This *Renaixença* (Renaissance) would in turn give rise to specific political, cultural and educational demands under the generic heading of Catalanism. It was a term which suggested that every issue in public life had a specifically Catalan dimension, with the implication that no solution would be acceptable if it did not recognise that dimension. The implications of that position are still being worked out.

The third and final problem which was to grow, flourish, transmogrify and pervade the nineteenth and twentieth century was the issue of social class, and in particular the relations between social classes. At one level, the Catalan bourgeoisie was a progressive force, agitating for change in the social and economic field in a country that was by and large backward and poor, and had recently lost the vast majority of its American empire. But at another level it was extremely reactionary. Its attitude to its workers was very much modelled on England — poor wages, worse conditions, exploited child and female labour, and little or no attention to the social needs (housing and welfare) of the industrial working class it had created to serve its purposes. The cultural renaissance was not for them, although they used Catalan as their daily language and considered themselves to be as Catalan as the participants in the Floral Games.

The callous indifference of employers tended to bring together the skilled workers and artisans with the unskilled working class, despite the latter having indulged in machine-breaking as an alternative protest weapon when they ran short of churches to burn in 1835. In the 1850s they also resorted to torching several factories that were attempting to increase productivity by introducing semi-automatic machinery — the *selfactines*. The authorities alternately tolerated and tried to stamp out the mutual aid societies and trade unions set up by the workers. By the second half of the nineteenth century, Catalonia was fertile ground for anarchism, and the ideas of Charles Fourier. If the labour of the working class was the true source of wealth, could not the working class refashion society for its own ends? What need was there for church, state and capitalism?

While the bourgeoisie adopted many of the trappings of medieval Catalan culture, the working classes stuck more closely to that long tradition of common action which runs through Catalan history. Alongside trade unions and political parties, this meant adult education and cultural centres, workers' choirs and sports clubs, libraries and co-operatives. Far from the popular image of bomb-throwing extremists, Alba describes the Catalan working class as 'sober and petit bourgeois in its habits, even among its most passionate anarchists.' The move from bomb-throwing to industrial organisation was confirmed by the establishment of the anarcho-syndicalist trade union, the CNT, in 1907. But the workers did not ignore the call to arms when it came. In 1909 there was a whole week of general strike and riots — the *Setmana Tràgica* (Tragic Week) — against the sending of Catalan reservists to fight a colonial war in Morocco. Some eighty churches, monasteries and religious schools were destroyed. The death-toll reached 83. The government needed a scapegoat, and found one in Francisco Ferrer, the founder of a libertarian Adult Education School — the *Escola Moderna*. Despite an international campaign, he was tried by a military court and shot. Many more Catalans were to die violent deaths before the century was half over.

Chapter 5
The Spanish War 1936-39

War and Civil War

This chapter does not pretend to compete with the exhaustive accounts of historians of the Spanish Civil War, 1936–39, the outlines of which are now relatively well known by English language readers. Instead, it focuses on the relationship between Britain and Spain generated by the war, the sufferings of the Spanish and Catalan people, and the way in which the outcome of the war has affected the subsequent history of Catalonia. In particular, it is concerned with the various ways in which both British and Catalans have attempted to understand those terrible events in the 1930s.

The British people have every reason to be proud of their response to the Spanish war. Public support for the Republic was high. An early public opinion poll in 1937 showed 14% supporting recognition of Franco and 86% opposed. As late as January 1939, support for the republic was 71%, with 10% opposed and 19% backing neither side. (Buchanan, Britain and the Spanish Civil War, pp. 22/3) At a time when the fascist regimes in Germany and Italy (and, less enthusiastically, the Communist regime in the Soviet Union) were pouring support into Spain, the British government chose to support and promote the policy of neutrality or 'non-intervention'. Not so the people. From all four British nations, aid went to Spain. This mainly took the form of food aid and medical supplies for the republican armies and for civilian casualties of bombing. In 1937, when the republican government took the decision to evacuate large numbers of children from Bilbao and surrounding districts as the Franco armies approached, 4,000 children and a small number of adults were sent from Bilbao to Southampton. They were admitted by the reluctant British government on the express condition that they would be no charge on the public purse. Dispersed in families and small communities round the country, they were entirely cared for by donations from trade unions and co-operative organisations, and by private giving and support. Recently, their story has been told by Adrian Bell (*Only for Three Months: the Basque Children in Exile*) based on the memories of those who came and those who cared for them. Some lost contact with their families, caught up in the destruction and confusion of war. Some never returned and lived out their lives in Britain. A few are still living here.

The exploits of the International Brigades, who went out to fight for the Republic, are better known. They are often referred to as the 'men' who went to Spain, but the first to die was Felicia Browne on 25 August 1936, only five weeks after the outbreak of war. She had found herself in Barcelona for the alternative People's Olympics for athletes who opposed the holding of the 1936 Olympic Games in Berlin. She volunteered immediately and fought on the Aragon Front. She was a sculptress who had trained at the Slade School. A book of her drawings was sold posthumously in support of Spanish Medical Aid. Women also saw distinguished service in the ambulance corps and in hospitals. Despite the official policy of non-intervention, volunteers found their way to Spain, especially if they were members or supporters of the Communist Party which was the best organised recruiting agency for the Republic. South Wales, where the Communist Party had a strong local organisation and presence in local government, sent a number of men to fight in Spain. For many years there had been strong links with Spain because of the presence of highly political Spanish miners in the Welsh valleys, in particular at Dowlais near Merthyr and at Abercrave in the Upper

Swansea Valley. There were close connections between a number of political themes in the 1930s, in particular agitation against the endemic unemployment within the capitalist system and opposition to the rise of fascism in Europe (including Mosley's blackshirts in England). The men and women of the International Brigades are well remembered. At the last count there were 52 memorials in England, Wales, Scotland and Ireland, from Achill (County Mayo) to St Albans and from Aberdeen to Rottingdean. The best known is in Jubilee Gardens on London's South Bank which in less than 20 years has survived the demolition of the Greater London Council and Inner London Education Authority, the building of the Jubilee Line and the erection right next to it of the London Eye as part of London's Millennium celebrations.

Walter Gregory, whose memoir of the Spanish war was published only in 1986, traced his own political radicalisation in the East Midlands to his decision to join the Tyneside Hunger march of 1934. Two men stood out in his memory — Bobbie Elliott and Wilf Jobling:

> Bobbie's immediate subordinate on the march was Wilf Jobling. Wilf was an extremely attractive personality. He was athletically built, with a powerful voice, which was ideal for addressing open-air meetings, and a wonderfully persuasive magnetism. Tirelessly Wilf would walk up and down the length of the marching column of shabbily dressed and weary men, urging them on with words of encouragement and offering advice on how to treat tired and blistered feet. Like Bobbie, Wilf was to fight in Spain against the Nationalists and it was a great loss to the cause of working class radicalism in Britain that both of them were killed in 1937 within a few months of each other: Wilf at Jarama in February, Bobbie at Brunete in July. (Gregory, The Shallow Grave, p. 168)

Gregory was certain, too, that the war could not be seen as an exclusively Spanish affair, as the term civil war suggests. He wrote:

Although the war was fought exclusively on Spanish soil, I never saw it as a domestic conflict. To this day I cannot view it except as part of the struggle between the forces of fascism and democracy that was being fought out throughout Europe. When I served in the British Navy from 1941 onwards . . . I always considered that I was simply engaged in a further round of the fight against Fascism which I had entered in 1936.

For precisely this reason, the use of the term Spanish War is preferred in this book to the common English phrase Spanish Civil War. There is no doubt that without foreign intervention, the course of the war would have been very different. Without Italian and German support, it might not have begun, for the crack fighting force at the disposal of the rebels was the Army of Africa, which had to be brought over to Spain in August 1936 by German military aircraft (the Junkers 52s) and a fleet of merchant ships protected by Italian military aircraft. There is also no doubt that other international events influenced the progress of the war. Most noticeably, Soviet aid became even more half-hearted after Chamberlain's return from Munich in 1938 announcing 'peace in our time'. Aware of the probable need to do a deal of at least temporary nature with Hitler, Stalin came to see the Spanish War as having little interest for Mother Russia.

Spanish Labyrinth: Catalan Maze

Catalonia was a complex place politically at the opening of the twentieth century. The Republic which was established in 1931 was always an uneasy compromise between middle class reformist politics and working class revolutionary politics. It might help to begin by reviewing some of the major groupings which were to play a part in deciding Catalonia's destiny between 1931 and 1939.

Confederación Nacional del Trabajo (CNT)	The Anarchist (or anarcho-syndicalist) trade union which was the most powerful Catalan working class organisation in the 1930s. More members than socialist-communist UGT.
Esquerra Republicana Catalana (ERC)	Welded together a number of small centre left Catalan parties after 1917 General Strike. Became dominant party in the Catalan government (the Generalitat) after 1931, first under Macià, then Companys. Still exists, and now part of ruling coalition in Generalitat.
Falange	Spanish fascist organisation. Together with church and big business was the main supporter of Franco's military rising in 1936. Remained important throughout Franco period.
Nationalists	The term usually used for supporters of General Franco in the war, as opposed to 'Republicans'.
Partido Obrero de Unificación Marxista (POUM)	A left communist political party denounced by the communists as 'Trotskyist'. Involved in street fighting in Barcelona in 1937.
Partit Socialista Unificat de Catalunya (PSUC)	Catalan Communist Party, formed from a number of smaller communist groups in 1936.
Republicans	Those who supported the legitimate Republican government after the 1936 military rebellion.

The Republic began badly, at least in Barcelona. Macià, the Catalan leader, declared not the Spanish Republic but the Catalan Republic. The re-establishment of the

Generalitat in 1931 was a compromise, suggested by Spanish socialist Minister of Justice, Fernando de los Ríos, to deal with that fact. To the officer corps in the army and to the small but growing adherents of the fascist Falange, this was anathema. Spain was 'one, great and free', and 'one' meant precisely no concessions to Catalans and Basques. The Republic struggled from the beginning to deal with both the political question of Catalan rights and the ferment of agitation in society — in the countryside the conflict between anarchist peasants, the landowners and the church, and in the cities between industrialists and trade unions. Gerald Brenan's *The Spanish Labyrinth*, first published in 1943 and much reprinted since, remains an indispensable guide to the politics of the 1930s. As he puts it in a striking comparison: 'The Spanish Republic can be compared to the League of Nations. It was an attempt to found a regime of law and justice and comparative decency in a situation where hitherto only injustice and violence had prevailed.' (Spanish Labyrinth, pp. 261–2)

The situation became more complicated still in 1934. Macià died on Christmas Day 1933, just after the Right had come to power in national elections. The new Catalan president, Lluís Companys, then won the elections for the Catalan parliament and set about the issue of land reform. Companys had an impeccable Left background, having worked for the anarcho-syndicalist trade union CNT as a lawyer, and having set up the union of the *rabassaires*, the Catalan peasant grouping within ERC. With their co-operatives, credit unions and mutual aid societies, the *rabassaires* were a potential model of agricultural reform for the whole of Spain. For precisely that reason, the right-wing government in Madrid resisted the moderate law of agricultural reform passed by the Generalitat, which gave tenants rights to acquire land they had rented for fifteen years. The Spanish government declared the law illegal; Companys responded by upping the stakes, declaring to the people from the Generalitat Palace in Barcelona: 'The government over which I am presiding assumes all the faculties of power in Catalonia, (and) proclaims the Catalan State of the Spanish Federal Republic.' After brief but intense fighting, the Generalitat was suspended, while Companys and his fellow ministers ended up in jail. It would not be Companys' last experience of prison.

In 1934 it was the Left in Spain (most noticeably in the Generalitat and in the revolt among the Asturian miners put down with great brutality by the rising star of the Spanish Army — Francisco Franco) which was not prepared to accept the legitimacy of the Right in government. In 1936 the situation was reversed. A Popular Front government was elected and the Generalitat was reinstated. The Right prepared to take action, now reinforced by a growing fascist party, the Falange, and the willingness of Franco and other army officers to assume a political role. When the military rising began, on 18 July 1936, Spain was divided. Roughly half the armed forces declared for the legitimate government, roughly half for the rebels. Franco, crossing the Straits of Gibraltar the following month with the battle-hardened Army of Africa and German and Italian support, was set to make the difference. The policy of non-intervention followed by the European democracies, meant that the Republic received little support other than from the Soviet Union and the volunteers of the International Brigades.

War and Revolution

In Barcelona, effective power fell into the hands of the anarchists. Andreu Capdevila, a CNT textile worker interviewed in the 1970s by Ronald Fraser for his oral history of the war, published as *Blood of Spain*, said of the seizure of arms by the workers:

Ten thousand rifles, I calculate, as well as some machine-guns, were taken. That was the moment when the people of Barcelona were armed; that was the moment, in consequence, when power fell into the masses' hands. We of the

CNT hadn't set out to make the revolution but to defend ourselves, to defend the working class. To make the social revolution, which needed to have the whole of the Spanish proletariat behind it, would take another ten years at least, we believed.

Into this chaotic situation came George Orwell, upper class, well educated, with a strong social conscience and a keen sense of right and wrong. What he found in Barcelona was not just war, but revolution. Given that Orwell's views on Catalonia have become well known, even notorious, with the passage of time, they are worth quoting at some length. Not the well-known lines from *Homage to Catalonia*, but Orwell in reflective tone, from a 1939 article for a Workers Educational Association in-house magazine:

I was in Catalonia and Aragón from Christmas, 1936, until about the middle of the following year. To be in Spain at that time was a strange and moving experience, because you had before you the spectacle of a people that knew what it wanted, a people facing destiny with its eyes open. The rebellion had plunged the country into chaos and the Government nominally in power at the outbreak of war had acted supinely; if the Spanish people were saved, it had got to be by their own effort. It is not an exaggeration to say that practically the whole resistance of the opening months was the direct and conscious action of the ordinary people in the street, via their trade unions and political organisations. Transport and major industries had devolved directly into the hands of the workers; the militias which had to bear the brunt of the fighting were voluntary organisations growing out of the trade unions. There was plenty of incompetence, of course, but also there were astonishing feats of improvisation. The fields were tilled, trains ran, life away from the fighting line was for the most part peaceful and orderly, and the troops, though poorly armed, were well fed and cared for. With all this there was a spirit of tolerance, a freedom of speech and the press, which no one would have thought possible in time of war. Naturally the social atmosphere changed, in some ways for the worse, as time went on. The country settled down to a long war; there were internal political struggles which resulted in power passing from the hands of socialists and anarchists into the hands of communists, and from the hands of communists into the hands of radical republicans; conscription was imposed and censorship tightened up — two inevitable evils of modern war. But the essentially voluntary spirit of the opening months has never disappeared, and it will have important after-effects. (*The Highway*, March 1939)

Orwell was not alone in emphasising the revolutionary fervour of Barcelona in 1936. Looking back on it fifty years later, Walter Gregory exclaimed 'What a city! It was just like a volcano, erupting in all directions at the same time. A breath-taking, awe-inspiring and heart-warming spectacle of noise, enthusiasm and gaiety. A revolutionary city in the full flood of revolutionary zest and zeal; an unforgettable sight.' For Orwell, Catalonia in 1936/37 was about class, no more and no less:

The hatred which the Spanish Republic excited in millionaires, dukes, cardinals, play-boys, Blimps and what not would in itself be enough to show one how the land lay. In essence it was a class war. If it had been won, the cause of the common people everywhere would have been strengthened. It was lost, and the dividend-drawers all over the world rubbed their hands. That was the real issue; all else was froth on its surface.
(*Orwell in Spain*, p. 357)

It is pertinent to dwell on this for a moment. 'Froth on the surface' included the appalling excesses of over-enthusiastic anarchists burning churches and shooting anyone considered by them to be an enemy of the working class. The anarchist notion of redemption through violence is well summed up by Buenaventura Durruti, who died at the front in 1936: 'We are not afraid of ruins, we are going to inherit the earth. The bourgeoisie may blast and ruin their world before they leave the stage of history. But we carry a new world in our hearts.' Anarchist executions may have been high-minded but they were nevertheless

93

summary and did justice neither to the anarchists' utopian visions of a peaceful, co-operative society or the real social achievements of the Spanish Republic. In Orwell's account, such scummy 'froth on the surface' was ignored. The one piece of froth which Orwell did not leave out was the 'war within a war' — the events of May 1937 in Barcelona. Subsequently this became the basis of his anti-communism.

In essence, Orwell was right: there is little doubt that the communists, encouraged by Moscow, set out to destroy their political opponents in the spring of 1937. The policy of Popular Front socialist-communist alliances was being put at risk, as Moscow saw it, by exactly the kind of social revolution that George Orwell and Gerald Brenan witnessed in Barcelona. Their preferred target would have been the anarchists, but the anarchists were numerically far stronger than the communists. The proxy target, then, in 1937 was POUM, the left communists closely linked to the Independent Labour Party in Britain, and in whose militias Orwell found himself fighting. Orwell was no dispassionate observer in Barcelona in May 1937 but a man whose life was in danger. In police files, he and his wife Eileen (who was working in the ILP office in Barcelona) were identified as 'known Trotskyists . . . linking agents of the ILP and the POUM'. (Buchanan, Britain and the Spanish Civil War, p. 165)

Gerald Brenan's account is very close to that of Orwell, but other observers were less sure. John Langdon-Davies, in the early stages of a lifelong love-affair with Catalonia, tended to support the communist view of the need for order to conjure international support for the Republic — a reasonable view but unrealistic since non-intervention remained firmly in place throughout the war. His review of *Homage to Catalonia* was one of a number of less than enthusiastic accounts, and it is difficult to believe in view of its subsequent fame that only 683 copies of the first print run were sold. At the same time, it is not necessary to look at history through Stalin's prism to recognise the need to inject some sort of order into the revolutionary enthusiasm which could spill over at into bloodshed at a moment's notice. To some extent POUM and the anarchists were architects of their own fate, given their refusal to take political power when it was there to be taken. But like Orwell, many have questioned whether further bloodshed against anarchists and left communists was the best way to re-establish order. So the argument swings backwards and forwards. Subsequently, Orwell's reputation as standard-bearer of anti-communist liberal democracy has grown and grown and only in very recent years has this reputation been dented. Firstly by revelations about his involvement in the Cold War activities of the British secret service. Secondly by the publication in an article by Andy Croft in the *New Statesman* (18 March 1994, p. 57) of his homophobic outburst against 'fashionable pansies like Auden and Spender'. Thirdly by his bizarre political analysis that 'Fascism is being riveted on to the Spanish workers under the pretext of resisting Fascism.' It is difficult to understand why Orwell's anti-communism dwells so insistently on the street-fighting of May 1937 in Barcelona rather than, for example, Stalin's activities back in the Soviet Union or the cynical non-aggression pact with Germany in 1939. Pierre Vilar has written in his monumental history of Catalonia, published in 1987: 'I do not believe that Orwell understood very much about the meaning of the struggle he had wanted to take part in.'

Orwell's translation from supporter of revolutionary socialism in the 1930s to Cold War Warrior in the 1940s is certainly a curious story. No doubt an important motive for a decent man with a strong belief in justice and truth was the attempt to conceal a crime within the confusion of May 1937 — the murder of the POUM leader Andreu (or Andrés) Nin in prison. Victor Alba, himself a member of POUM in the 1930s, suggests Nin may have died under torture at a house near Madrid belonging to the NKVD, the Soviet secret police, but there is no conclusive evidence. The other leader of POUM, Joaquín Maurín survived by the curious chance of being incarcerated in a fascist prison for the duration of the war, and lived on until 1973. Other leading POUM supporters were arrested and tried. But given the widespread international publicity given to the suppression of POUM it was always unlikely that they would be found guilty of treason and espionage. Although the events of May 1937 had been directed at POUM rather than the anarchists, they did succeed in bringing down the broad coalition government of Largo Caballero. The new government was noticeable for the absence of CNT ministers, and although they were to reappear briefly between April and August 1938, May 1937 marked the beginning of the end for what is probably the closest flirtation by anarchists with government in history. Two views of the revolution had clashed, and the more attractive (in emotional terms) had been defeated. Here is Nin, speaking in 1937:

> The reformists, the republicans also say they want to make the revolution. But they tell you they want an orderly, well-made revolution; Lenin also came up against people who wanted a revolution in Russia made by well-educated, clean workers. These people think the revolution is like a train which arrives on time at the station, and then the station-master says: 'gentlemen, we have reached the social revolution.' Revolution is not, cannot be, like that . . .
> (quoted in Fraser, Blood of Spain, p. 335)

1937 also marked the closer integration of Catalonia into the Republic. Initially, the outbreak of the war had loosened the ties between Madrid and Barcelona. Thus the advance of the anarchist and socialist militias into Aragon in 1936 was never officially sanctioned by Madrid. Given the imminent threat of the fall of Madrid to the Nationalists, the Generalitat was able to take over with little difficulty customs, railways, docks, hydro-electric plants, and even the right to print money. Under the Catalan statute of autonomy, all such duties rested with

96

the Spanish government. Hugh Thomas, in his exhaustive history of the Spanish War, mentions the view of Josep Tarradellas that 'since Catalonia had successfully defended herself against the military uprising, she could wash her hands of Spain.' That position changed after May 1937. Control of the police passed to the central government. While the Catalans had been concerned with their own affairs, Málaga had fallen, to be followed in June by Bilbao. Once the industrial areas of Asturias and the Basque Country had fallen to the Nationalists, the dependence of the Republican war effort on Catalan industry was clear. The central government moved to take control of the war industries. Then in October 1937 the central government moved from Valencia to Barcelona: the forces of order and moderation had arrived in the home of social revolution, but the social revolution was not at home.

The Home Front

If the first two years of the war in Catalonia were dominated by the efforts to secure a social revolution, the departure of large numbers of fighters for the front, and the usual disruptions of everyday life that affect a country at war, the last twelve months of the war involved Catalonia much more directly. In October 1937, the Republican government, already in Valencia, moved to the relative safety of Barcelona. By now the strategy of the Republican army, heavily outnumbered and out-gunned by the Nationalists, was increasingly reduced to a series of brilliant counter-offensives which delayed but did not prevent a fascist victory. These offensives involved heavy fighting in which many thousands of men died. In April 1938 the Nationalists, advancing down the western side of the Ebro valley had chased the Republican armies back across the great river into Catalonia and reached the sea at Vinaroz, a little further south. This meant that the last two Republican enclaves — Catalonia and Valencia — were separated from one another. Supplies from the Soviet Union, plagued by submarine attacks in the

Mediterranean, were drying up. A further problem was that Barcelona and Valencia could now be bombed not just from warships at sea but by bombers flying from rebel-held territory. The second half of 1938 was dominated by the heroic, doomed counterattack by the Republican army, with the International Brigades to the fore, across the Ebro, to which we shall have cause to refer back. The war was on Catalonia's doorstep, and the outlook bleak.

Victor Alba describes the growing impact of the war on the Catalan people: food rationing, power cuts and fear of bombing. Xavier Muñoz, one of the leading socialist figures in the transition to democracy in the 1970s and 1980s, came from a bourgeois, family background of textile manufacturing and retailing in Barcelona. His account of the war years from a child's point of view is fascinating. For the middle classes, survival meant both dealing with shortages and making occasional deals in the black market, but also not provoking the wrath of the various armed militia groups. Porridge is not a dish that springs to mind when writing about Catalan cuisine, but it kept this family alive during the war. It was prepared by roasting maize and then grinding it in a hand-held coffee grinder. Lack of food and poor diet killed people. Those who survived got by as best they could. Instead of school, young children like Xavier occupied their time keeping a place in queues. He uses this experience of queuing, which went on for many years after the end of the war, to explain the often noted Catalan reluctance to form a queue. He contrasts England, where queuing seems to be about order and fairness, with Catalonia where it simply brings back memories of scarcity and war.

Added to illness and hunger was bombing. Already, on 26 April 1937, the German air-force had destroyed the small Basque town of Guernica. The town had no air defences, and was crowded with refugees and retreating soldiers from the Nationalists' assault on Bilbao. Thomas suggests that only 10% of the town was left undamaged and puts the death-toll at 1,000 in a town whose normal population was 7,000. Those are the stark facts behind Picasso's 'Guernica', one of the great emblematic paintings of the twentieth century. On 28 January 1938, the Italian air-force launched a massive raid on Barcelona from Majorca, which had long been in the hands of the Nationalists. The city was poorly prepared. The Italians attacked again on 30 January. Two uncles of Xavier Muñoz died in this raid, vainly seeking shelter in the church of Sant Felip Neri in the old city, not knowing that it had been destroyed by bombs a short while before. The bombers came again on 16 March, and the German ambassador to Spain reported to Berlin that 'All parts of the city were affected. There was no evidence of any attempt to hit military objectives.' (in Thomas, The Spanish Civil War, pp. 806/7) On the morning of 17 March, Júlia Gay, mother of the novelist Juan Goytisolo and the poet José Augustín Goytisolo, was killed by a bomb while out shopping. These bombing raids were undertaken without consultation, mainly by Mussolini but with support from the Germans and Ramón Franco's nationalist air force. Bizarrely Franco himself asked for them to be stopped, concerned about the possible effect on non-intervention if they were continued.

Casualties were 1,300 killed and 2,000 injured. For Josep Trueta, chief surgeon at Barcelona's main hospital, the raids were like Guernica, 'meant to test the population's capacity of resistance. By the time they ended, there were 2,200 casualties in my hospital.' Trueta had developed striking new ways of treating war wounds. In Britain, after 'their' war had become 'our' war, his new techniques saved the saves of countless British soldiers and civilian casualties. Such humanitarian advances mark out some of the ironies of the cruel twentieth century: 'our knowledge cannot save all of you from war, famine and disease, but we may be able to save some of you — with our knowledge.'

By the following January, such considerations no longer mattered. France had opened the border for the passage of military supplies from Russia but the Republican army was now in headlong retreat. Barcelona was bombed daily, especially the port area, to prevent any orderly evacuation. The Nationalists reached Barcelona on January 26 and found the streets full of litter, torn newspapers, union cards and posters, anything that might draw attention to a family's Republican sympathies. For those supporters of the Nationalists who had laid low during the war, it was time to come out into the streets and rejoice. Xavier Muñoz remembers his father breaking into a cache of *cava* (Catalan sparkling wine) stored away in anticipation of this very day. Years later, his own family, like many Catalans, were to keep a special bottle of *cava* in the refrigerator against the day of Franco's death. Which was a long time coming. As Xavier writes, 'The war had finished, but peace had not arrived.' Twenty-five years later, the observation by Aureli Escarré, Abbot of Montserrat, that the years from 1939 to 1964 had been 25 years of victory rather than of peace, was to cost him his job and send him into exile. For Xavier, the long march 'From Right to Left' (the title of his autobiographical book) had begun.

It is useless to attempt to estimate exactly how many people died as a result of the war. Francoist Spain tended to use the round figure of one million; subsequent estimates by more detached writers might suggest something in the region of half that number, even taking account of those who died in air-raids or as a result of political reprisals on both sides. But in addition to those who died during the war, it is also necessary to take account of those who died after the war. Paul Preston, Franco's biographer, estimates 200,000 prisoners executed between 1939 and 1943. The dubious legal basis of this was the Law of Responsibilities passed in early 1939. 'Crimes' included crimes of commission (membership of left-wing parties and Masonic lodges) but crimes of omission too ('those . . . who have opposed the National Movement by either deed or grave passivity'). With the rest of Europe now involved in the Second World War, Franco could do much as he liked. The occupation of France by the Nazis in 1940 produced further problems for those who had opposed him. Some 400,000 Republicans had fled Spain in 1939, most of them keeping just ahead of the advance of the Nationalist army through Catalonia. The confusion, misery and human suffering of those going into exile can only be imagined. Some were fortunate enough to move on — a few to England, even more to Latin America. Others were still in France when Hitler's armies arrived. Some were lucky and escaped again to third countries, others were unlucky and ended up doing forced labour in factories. Some were seriously unlucky and ended up in either in Nazi concentration camps or being returned to Spain to face Franco's 'justice'. The fate of the Catalans who ended up in the camps has been well documented by the Catalan writer Montserrat Roig in a book[1] which includes much testimony from survivors. Numbers were considerable. No less than nineteen people from the industrial town of Manresa ended up in Mauthausen. Thirteen of them died there.

Among those who were returned to Spain was Lluís Companys, still President of the Catalan Generalitat, although in exile. The seizure of Companys by the Gestapo, his hurried return to Barcelona, the secret trial at Montjuïc Castle on 14 October 1940, and the summary execution and burial in a common paupers' grave on 15 October were supposed to set an end to an epoch. But it was too awful a fate, too powerful a story, to remain a secret. The writer Juan Goytisolo knew the story, and he was not the only one. Goytisolo is a Catalan writer who writes in Castilian, a Catalan who grew up in Barcelona but has lived most of his life in Paris. In *Señas de identidad* (translated as *Marks of Identity*), first published in Mexico in 1966, Goytisolo ends with a confrontation on Montjuïc. The violence is all inward, a writer preparing for

---

[1]*An extract is available to English language readers in J.M. Sobrer, Catalonia: a self-portrait, pp. 127–145.*

101

exile while the official guides peddle lies about the recent history of his country. The words Salida/Sortie/ Exit/Ausgang recur as a motif in the final obsessive pages of the novel. He slips a one hundred peseta note to a gardener who silently leads him to the spot where President Companys was shot in October 1940.

The Grace of Democracy — and the Forgetting

In Tortosa, near the mouth of the River Ebro is a monument. More precisely, the monument is on a small island in the Ebro. It is dedicated (in Spanish rather than Catalan) to 'those who found glory in the battle of the Ebro'. It is extraordinary that such a monument, inaugurated by Franco himself, has managed to survive the transition to democracy in Catalonia. It is of course not a monument to all those who died, but to those who died fighting for the 'right' side, those who had God on their side. Older people think their own thoughts and do not always want to share them. One suspects that most people treat this monument like a pile of rubbish in a rural beauty spot, something that can be more easily ignored than analysed. The fighters of the International Brigade who died at the Ebro — fighting for freedom in any and every language — have their own memorial. It is very hard to find, hidden away on 'Hill 666' in the Pàndols mountains beyond the river, where Percy Luddick and his sappers left a memorial built of simple blocks of concrete which managed to outlive Franco himself.

There has been no Truth Commission, no War Crimes trials in Catalonia, no cases referred to the International Court. When Franco finally died in 1975 and dictatorship gave way to democracy, there was a general agreement to let sleeping dogs lie. It was as if the success of the Transition (from dictatorship to democracy) depended on a collective amnesia which was the necessary price of 'peace' and continuity. People have been too keen to get on with their everyday lives, too keen to make democracy

102

work, to make the statute of autonomy an effective form of political devolution, to enjoy the standard of living which they now have, far exceeding anything which might have been dreamt of at the time of the Spanish War. With a very few exceptions, the politicians of the new Spain and the new Catalonia have been women and men with no direct experience of pre-1939 politics. What they did have of course was plenty of experience of Franco's Spain, of clandestine organisation of political parties and trade unions, and in cases such as that of Jordi Pujol, the first democratically elected President of Catalonia since Companys, of Franco's prisons. As early as the 1960s, the French film-maker Alain Resnais made a controversial film called *La Guerre est Finie* (The War is Over) which suggested the increasing distance, psychological as well as in space and time, between the life of exiles and the 'real' Spain in which people had made their accommodation with the Franco regime. The screenplay was by Jorge Semprún, himself a political exile. It is a multi-faceted film which plays games with public history and personal memory. The title acts as a reminder of Franco's declaration to the people of Spain on 1 April 1939 that the war that he had started was indeed over ('la guerra ha terminado'). It is also a reminder that the normality of Franco's Spain was an <u>abnormal</u> normality in which many of the freedoms enjoyed in other Western European countries were unavailable.

People have turned their backs on the past, but the past will not go away. People forgot not just because time passed but because the regime commanded forgetfulness. The poet Salvador Espriu expressed this sense of internal exile in his 'Cançó de Capvespre' (Evening Song):

Però ara és nit.	But now it is night.
i he quedat solitari	And I've been left alone
a la casa dels morts	In the house of the dead
que només jo recordo.	Whom only I remember

103

The singer Raimon set this poem to music in the 1970s. As Vázquez Montalbán puts it, 'In this context Espriu's verses came to express, whether the poet intended it or not, the melancholy which accompanied the prohibition of memory', although for Espriu it has a deeper spiritual sense of isolation and despair (Barcelonas, p. 140). It is as if history has contradicted Espriu: memory has endured and is not satisfied. The past will not go away.

If the war involved many people from outside of Spain, its aftermath was a uniquely Spanish tragedy. The Spanish War is not celebrated by Catalan nationalists as part of their heritage. Often, it is in films and books that these issues are addressed. For the two generations of Spaniards who had lived their lives under Franco, there were still so many unanswered questions. Books and films about the Spanish War, often with an innocent child's-eye point of view, have been an important way in which people, individually and as a society, have begun to come to terms with what happened. Commercially they are very successful. On the one hand they tug at people's emotions, tell strong stories and look good on the screen. For similar reasons, they travel well, too. But on the other hand, there is little doubt that people of all ages need to understand how and why Franco came to power, and why the best efforts of opposition within and outside Spain failed to shift him, the only fascist dictator to die in bed attached to a life-support machine.

Despite a number of other excellent films with the Spanish war as subject-matter, it is Ken Loach's *Land and Freedom* (1995) which confronts the key issues of what was at stake socially and economically in the war, and the methods used to achieve those ends. In placing the theme of social revolution in the foreground, Loach follows Orwell, though the detailed village discussions about collectivisation and the feminist positions put forward by the militiawoman Blanca go far beyond anything in *Homage to Catalonia*. But whereas Orwell joined POUM through naivety, Dave Carr in Loach's film is a member of the

Communist Party. So what he comes to recognise is not just the primacy of revolution but the extent to which the Communist Party is an obstacle to it. He writes to his girl-friend at home in Liverpool: 'The Party stinks . . . it is evil and corrupt . . . Stalin is just using the working class like pieces on a chess-board to be bartered, used and sacrificed.' The film ends with Spanish soil carefully wrapped in a red flag and kept by Dave scattered on his own tomb in Liverpool as his grand-daughter reads lines by William Morris:

Join in the battle
Wherein no man can fail
For whoso fadeth and dieth
Yet his deeds shall still prevail

It was suggested that *Land and Freedom* was the film that the Spanish were unable to make. One novel, since made into a film, does stand out though. For Javier Cercas, a novelist who lives in Catalonia and sets his novels there, but writes in Spanish, the years since the death of Franco, the years of the transition to democracy, have been the years of forgetting. Interviewed by this author in 2002, tired and drawn and just back in Girona from shooting the film version of his novel *Soldados de Salamina* (Soldiers of Salamis), he said:

"And the Transition . . . was a pact between winners and losers not to look behind them, but to build a democracy. And that had a lot of positive aspects, concretely, that Spain became a democracy, it has grown, it has become wealthy, that's for sure. But it's also had negative aspects, for example the Forgetting. For example, that people have not spoken about very important things, about the past, about the post-war period, about the war, it's been covered up."

After 1975, the church, the army and right-of-centre political parties continued to make comfortable homes for men and women who had been involved in human rights abuses in the Franco years. People preferred to turn their backs on 36 years of history. The very word collaboration sounded curious. Everyone in Franco's Spain 'collaborated'. The Forgetting encompassed not just the Franco years but the crimes of the War itself. And Cercas has reminded Spain about the many crimes committed in the name of the Republic, against priests and members of religious orders, conservative politicians and businessmen.

Cercas admitted to being of a younger generation — his parents were not involved in the war, did not get shot or bombed — and he can look at the War from a greater distance. He takes the true story of Rafael Sánchez Mazas, one of the founders of the Spanish Falange (fascist movement). In the confused last days of the war and the retreat to France, Sánchez Mazas escaped mass execution by his Republicans captors and hid in the hills near Girona. Here he was spared by a Republican soldier who finds him, and much of the second half of the novel reconstructs the later life of this man (Miralles) fighting for France, for democracy in the African desert during the Second World War, and ending up in an old people's home in Paris. But if there are real lives, real people in the novel, there is also much literary ambiguity. Cercas said that

> ". . . the book starts out from an obsession, a simple story, one man looks at another, he's supposed to kill him, but he doesn't. That's the starting-point. I don't know what that means, I just know it fascinates me. Is it a pacifist attitude? Maybe, but it's also true that Miralles is fighting a war, raising the standard of Free France, a country which is not his country. And that period at the end of 1941 is crucial for European history. All of Europe under the Nazis. And he's there, not because he wants to be there, but by chance. Miralles is in no way a man of rigid principles. He just wants to live, that's all. A saint, I see him as a saint, a hero."

If Miralles is a saint or a hero, then he is certainly one for sceptical times. The extraordinary success of the novel, which has already gone through more than twenty editions, suggests that Cercas has struck a chord, especially with younger people who wonder about their parents, their grandparents.

Part 2:

The Cultures
of Catalonia

Chapter 6:

Muslims, Christians and Jews

Living Together Apart

In the Cathedral Museum at Girona is one of medieval
Catalonia's most attractive works — the Tapestry of the
Creation. It is probably unique, a colourful piece of
embroidery dating from the eleventh or twelfth century in
a remarkably good state of preservation. The anonymous
craftworkers, for it is impossible to imagine a work of this
size and magnificence made by one person, solved the
problem of subject by choosing creation itself, the whole
created world as it appeared to medieval Catalan
Christians, with the sun and the stars, the winds, the cycle
of the months and seasons, the plants and fishes and animals. And at the centre of it a rather friendly, rather
humble looking God, looking almost embarrassed at the
wealth and variety of created nature. The words 'And God
said "Let there be light", and there was light' are embroidered around the creator. The abstract principle of light
modulated and transmogrified into physical being. The
great cake of creation is divided into slices, with the upper
ones representing the inhabitants of heaven, and the
lower ones those of earth. There is Eve, emerging from the
side of a naked, puzzled Adam. There are the birds of the
air and the fish of the sea. There is Adam again, surrounded by a merry throng of animals. The circle of
creation is then fitted into a square, with at each corner
the symbolic figures of the four winds sitting on their
gigantic wind-bags. They are not classical mythological
figures but 'green men' from the shared folk-culture of

pagan, pre-Christian Europe. Outside this again the borders of the tapestry made of square panels depict the routines of the agricultural year — ploughing, sowing and reaping. Not surprisingly, after 900 years the tapestry has become frayed at the edges, and some of the border panels are missing. The miracle is that these vivid images of the Christian cosmos have survived so well.

The problem with understanding medieval Catalan culture is that the physical evidence is overwhelmingly of a Christian culture, while the Jewish and Muslim elements in Catalan culture have left far less evidence in bricks and stone. There is also much potential for confusion. Girona makes much of its 'Arab Baths', but they are certainly not Muslim in the sense of dating from the period of sixty years in the eighth century when Girona was under Muslim rule. The Romans had built baths in North Africa, the model had been adopted by Muslims, for whom water and bathing were both exquisite luxuries and part of religious ritual, and copied by some of the more enlightened Christian rulers. These particular baths were destroyed by the French in 1285, rebuilt in the late thirteenth century and rebuilt again in modern times, incorporating a horseshoe entrance arch which suggests a rather spurious 'Arab' presence. In Tortosa, the Street of Jerusalem in the heart of what was once the Jewish ghetto (*call* in Catalan) refers not to dreams of a Jewish homeland but to the crusading Order of the Knights of the Order of Jerusalem who owned land in Tortosa. Again in Tortosa, the splendid *parador* (part of a chain of state-run luxury hotels) is built within a Christian fortress built upon the Muslim fortress — the *Suda*. A little more history is perhaps in order ...

Muslims arrived in Spain in the early eighth century. They established themselves in the country from then until finally expelled from Granada in 1492. We shall use the term al-Andalus to refer to those parts of Spain under Muslim control at any point in time, and to avoid getting into the complex political history of Muslim rule. While conservative, Catholic views of Spanish history use the term reconquest to describe the 750-year process by which Christian rulers gradually extended their power over the whole Iberian Peninsula, the reality was far more complex. Here we shall deal with Catalonia alone. Old Catalonia, north of Barcelona, was never securely under Muslim rule. New Catalonia, on the other hand, west and south of Barcelona, remained in Muslim hands until the middle of the twelfth century. Farther south, Valencia was secured by the Aragonese-Catalan crown in 1238. This means that in New Catalonia Muslim rule lasted for some four hundred years. From then until 1525, a Muslim presence was continued, and these Muslims living under Christian rule are known as *mudèjars*. From 1525 until 1610, the date of their final expulsion, groups of converted Muslims, known as *moriscos*, continued to preserve privately their culture and their religion. In Andalusia and in Valencia their history is well documented. But for Catalonia, detailed information is not easy to come by. English language readers are greatly indebted to Mark Meyerson's study of Muslims in Valencia during the reign of the Catholic Monarchs — Ferdinand and Isabella — for the side-light it casts upon the situation north of the Ebro. This makes it clear that by the fifteenth century, 30% of Valencia was still Muslim, against 20% in Aragon and a mere 5% in Catalonia. But of course that 5% was concentrated in the southern areas of New Catalonia, and Tortosa and Lleida were both important centres of Muslim communities.

It is harder to pin-point the arrival of Jews in Catalonia, since they came not as conquerors but as traders, craftworkers and financiers. It is probable that their presence was significant from the earliest days of the re-establishment of the Christian counties of pre-Catalonia, and their high point was reached in the period between about 1200 and 1400. If Girona was the greatest of the Catalan Jewish communities, even small Catalan towns such as Besalú, La Bisbal and Olot had their *call*. Barcelona and Perpignan were both important Jewish centres. Estimates of the pop-

113

ulation vary considerably, but any figure above 5% is considered unlikely. In numerical terms this would mean about 10,000–12,000 Jews living in Catalonia in the mid-fourteenth century. But in urban areas where they were most numerous, this figure could easily reach 10%. Jews were active in crafts such as textiles, book-binding, gold and silver, in trading food and silk, in financial services, and as doctors and lawyers. From the thirteenth century, a small group of Jewish civil servants played a key role in the state affairs of Aragon.

Until 1975, when Franco died, there was silence on the Jewish and Muslim past of Catalonia, but that situation has changed very rapidly. There are a number of preliminary observations to be made about this. First and most importantly, the word *convivència* (living together) is often used to describe the circumstances under which Christians, Muslims and Jews shared in Catalan life in the Middle Ages. In so far as it suggests harmony, this is wrong, and the colloquial English 'rubbing along together' perhaps would be a more accurate description. And as with any rubbing along, there was friction. The Muslims of al-Andalus had been forced to relinquish control of their Catalan lands by force. Those who chose to stay behind were in the same position as the Jews — second-class citizens who were not entitled to the same treatment as Christians. While at one level both communities were protected by the royal authorities, at another level they could be taxed more severely, forced to wear distinctive clothing, and be subjected to daily discrimination. In some ways, this is not unexpected — the Muslim authorities of al-Andalus treated their Christian and Jewish minorities the same. The Jews in particular had to suffer the attentions of the Dominican preachers who propagated the doctrine of Jewish culpability for the death of Jesus, and pogroms happened in mediaeval Catalonia just as they did in Central and Eastern Europe in more recent times. Meyerson refers to a 'latent ideological antagonism ... this ever-present potentiality for religious and ethnic violence.'

Yet there was sharing too. If Arabic and Hebrew were the languages of religion and scholarship, Catalan was the language of translation and it is probable that both Jews and Muslims spoke Catalan on a day-to-day basis. It is the abundance of evidence of the efforts made by the authorities to keep the communities apart which reveals the extent of interaction in the daily round of work, shopping and popular entertainment. It was bad enough when men and women from the two communities had sex with one another. In cases of Christian men having sex with Muslim or Jewish women, it was normally only the woman who was punished, unless of course she was a registered prostitute. In the case of Jewish or Muslim men having sex with Christian women, both partners were severely punished, usually by death or enslavement. Religion was another matter altogether. Towards the end of the fifteenth century, Ferdinand of Aragon was shocked to find that the church of La Ràpita in Tortosa was being used for gatherings by Muslims from Catalonia, Aragon and Valencia on Muslim holy days. There were threats of large fines, of capital punishment for the key-holders if they allowed the crime to be repeated, and of death or slavery for any Muslims found in the church.

Yet the last thing Ferdinand wanted was a mass exodus of Muslims. They were too important to the economy of his lands. In 1492, on the successful completion of the war against the Granada enclave of al-Andalus, he welcomed fleeing Muslims to his lands in Valencia. In 1499-1501, during the panic following the Muslim rising in the Alpujarras to the south of Granada, Ferdinand expressly prohibited *mudèjars* from embarking on boats at Tortosa to seek a new life in North Africa. He went along with the expulsion of the Jews in 1492 because, as we shall see, there were already pitifully few Jews left in Catalonia. But throughout his lands he opposed expulsion and forced conversions of the *mudèjars*, until the Christian unrest in Valencia in the 1520s made that policy of conversion politically unavoidable. While in many ways, the link with

115

Castile represented by the marriage of Ferdinand and Isabella may be seen as a prelude to the greatness of imperial Spain, it also set a precedent for the future. Spain became one monolithic culture from which it is still trying to escape. The re-emergence of Catalonia as an autonomous nation raises once more those issues of multiculturalism with which Ferdinand was struggling before and after 1500.

Catalan Jews

Girona's Jewish past is now vigorously promoted as part of its heritage. Colm Tóibín has suggested, perhaps mischievously, that this may be part of the Catalan desire to disassociate themselves as completely as possible from the rest of Spain, where the Muslim presence was both longer and more thorough than in Catalonia. It would not, however, be a popular policy with those who promote the cause of a wider definition of Catalonia as the 'Catalan lands', including Valencia where Muslim influence was much stronger for much longer, as we have seen. Or in the border lands of Tortosa and Lleida where any visit to the local baker to taste the traditional spiced cakes of the region offers evidence of a deep and long Islamic past. Promoting the past of Girona's Jews is, however, a struggle. Not against discrimination or hostility but against a certain forgetting, a loss of public memory, and more important the loss of written sources and cultural and religious objects. The history of the *call*, the ghetto, must be read and interpreted from largely Christian sources, despite the fact that the *call* existed for 600 years. Its final location is clear — a jumble of narrow little alleyways and tall dark houses opening off the Carrer de la Força (the old Imperial Roman Via Augusta) in the old town, sheltering beneath the Cathedral in symbolic acknowledgement of the royal protection (and restrictions) under which the Jews lived. It is here that the city authorities have established their Jewish museum and archive. But at its peak in the thirteenth and fourteenth century the *call* occupied a considerable further area between the Força and the River Onyar.

Jewish communities (*aljamas* — confusingly the same word is used for both Jewish and *mudèjar* communities, and also for the areas where *mudèjars* lived) were legally constituted entities with their synagogues, cemeteries, baths, bakers and butchers. They were governed by their own mayor and aldermen rather than by the town council. Often we find in Christian documents the Jewish and *mudèjar* communities referred to as 'laws', because of their separate legal status with their own legal officials. The Jews in Girona worked as gold and silversmiths, cobblers and tailors, with workshops both inside and outside the *call*. Others worked in traditional, stereotypical Jewish occupations as doctors, moneylenders or pawnbrokers, or as rent and tax-collectors for the royal authorities. Towards the end of the fifteenth century war of the *remences* between the Catalan peasantry and the nobles, it was a Girona Jew who loaned money to the leaders of the revolt to attend the court and enter into negotiations with the king, who was equally keen to curb noble power but had no desire to inflame the revolt any further. This happened in 1485, just seven years before the final expulsion of the Catalan Jews. Of Jewish women, we know less even than of their men, though some certainly were in great demand as midwives, while middle-class Jewish women were often active in financial business.

There is considerable debate about the cultural and intellectual affiliation of the Catalan Jews. The culture of the original Sephardim (the Jews of Iberia) had been profoundly influenced by contact with Muslims throughout the Mediterranean world. We saw in chapter 3 how Ramon Llull dreamed of reuniting Islam and the Jews with Christianity by force of argument and logic. He could, of course, only do so because of what the three religions shared as well as what pulled them apart. Just as the Muslims introduced advanced medical practices into

117

Spain, building on classical Greek beginnings, so in Catalonia medicine and midwifery were two preferred Jewish careers. Intellectuals maintained a knowledge of Arabic while using Catalan as their language of translation. There was intellectual contact between communities, as well as across the border with al-Andalus and the broader networks of Jewish and Muslim scholars around the Mediterranean. But from about 1200, Jewish communities in Catalonia were also heavily influenced by Jews fleeing persecution in Provence. This wave of Jewish refugees brought with them the teachings of the Cabbala, which proposed, in essence, a rationalist and mystical interpretation of the Hebrew Bible (the Old Testament). This led to the flowering of Girona as a Cabbalist centre, led by Moses Ben Nahman (or Nahmanides) whose Catalan name was Bonastruc ça Porta. Born in Girona in 1194, doctor, philosopher, poet and later Grand Rabbi, in his writings he seeks to illuminate the 'real meaning' of obscure biblical passages, and the 'common flame that illuminates the heart'. So much for more lurid explanations of the Cabbala, which mix anti-Semitism and pure fantasy in equal quantities.

By 1400, the Jewish community in Girona, as in most of Catalonia, was in crisis. There had been anti-Jewish demonstrations in Girona in 1331. There had been conversions to Christianity, a few maybe from conviction but most from fear. Jews were used to having to move on. England had expelled her Jews in 1290 and France in 1306. If the communities rubbed along on a day-to-day basis, there were always those prepared to fan the flames of popular anti-Semitism. One such was Pau Cristià, a Dominican friar. In 1263, at the height of the Girona *aljama*, Nahmanides was summoned from Girona to Barcelona by the king, Jaume I, to debate with Cristià and a converted Jew the status of Jesus as prophet or son of God, and the 'blood guilt' of the Jews for the death of Christ. The gentle philosopher may have won the intellectual debate, but it was the fanatical priest who was the real victor, with fresh outbreaks of violence in 1276, 1278 and 1285. There was more trouble in 1348, the immediate cause of which was the accusation that Jews had been responsible for the Black Death. In England popular unrest climaxed in the Peasants' Revolt of 1381. In Spain and Catalonia it culminated in the pogroms of 1391. The next twenty years were critical: in 1391 there were 25 *aljamas* with a Jewish population of 10,000 in Catalonia. By 1419 there were only 14 *aljamas* and 2,000 Jews. This figure changed little by 1492 and the final expulsion when there were 15 *aljamas* with a population of 1,500. The Girona *aljama* consisted of only 20 families when the expulsion order was published on 31 March 1492, effective from 31 July that same year. A tragedy, but the image of thousands of weeping Jews leaving their beloved Catalonia in 1492 is false: most had already gone or sought the dubious protection of conversion to the majority Christian faith.

It is not the intention here to suggest that only extremist, populist agitators were involved in anti-Jewish activities. In Tortosa, for example, it was the Pope Benet XIII who summoned the Disputation of Tortosa in the Cathedral which lasted from February 1313 through into 1314. The Jews were compelled to attend, and all but two of their rabbis converted. This led to mass conversions and persecutions of those who did not convert. Worse was to come. The converts were in a cleft stick: at one level they had renounced their religion; at another level they continued with cultural practices, maintained contact with friends and family members who had not converted, and were therefore continually suspected of secretly clinging to their religion. The adjectives *convers/pervers* (Spanish *converso/perverso* and English convert/pervert) became inextricably linked, like poison ivy draining the lifeblood from a great tree. The 'solution' was the Inquisition. While Fernando resisted strongly the introduction of the Inquisition into Catalonia from Castile, he was only able to delay the inevitable. Where the Inquisition was active, as in Girona in 1489, 1494–5 and 1504–5, it has been suggested that economic motives, (i.e. the confiscation of convert property), were uppermost. For example, fourteen members of the wealthy Falcó family suffered at the hands of the Inquisition. In 1402 the City Council of Barcelona had voted not to allow either Jewish or Muslim converts into trades and professions; in 1495 they were complaining to the king that after years of civil war, almost the only economic activity taking place in the city was in the hands of converts, some of whom were fleeing in fear of the Inquisition. But whatever hopes the Catalan economy might have had of recovery, within the new Spain turning to face the Atlantic and America, they were certainly not helped by persecution of Jews.

While it is slightly beyond the scope of this book, the case of the Majorcan Jews both supports the argument put so far and also adds some weight to the question of the extent to which Judaism, and in particular its cultural practices, may have persisted in Spain until modern times. Gil Sánchez Muñoz, Pope-in-exile as Clement VIII at Penyíscola down the Valencian coast from Tortosa, resigned in 1429 and became bishop of Majorca as a reward for his role in solving this thorny papal problem. He determined to make his name by securing the conversion of the remaining 200 Jews — most had converted after the killings of 1391. In 1436 sixteen Jews were arrested and accused of sacrilege. Four — leaders of the *aljama* — were condemned to be burned or, if they accepted conversion, death by hanging. They converted and the city authorities then let it be known that they would be spared if the rest of the Jewish community converted. It was agreed, and a solemn Te Deum sung in the Cathedral at Palma. But over the years, the converts, *xuetes* as they came to be known on the island, became a feature of the life of Majorca. 99 of them perished at the hands of the Inquisition between 1489 and 1535 but many others continued to live publicly as Christians and secretly as Jews. But because it was in secret, and because the

Inquisition fabricated evidence, we do not know, can never know, how many continued this secret Jewish life and the balance between cultural practices (food preparation, the celebration of family meals on feast-days) and actual religious belief. There was sufficient evidence, however, for 37 of them to be burned in 1691, though again the balance of economic jealousy and religious motives is hard to estimate. Despite the attempt by enlightened Spanish monarchs to regularise their position at the end of the eighteenth century, an element of social stigma continued to attach to these families, ignorant of Judaism, yet still paying for the supposed 'blood guilt' of their Jewish ancestry. In the words of the historian Carl Gebhardt they became 'Catholics without faith and Jews without knowledge' (in Kedourie, Spain and the Jews, p.17).

Catalan Muslims

Tortosa has giants, as do most Catalan towns. These enormous, ornate figures are a feature of Catalan popular culture. Twelve to fifteen feet high, they are elaborately dressed figures draped over a wooden frame carried by a single person. Every town of any size has its own giants, and they take part in processions of all kinds and generally preside at public events, keeping a watchful eye on the Catalans at play. They are usually stored somewhere around the town hall, and a friendly enquiry at reception normally leads you to them. In Tortosa, they preside over business in a tall atrium behind the main entrance and the elegant facade, perhaps once a patio which at some time has been glazed over. People come and go, paying their taxes, enquiring about the usual local government issues of housing, water and sanitation, social welfare and street-cleaning. The giants witness everything in silent detachment. There are eight of them, a generous supply even in a town of Tortosa's size and importance. Four are Christian, two representing historical characters from Tortosa's past and two fairy-story characters, two are

Jewish historical figures, and two are Muslim figures from Tortosa's past.

The balance seems about right. If Tortosa is maybe the last town in Catalonia to conserve a fascist monument — the bizarre metal construction in the centre of the river to those who died at the battle of the Ebro in 1938 — it is also a town which has thought about its history. Most of its tourist literature bears the slogan 'Mediterranean City of the Three Cultures', and there are fascinating itineraries to pursue around the sites of the Muslim *aljama* and Jewish *call*. On a hot summer's evening, in the narrow alleyways and tiny squares, it is possible to imagine oneself back in old medieval Tortosa, with its social castes and hierarchies, and the shared experience of poverty and squalor of Christian, Jewish and Muslim poor alike. The dispossessed of today in these narrow streets are Castilian-speaking workers from the south of Spain, immigrants from North Africa, a few Bosnian refugees, some Roma. Hard up against the castle walls, a paved square has been created, named after Menhamen ben Saruk, a Jewish trader, poet, lexicographer and linguist, who managed the difficult task of producing a Hebrew grammar based on Arabic. He died amid the splendours of Muslim Cordoba some time in the tenth century. Languages seem to have been something of a speciality in Tortosa: a tombstone in the Cathedral, dated as early as the sixth century, is in Hebrew, Latin and Greek, and records the life of Melissa, daughter of Judas and Mary. In this scholar's square, family groups sit out on dining-room chairs, watching their children at play, raising their heads as the swifts perform noisy acrobatics above them.

In *call* and *aljama* there are well-kept houses with pretty flower-decked balconies, but others with pealing plaster and a few tumbledown. There is work to do in Tortosa and not enough money to do it. If it is hard to reconstruct an accurate view of Jewish life in medieval Catalonia, it is even harder for Muslim Catalonia. And there is the further issue of Jewish life within Muslim

Catalonia. For example, the location of the Jewish *call* is known for Christian Tortosa, but not for Muslim Tortosa. The massive size of the castle — the *Suda* — reflects the fact that although the Muslims stayed in Tortosa for over 400 years, this was always frontier land. And that applied not just by land but also by sea, with Christian raids on the coast and attempts to intercept Muslim trade just as in later centuries the pirates from al-Andalus and North Africa would attack Christian coastal towns. Fortified as it was, Tortosa may not have had the splendour of Cordoba, but nevertheless shared in the life and culture of al-Andalus. It had a mosque, the centre of religious life, it had poets and philosophers, scholars and musicians.

Muslim society, of course, was no less unequal than Jewish or Christian communities. In both the al-Andalus period (up to 1148) and among the *mudèjar*s, those who chose to continue to live as Muslims in a Christian society, there were class and ethnic divisions. The Arabs consti-tuted a privileged class, while North African Berbers were looked down on, as evidenced in chronicles. The Arabs, who could trace family kinship to the prophet, tended to live in urban areas. Arabs described Berbers in similar terms to those they used about the Christians, noting a shared lack of intellectual ability, an anarchic spirit and a tendency to disorder and violence. But there are also numerous examples of Berbers filling important public offices in Muslim Catalonia. The most extensive group in Muslim Catalonia were the *muladins* — Christians who had become Islamicised. There were also slaves. Apart from Jews who lived as Jews, there were also Islamicised Jews — often active in the political and diplomatic field, in relations between Al-Andalus and Christian courts.

Muslim Tortosa also had a rich material culture, and the origins of irrigation in the lower Ebro valley can certainly be traced back to the Muslims, while in later centuries it was the skills of *mudèjar*s and *moriscos* (Muslim converts, post-1525) who maintained the dams and canals and dykes. The waters of the Segre, Ebro, Segrià and Francolí

123

were used for irrigation and for mills. Lleida was already an important fruit-producing area in the Middle Ages. *Mudèjar*s also farmed intensively the lower Ebro valley between Xerta (just north of Tortosa) and Amposta. Balaña comments that it is significant that 'the first documented public official in 1165, shortly after the reconquest of Tortosa by the Christians, was the *cavasequia* or inspector of waters in the community of Horta de Sant Joan, a basic job in the organisation of irrigation in the previous Muslim regime.' He notes the large number of Arabic words still in regular use in Catalan agriculture, and the use of spices such as cumin and aniseed in Tortosa cakes as further evidence of Muslim influence. Tortosa's importance as a trading centre remained constant. This trade was between the areas up-river from Tortosa under Muslim control and the rest of al-Andalus, by sea and land. In addition, relations between Muslims and their Christian neighbours were not just limited to times of war, whatever films like *El Cid* may have suggested. They were also based on frequent and profitable commercial, diplomatic and cultural exchanges. Much of this contact centred on Tortosa which traded extensively with al-Andalus, North Africa and beyond. It was claimed that wood from Tortosa was used in the building of the Mosque at Cordoba. Slaves, cotton, spices, sugar and gold are also documented as passing through the docks. A vital port for both trade and defence, Tortosa boasted extensive shipyards which after the Christian reconquest of 1148 were drained and became the new home of the Jewish *call*.

Lleida, which fell to Christian rule in 1149, was the other important centre of Muslim Catalonia. Again, for over 400 years it enjoyed prestige as a important city, while the irrigated plains that surround it bear witness once more to the skills of Muslim engineers and farmers. All through this area, the survival of an obviously Arabic place-name or a sudden eruption of abstract *mudèjar* decoration on a Christian church bear witness to the Muslim heritage. But there is no Alhambra (Granada), no Giralda

(Seville) or Mosque (Cordoba) to remind us of the splendours of al-Andalus. And despite some local initiatives, the official version of Catalan history in publications of the Generalitat still continues to ignore the Muslim past. A Roman town in origin, Muslim Lleida, like Tortosa, had its Jewish and Christian quarters, and a similar kind of harmony without equality. After the break-up of the great Caliphate of Cordoba in the early eleventh century, it became the capital of an independent *taifa* (statelet), but in the next century fell into the hands of the Almoravids, Muslim warriors from the Sahara who surged through al-Andalus with their particular intoxicating brew of religion, violence and misrule.

Lleida has had a difficult history. Although now again a thriving city, its population in 1900 was a mere 1,000, less than it had been in 1400. While Tortosa remained an important port in the united Spain of post-1492, a favourite city of the emperor Charles V with perhaps the best (the only?) Renaissance palace in Catalonia, Lleida was a strategic centre repeatedly besieged, bombarded and destroyed. A gunpowder explosion during the Napoleonic wars put paid to most of the remainder of the castle (successively Muslim, Christian, Hapsburg, Bourbon) and a whole suburb of the town as well. The miracle is that the Old Cathedral, the *Seu Vella*, survived, located on the site of the mosque to one side of the *Suda*, the Muslim fortress on the hill overlooking the town. It is worth the climb. Built in just 75 years between 1203 and 1278, the Cathedral's ecclesiastical days effectively came to an end after the 1707 siege. The whole area was occupied by the military and rebuilt as what the Muslims had originally intended — a fortress. The building was subsequently used as a warehouse, prison, military quarters and a hospital. Meanwhile a neo-classical cathedral was built in the town below. In 1949 work began on the reconstruction of the *Seu Vella*, not least to remove the many changes made since 1707, which included a false roof, the division of the nave into rooms and the opening up of new doorways. For a building with such a bizarre history, there is much to see and admire. In the chapel of Sant Tomàs are thirteenth century wall paintings in the upper parts and tympanum, but more remarkable are the intertwining patterns of the *mudèjar* work on the lower walls. These Muslim craftsmen, living and working in Christian Lleida, produced work the equal of any Christian artists or craftworkers of the period. Their work marks a clear break with the moralising, storytelling tradition of the Romanesque. Over three quarters of all the capitals at the *Seu Vella* are purely decorative. And then there are the cloisters. We tend to think of cloisters as quiet, intimate, secluded places. But not at Lleida. The monumental cloisters are placed before the church, and right on the edge of the hill, where it falls away to the fields and orchards to the south. With the slanting evening sun lighting up the orange-brown stone, the distinctive style of these cloisters seems to embody three design traditions: intertwining, abstract forms in the Islamic tradition; plant forms of leaves and fruit and flowers; birds and animals and figures passed down from the Romanesque to the Gothic.

But the grand finale of this temporary union of east and west, of Christianity and Islam, of revealed religion in two of its major forms, is the great west porch of the parish church of the little town of Agramunt, stranded miles from nowhere in the alternating landscape of arid dryness and rich, irrigated lands that stretch as far as the eye can see from the summit of the Suda in Lleida. Agramunt is a cheerful little market town, with an open-air market completely filling the area in front of the church and spreading along the little arcaded streets in the town centre. To see the porch at all is to strain and stretch above the throng of cheerful shoppers, the market stalls piled high with fruit and vegetables, plants, pots and pans, and North Africans travelling salesmen with their radios and watches, their rugs and carpets. The bustle of the people below is matched by the busy house martins above who have colonised this porch. Again, there is that perfect combination of east and west, of representation and decoration, of animal and vegetable, of the divine and the secular. And each archivolt has its own character, whether it be abstract decoration or wild beasts, or figures of the Christian saints. The columns are slim and graceful with delicate foliage in the capitals. It is as if a little of the life of Muslim Cordoba and Granada had come to share the day-to-day life of this down-to-earth agricultural community.

It was not to last, of course. In 1610 the Spanish state decreed that the *moriscos*, the direct descendants of those Muslim craftworkers, and of the people who had come from Arabia, from North Africa all those centuries before, were to be expelled. Yet even then, the expulsion was not uniformly welcomed. In the Ebro valley, the bishop of Tortosa complained that his *moriscos* were well integrated and good Christians. He knew that it would take centuries to rebuild the knowledge of agriculture and crafts that they would take with them, that neither the economy nor the culture of New Catalonia would ever be the same again. Perhaps in his Christian heart there may have been a gleam of sympathetic understanding of Islam. Or was he just another hard-headed Catalan ecclesiastical businessman? Who knows? Yet this argument from history and culture matters. It matters to Catalonia today. Is Catalan culture one culture, based on the language, the *sardana*, the red roses of Saint George's Day and the fire-crackers of countless local festivals? Or is it something more complex, a mingling of cultures twisting around one another like that decoration on the porch at Agramunt? They are real questions, and will recur before we reach the end of the book. The cultures of modern Catalonia (like those of medieval Catalonia) are many and varied, popular and classical, religious and secular, local and international. No Catalan, no book about Catalonia, can ignore the existence of large numbers of people born in Catalonia but whose parents come from elsewhere in Spain. Or of other newcomers, from North Africa and Latin America, from other parts of Europe, professional people coming to make the most of the vibrant economy and cultures of Barcelona, the poor of the earth seeking any way out in a world tragically divided between rich and poor.

Footnotes to a History

Daniele Conversi, in his fine book on the rather different recent histories of the Catalans and Basques in Spain, picks up on an historical oddity. Spain's Jewish community had disappeared centuries ago. But for one man, for one ideology, in the twentieth century, Catalans were Jews. The man was Franco, the ideology fascism. Jewish-Catalans was a favourite Falangist term to abuse the Catalans at the end of the Spanish War. But as the Second World War progressed, Franco, crafty as ever, was already distancing himself from Hitler, his one aim, as it would be for thirty more years, power and clinging to power. Anti-Nazi refugees and several thousand Sephardim from the Balkans were given sanctuary or transit visas. Some eventually became full citizens. It is one more curious footnote of history.

Another man, a Catalan, thought of the Jews too, and used obscure Old Testament language to hide his real poetic intentions. That man was the poet Salvador Espriu, probably the best of many fine twentieth century Catalan poets. He used the ancient term 'Sepharad' for Spain in his book *La Pell de Brau* (The Bull's Hide — an analogy often used for the map of Spain). His home town of Arenys de Mar, still a popular little holiday resort and fishing village, became Sinera. In this way he was able to make direct comment on the fate of a nation that found itself still caught up in the clutches of fascist dictatorship, where to argue directly for difference, and for community across difference, was anathema. Conversi observes that 'As the name 'Sepharad' suggests, Spain could be emulated and desired only in its pre-1492 form'. As Sepharad, it 'might one day recognise that pre-1492 form to be one of

128

cultural dialogue and exchange, but now recast in the image of democracy and equality' (Conversi, <u>The Basques, the Catalans and Spain</u>, p. 122). Espriu wrote:

> Always remember this, Sepharad.
> Keep open bridges of dialogue
> And seek to understand and love
> Your children's desires and languages . . .
> That Sepharad may live forever
> In order and in peace, at work
> In difficult and deserved freedom.
> (author's translation)

There are once again Jews and Muslims in Catalonia. But there are also many other groups of people who find joy in being different, and in sharing that difference with others who feel the same way as they do. The argument is put from a different angle, because our world is different from that of the 1940s and 1950s. But we owe a debt to Espriu for keeping that ideal alive, in a mythical little fishing village called Sinera.

Chapter 7

Barcelona — the Nineteenth Century Heritage from Cerdà to Gaudí

A City of Conflict

Chapter 5 of this book outlined the beginnings of the spectacular growth of the Barcelona area as an industrial region in the nineteenth century. It was a process that put Catalonia on a collision course with backward, rural Spain with its dominant figures of the village priest and the landlord (often absentee), its churning poverty and its antipathy to industry. This clash between a relatively closed, traditional Spanish society and the relatively open society of Catalonia with its commitment to economic growth and material prosperity was worked out in the relations between the Madrid government and the Catalan bourgeoisie and the nationalist political groupings it generated. From the middle of the nineteenth century this class pursued its economic and political interests with single-minded zeal. Factories were established, and the Catalan bourgeoisie became a potent political force in Spanish politics, arguing for tariff protection for its fledgling industries and feeling its way cautiously towards a programme of regional autonomy, finally crystallized in the *Bases de Manresa* (1892). Convened by the Unió Catalanista, itself a grouping of various conservative Catalanist organisations, it devised a programme of political autonomy which still reserved for the Spanish state responsibility for foreign policy, postal services, railroads, customs and Church-state relations.

131

As in so many European cities, industrialisation brought with it social conflict. The necessity to create a new class of industrial workers, working closely together on the production process in factories, always entailed the risk that this new class would combine together in defence of interests that were different from those of the thirty or so great families who dominated the Catalan manufacturing of textiles and metal. The conflict was played out in the division between the old city where most of the working class continued to live, subject to overcrowding and disease, including outbreaks of cholera, and the middle classes who took up residence in the new town that grew beyond the confines of the old city walls. From the mid-nineteenth century onwards, Barcelona erupted in periodic fits of violence. This is the *Rosa de Foc* (Rose of Fire) which Manuel Vázquez Montalbán describes in his book *Barcelonas*, a book that is available in English translation. It is one 'Barcelona', but an important one, and its identification should not be lost in the description of that other Barcelona of spacious avenues and *Modernista* masterpieces.

At times, the one Barcelona enters into the life of the other, as in the anarchist bombs of the 1870s, 1880s and 1890s. For the working class, the ostentatious lifestyle of the Catalan bourgeoisie was a constant provocation and a target. What purpose did wealth have if it could not be flaunted? But if it had to be flaunted, how was it possible to defend it against those who had nothing to lose but their own lives of poverty and insecurity? It did not need a sophisticated political philosophy to recognise that the wealth of the thirty leading Catalan families was built on the exploitation of the workers. It did not need a Darwinian theory of human motivation to understand that the bourgeoisie would never give up its privileged lifestyle unless forced to do so. It is the way that cities lie posed between such questions and their answers that makes them social documents of such importance. We look, and we see not just wealth and squalor but political antagonisms and ideologies being worked out before us.

For the middle classes, these ideologies ranged between liberalism and conservatism, between Monarchy and Republic, between Spain and Catalonia. Catalans were engaged in Spanish politics, as they have always been, and at least until the *Bases de Manresa* in 1892 it is not possible to identify unambiguously a single dominant tendency in Catalan political thought. Equally for the working classes, anarchist outrages were not the only politics. Others stressed the importance of the developing trade union movement in negotiating improvements in pay and conditions, or the development of autonomous working class cultural and educational organisations.

Barcelona was in full-scale revolt with especially bloody results and bloodier reprisals in the *Setmana Tràgica* (Tragic Week) of 1909. In 1909, the governor of Barcelona wrote about the events of the *Setmana Tràgica*: 'In Barcelona there is no need to prepare the revolution simply because it is always ready. It leans out of the window on to the street every day and if the atmosphere is not right it goes back in.' The *Rosa de Foc* again. It was the same city which was later to acclaim the 'Catalan' Republic of 1931 and to greet George Orwell with the unmistakable signs of social revolution in 1936. It was to take forty years of Francoism to bring the working and middle classes together in the tumultuous demonstrations of the 1970s that led to the statute of autonomy, and played their part in the transition from centralised dictatorship to decentralised democracy. By one of the frequent ironies of history, it was down the Passeig de Gràcia, the grand avenue of the nineteenth century extension of Barcelona that they paraded, their red and yellow banners unfurled.

The Barcelona New Town
Barcelona, as it grew, changed from a medieval city to a modern city. By the middle of the nineteenth century, it

had become impossibly cramped within its old city walls. As constructed in the eighteenth century they had always had more to do with Spanish state control over the Catalans than with rational urban planning. The density of population in the old town was four times that of Victorian London. Tearing these walls down was to open a new phase in Barcelona's history, as a dynamic new social force — the urban bourgeoisie — flexed its political, economic and cultural muscles. The decision to demolish the hated city walls in 1854 opened the door to a different, if uncertain, future. Cities are not just places to live in but symbols. If the medieval city with its labyrinth of streets and alleys and irregular little squares is somehow symbolic of the mystical quest of medieval religion (whether Christian, Jewish or Muslim), the grid pattern of the Barcelona new town (the Eixample) is a bold and proud statement of the human ability to control nature, to impose order and pattern. Yet only at one point, the Via Laietana plunging down past the Cathedral to the port, separating the quarters of Sant Pere and of Santa Maria del Mar from the heart of the old city, did the new building encroach on the old city, and this destruction was not completed until well into the twentieth century.

The designer of the new city was Ildefons Cerdà, engineer, rationalist and part-time socialist. He was also a politician to his finger-tips, being at various time between the mid-1850s and his death in 1876 a member of the Spanish parliament in Madrid and of the Barcelona Town Council. He was able to take advantage of a liberal phase in Spanish national politics to push through his 1859 plan (revised in 1863) for a vast grid plan extension to the city, with wide avenues and streets to carry the traffic which he foresaw the modern city bearing, and including plans for water supplies and sewage extraction. Cerdà wanted to improve the lives of workers by giving them access to good quality housing, to fresh air, light and hygiene. Yet in the hands of the property developers, the Barcelona Eixample became a substantially middle-class development, even using that term in its broadest possible sense. Thanks to the 2002 exhibition at the Royal Institute of British Architects in London, and accompanying publication by the Generalitat de Catalunya, we know much more of this remarkable man than we did before. But we also know that it didn't quite work out in the way he had planned. Where Cerdà intended his city as a social leveller, the Catalan middle-classes viewed it as an opportunity for social differentiation, profit and display.

Cerdà had compiled a statistical account of the unhealthy, cramped conditions in which the Barcelona working class lived. He had written a *General Theory of Urbanisation*, its principles applied to the specific case of Barcelona. His aim was a complete, integrated city which could respond to the movement, the bustle, the constant contact between people, of industrial society. From 1860, he attempted to turn theory into practice. His plan was a regular grid pattern with blocks which, taking account of road width, measured 133 metres each way (about 450 feet) with chamfered corners (that is to say, corners cut back at an angle of 45 degrees so that the street facades intersect on a diagonal· rather than at right angles) to assist traffic turning and loading and unloading. For the sake of comparison, the New York grid is 800 × 200 feet, and Melbourne 620 × 320 feet. On the Montjuïc side it is bordered by a diagonal avenue called the Paral·lel which runs from Plaça Espanya to the port and along which much of the city's old-fashioned nightlife — music-halls and review bars especially — is concentrated. Roughly parallel to this a grander avenue, the Diagonal, bites through the heart of the grid, with one modern extension up into the University City, and another reaching the sea at the site of the 2004 Universal Forum of Cultures. The other main axis is the Gran Via, three times wider than the average street, running roughly parallel to the sea just north of the Plaça de Catalunya, through the Plaça Espanya at the foot of Montjuïc, and on to the neighbouring city of Hospitalet at the Plaça Cerdà.

Rather than letting social development and social conflict run its course, Cerdà was convinced that rational planning was the answer. He wanted to unite working class and bourgeoisie, town and country. Each block in the grid would contain a cross-section of Barcelona society; the rigid geometry of the grid would be softened by parks and gardens. Only two sides of each block would be built upon. But this proved utopian in practice as soon as the property developers got to work. The commercial pressure of soaring property prices and the phenomenal growth of the city, with its continual pressure for more and more homes, meant that almost all available land was built upon. The blocks were built up on all four sides, permitted building heights were increased, and very often the central areas designed by Cerdà as gardens were filled in as well as the depth of building development increased. The occasional hidden garden is the exception that proves the downfall of Cerdà's vision, although viewed from the air, there are still more green spaces in the *Eixample* than in some of the newer working class housing estates on the outskirts of the city. Only an occasional green oasis, such as the Plaça Doctor Letamendi at the junction of Aragó and Enric Granados streets, with parrots squawking wildly in the palm-trees to drown out the traffic noises, a children's playground, lovers canoodling on the benches and a dog-toilet, suggests what might have been. It is a small but significant shrine in the busy city to Catalan sociability.

The architecture of the *Eixample* is an architecture of facades. This is inevitable, for it is only the facades that can be viewed from the street. This simple fact explains much, as does the desire of the Barcelona middle classes to have as little as possible to do with Cerdà's egalitarianism. As we have seen, much of the new wealth came from fortunes made in Cuba and Puerto Rico, and as in the more modest villas in provincial coastal towns, the decoration of the facades often made conscious reference to the flowers and fauna of the tropics. The decoration of facades was also the best way to let the world know of your social pretensions, and it is not surprising that the most remarkable facades, those that are still visited and admitted today, are in the streets around the broad Passeig de Gràcia. For a time, until the Barcelona-Sarrià railway which passes up the *Rambla de Catalunya* was covered in to create a pedestrian walkway, it was literally the 'right' and 'wrong' sides of the tracks. To the right were the wealthy, fashionable areas, to the left the less fashionable areas. This was not what Cerdà's egalitarian instincts had planned. As for the architecture of that more fashionable zone, it was the architecture of a confident middle class, nationalist in its politics but internationalist in its frame of cultural reference.

What the visitor sees today is in some ways rather arbitrary. Many of the buildings built between 1860 and 1900 were torn down to be replaced by taller, showier blocks as building regulations were gradually eased. In the years 1900-15 there was constant rebuilding of blocks and remodelling of facades in the Passeig de Gràcia. Given that this was the most fashionable area of the *Eixample*, and of highest property values, it was here that there was most pressure to change, innovate and generally show off. It was here that *Modernisme*, with its curving forms, its imaginative use of colour and decoration, became established as Catalonia's own version of art nouveau. But it is wrong to imagine the *Eixample* as *Modernista*. The driving principle of design moved beyond classicism but only to wallow in eclecticism. Most of the design tendencies that flourished in Europe either side of 1900 can be found in the busy streets of the *Eixample*, as the local architects felt their way out of style as straightjacket and into style as self-expression and commodity. If Cerdà's plans show ambivalence between the rational classicism of the geometric layout and the Romantic utopianism later to find its expression in the Garden City, the outpourings of Catalan architecture and design fit clearly into an historicist framework in which neo-Romanesque, neo-Gothic, neo-Arab jostle for pride of place. It was the despised

137

crafts, as much as sophisticated art and architecture, which showed the way forward. The neo-Romanesque style adopted by Josep Puig i Cadafalch fitted his conservative politics, but also implied the use of materials such as iron and ceramics to decorate facades and interiors in ways consistent with Catalonia's past. The *Renaixença* (the Catalan cultural rebirth which coincided with the first buildings of the *Eixample*) had been a rediscovery of national cultural and political identity. *Modernisme* was to be the apotheosis of the dream of nationhood, and the apotheosis of *Modernisme* was to be Antoni Gaudí, born at Reus in 1852, and destined to become a national symbol. He was fortunate in enjoying the patronage of the rich industrialist Eusebi Güell whose family had used wealth initially built up in Cuba to found Catalonia's first great industrial empire. Gaudí was especially fortunate in finding a man who was both immensely wealthy and also prepared to share the architect's idiosyncratic views about design.

The best place to start a tour of the *Eixample* is still, without doubt, the *Mançana de la Discòrdia* (block of discord) outside Barcelona's town centre Passeig de Gràcia railway station. The name comes from the contrasting style of the three principal buildings: the Casa Batlló (Gaudí, 1904–06), the Casa Ametller (Puig i Cadafalch, 1898–1900) and the Casa Lleó Morera (Domènech i Muntaner, 1902–06). For many years, all but the favoured few have seen only the facade of the Casa Batlló and most have assumed that that is all there is to see. Evelyn Waugh got inside and dismissed it, remarking with a characteristic touch of old-fashioned English racism that it was no doubt suitable for its occupant — the Turkish consulate. Robert Hughes got inside and was impressed. In 2002, declared the Gaudí Year by those who market Barcelona to the world, far more people got inside, with the whole of the first floor open to visitors. The Casa Batlló is not just facade. Gaudí treated the whole house, rebuild job that it was, as a single design, and put as much care into the moulded ceilings, the lift, the furniture, the terrace garden at the back, as into the jewel-studded mosaics of the facade. The other surprise is the practicality of Gaudí's design, and the detailed attention that he paid to matters such as lighting, door handles and hinges and the circulation of air through the building. Many of the virtues of the building at close quarters are those of English Arts and Crafts, however different the result. Just as there is one logic that goes from William Morris to the international modernity of the 1920s and 1930s, so there is another development line of arts and crafts that profoundly influenced the various national forms of art nouveau in the 1890s and early 1900s. The building works at a number of levels. For most people, it is entirely a question of line and fantasy, but there is also a religious and patriotic 'reading' of the building as a symbolic treatment of the legend of St George, patron saint of Catalonia, and the dragon. In this reading, the bulging roof with its green tiles becomes the scaly back of the dragon and the mask-like window balconies represent the skulls of the dragon's victims. At times, Gaudí seems to take his own playfulness rather too seriously.

Next door, and the earliest of the three key buildings, is Puig i Cadafalch's Casa Ametller. The success of this building is that it gives the illusion of being a small Gothic palace, rather than the block of flats it has always been. There is elaborate tracery and carving on the lower floors, and a more fanciful tiled and stepped gable above, which gives the illusion of a Dutch town-house from Delft or Alkmaar transported to the south and acquiring just a hint of an Arabian palace en route. The Gothic, in any case, is of the most eclectic, including, for example, carvings of monkeys around the windows which are a reference to the client's status as a cocoa merchant. Hot chocolate has always been a popular drink in Barcelona. This is Puig i Cadafalch in relaxed mood — as an architect he is perhaps better known as a formal exponent of the Romanesque as Catalonia's national style, while as a politician he was, like Domènech i Muntaner, a leading member of the big business party of Prat de la Riba — the Lliga Regionalista (later Lliga Catalana). In him, more than any other Catalan at the turn of the century, there are explicit links between historicism in architecture and design, conservative nationalism in politics, and hard-nosed capitalist economics designed to squeeze the workers as much as possible. Despite his respectable bour-geois credentials, Puig i Cadafalch's nationalist politics made him a victim, like many of those workers, of being on the wrong side in the Spanish War. He was forbidden to practice as an architect from 1939, and lived mainly in Catalunya Nord (French Catalonia) where he pursued his academic researches into the Romanesque.

The third building is the corner block of flats known as the Casa Lleó Morera by Lluís Domènech i Muntaner, another re-build of an earlier construction. A decade or two ago it was described as 'badly mutilated', but since then has undergone extensive repairs which have returned it to something like the graceful elegance of its original state. Again, access is a problem. During the 1980s and 1990s, the Barcelona Tourist Board had its offices on the first floor, the perfect excuse to go in and admire this arts and crafts paradise. By the end of the cen-tury, this happy situation had been replaced by a fierce porter able to spot a tourist at fifty paces and quite deter-mined that access to the building should remain limited to its tenants and their legitimate visitors. The external stone-work is elegant and complex, exploiting to the full the potential of the chamfered corner site. On the second floor are female figures symbolising technical innovations such as the electric light, gramophone, camera and tele-phone; Domènech is one of those happy architects who is able to look both backwards and forwards in his work. Inside there is a small patio and staircase rather like those to be found in the medieval town houses of the Carrer Montcada, but here enlivened with stained glass, metal lamp fixtures, stone and wood carving. The public monkeys of the Casa Ametller are here replaced by private family pets. Above the staircase soars a glass roof in pink and mauve and yellow. The first-floor rooms, previously the Tourist Office, are the most elaborately decorated — the convention was for the first floor to be occupied by the building's owners — and here there are mosaic murals of family life as well as the bright, cheerful stained glass that Domènech used in so many of his buildings.

These houses on the Passeig de Gràcia are at their best on a winter morning when the oblique sunlight shows off the delicate tones of stone work, ceramics and glass to full advantage. Those who are happy to tolerate the noise and the exhaust fumes which are now the daily staple of life in the *Eixample* can sit for a while on the benches beneath the wrought iron lamp standards and dream themselves back into the heroic days of the Catalan bourgeoisie at the opening of another new century, when money bought not just the conventional, but also the esoteric, the nostalgic and the outright perverse, all dressed up as the latest totems of urban progress. It is easy to imagine wealthy Catalans parading up and down this broad avenue in their fine clothes, flaunting their wealth before neighbours and friends, or in their boxes at the Liceu Opera House in the *Rambla*, taking more interest in the latest fashion and gossip, the tawdry business of marital alliances, and the political prospects of the Lliga, than in the latest production of Verdi or Wagner. In Victor Alba's opinion, the Liceu served as a kind of court:

Since Barcelona had no court, the bourgeoisie created its own substitute: the Teatre del Liceu, founded in 1844, around which revolved the social life of the country. To own a seat in the Liceu was almost a patent of nobility, as was membership in the Liceu Circle, the club housed in the same building as the opera. It is not without significance that when the Liceu was destroyed by fire in 1861, it was rebuilt within the year, and that the Liceu was chosen as the target of anarchist terrorism. (Catalonia, p. 62)

When the Liceu was again destroyed by fire in the 1990s, it was again rapidly rebuilt. There is change in Barcelona, an incessant seeking after the new, but there is also continuity. The right to flaunt wealth is a fundamental Catalan right.

The Passeig de Gràcia has always been, of course, the socially most elite street of the *Eixample*. Neither the richness of decoration as viewed, nor the financial wealth as imagined, applied to the narrower lives of the many humbler representatives of the Catalan middle classes (clerks, shop-keepers, professional people) who lived in the less showy streets of the *Eixample*. Although in describing their buildings in the Passeig de Gràcia, both Puig i Cadafalch and Domènech i Muntaner have been categorised as conservative Catalanists, the evidence from the buildings is that they were very different men. While to describe Domènech as a populist would probably be an exaggeration, two of his buildings — a concert-hall and a hospital — are among the most popular, in the best sense of the word, buildings in Barcelona. The Palau de la Música Catalana (Palace of Catalan Music) is perhaps of all the *Modernista* buildings in Barcelona the most perfect and the most accessible, assuming that we agree for a moment to set aside the 'special case' of Gaudí. Critical acknowledgement did not come immediately, however, and its present status as a World Heritage Site owes a lot to the international reassessment of *Modernisme* in recent years. The Palau was founded as the headquarters of the Orfeó Català (Catalan Choral Society), a role it continues to perform; in the 1980s it acquired an exemplary extension by Oscar Tusquets which included new offices for the choir, as well as improving the bar and box office facilities for the concert-hall. This remodelling took nearly ten years compared with the remarkable four years to build the original, between 1902 and 1906. The official guided tours of the building are popular and over-subscribed and curiously contradictory. While the film introduction, which takes place in the original cramped rehearsal room at the back on the ground floor, identifies the architect as individual genius, the guides tend to emphasise that the building was first and foremost the headquarters of a choir, and therefore itself part of a collective Catalan scheme of things.

The complex sculpture above the original entrance on the street corner represents the different social classes of Catalonia with their patron saint, Sant Jordi (Saint George) above. The Palau is one of the few *Modernista* buildings built within the old city walls and there are reasons for this. First of all, and bearing in mind that Domènech's client was a voluntary organisation, the Orfeó Català wanted to take advantage of the cheaper land prices here than in the *Eixample*. But equally important, they wanted to build in the old Sant Pere district because most choir members lived in working class areas of the inner city rather than in the *Eixample*. The seating for 2,000 represented the actual number of members of the society in the early years of the century. Millet, the founder of the choir, also had a flat in the roof area, and from the front of the stalls you can look up at a small glass ceiling, originally open so that he could listen to concerts from his own home. The removal of the church next door at the beginning of the twenty-first century has made the extraordinary lightness of the circle and balcony even more impressive, with a fine collection of stained glass and ceramics, much of it on symbolic Catalan themes. So the glass red-on-white St George's crosses are complemented by the ceramic pink and white roses of the ceiling, since the tradition of giving a rose to your loved one on April 23, St George's Day, was already well established by the early years of the twentieth century. Robert Hughes, like the present author, is an enthusiast for Domènech in general and the Palau in particular. 'Domènech,' he wrote, 'was a paragon of the architect as master of works. His friends compared him to an orchestral conductor. Under his baton you got to do well what you did best.' (Barcelona, p. 399)

143

The Palau has served Barcelona well. Even during the Franco years the concerts went on, in particular the Barcelona City Orchestra (now Catalan National Orchestra) concerts on Saturday nights and their repeats at 'popular prices' on Sunday mornings. Alicia de Larrocha played here at the age of seven, and again and again during the dictator's years. Jordi Pujol, President of Catalonia, was imprisoned for organising a demonstration here during a concert. For those of us who knew and loved the Palau in the 1960s, there is little to be ashamed of. The acoustics were awful? Well, they were not the best: John Langdon-Davies in *Gatherings from Catalonia*, no doubt influenced by the equally negative views of his friend the writer Josep Pla, described the Palau as 'the worst and most inappropriately conceived concert hall in the world'. An English architect living and working in Barcelona, David Mackay, sees it differently. For him, the Palau represents both the universality of music and the claims of the Catalan bourgeoisie to international recognition. His book *Modern Architecture in Barcelona (1854–1939)*, published in English by the Anglo-Catalan Society in 1985, is still a good read. Music is, after all, a universal language. And those who do not care for the acoustics have always had the option of admiring the architecture, which has always defiantly proclaimed Catalonia's pretensions to nationhood.

One of the many improvements that the Town Council has made in Barcelona is to pedestrianise a diagonal route now called the Avinguda de Gaudí from the north-eastern corner of the Sagrada Família to Domènech's second great public building, the Hospital de Sant Pau. This lies at the very edge of the *Eixample*, from where the ground climbs steeply towards the pretty Guinardó Park and the hills above the city. The Avinguda is maturing nicely as a promenade and as a place to eat, drink and relax. It is a relief to leave behind the coaches and tour parties and general din of the Sagrada Família. Maybe the plan was to lure foreign tourists up to the Hospital, but the truth is that it is still the sick, their visitors and medical students that the visitor is most likely to encounter. Gaudí's Sagrada Família towers, for all their polychromatic brilliance, for all their emblematic value as Barcelona's major tourist attraction, seem heavy and lumpy compared with the airy Gothic pinnacle on the hospital facade. Where the towers are earth-bound, the pinnacle hovers almost weightless against the blue Mediterranean sky.

Unlike the Palau, the hospital took a long time to build. Domènech planned it in 1901, the main administration building was completed in 1911, but a number of the pavilions were completed by his son Pere in the 1920s, faithfully following the father's overall design. A wrought-iron fence on brick and ceramic plinths surrounds the grounds and through this are enticing views of pavilions set in gardens. Domènech believed that a hospital should speak of health and well-being rather than sickness and created what is to all intents and purposes a little garden suburb, the many services required carried by underground pipework. Each department occupies a single-storey building with easy access to fresh air, sunshine and flowers. A less institutionalised setting for a hospital is hard to imagine. Some of the buildings, most noticeably the surgical block, are still in use for the purpose for which they were intended but the medical faculty of the Autonomous University has taken over other buildings. At the rear of the site, the hospital authorities have taken advantage of the sloping site to build a vast underground car-park. A programme of modernisation is in hand. But in general the hospital seems to manage very well to carry on twenty-first century medicine in an early twentieth century building.

Antoni Gaudí

The *Eixample* is all about facades. But one man, in one extraordinary building, contradicts completely that statement. The man is Gaudí and the building La Pedrera (the quarry), more formally the Casa Milà (1905–10). From the outside it appears like an enormous pile of stone, but this curvilinear stone facade is self-supporting and the building itself is on an iron frame. The design motif for the facade is marine — a shining white tidal wave of architecture about to immerse the city in which it has the good fortune to find itself a much loved guest. By 1905, Gaudí was a respected architect in Barcelona, and in view of the ambitious nature of his scheme, the urban by-laws controlling technical issues such as height and street-line were waived in this instance. As we have seen, they had previously been changed on a number of occasions to allow ever larger buildings to be put up. This was a large corner site near the top of the Passeig de Gràcia, where the ground begins to climb upwards towards the old village of Gràcia. The potential for display was considerable. The floors were planned around two polygonal light wells which illuminate the kitchens and corridors. Gaudí, as at the Casa Batlló further down the Passeig de Gràcia, combined the most exotic polychromatic effects in glass and ceramics with an engineer's sense of what was needed to make a block of flats work effectively, including an underground car-park, the first of many in the city. The Milà family disliked the building they had commissioned, at least from the point of view of having to live in it. Their dislike was intense, and in particular they disliked the finishes Gaudí applied to their own apartments on the first floor. In later years they removed the broken-tile decoration from the bathrooms and kitchen, and had the whole flat redecorated in French classical style. Only in recent years, with the purchase of the building by the Caixa de Catalunya savings bank has it been possible to recover the original Gaudí effects of this floor, which is now in use as an exhibition area. It is worth a look — in particular the complete freedom Gaudí gave himself via the rigid iron frame to create the most complex curvilinear forms, with walls and ceilings plastered in undulating, wave-like forms. It is also possible to visit the roof with chimneys and ventilation shafts decorated with coloured tiles, glass and mosaic and pulled into a variety of anthropomorphic shapes. But only some of them are finished in this way: when the Milà family found out what Gaudí was doing on the roof, he was asked to leave. Sometimes, just being Gaudí was hard work.

The Casa Milà was Gaudí's last civil building. For the rest of his life he concentrated on two religious buildings. The crypt of the church at the Colònia Güell, an industrial settlement outside Barcelona set among the fertile market-gardens and small-holdings of the Llobregat valley, was completed in 1915, but the church itself was never built. This was Gaudí's second collaboration with Eusebi Güell to build a model settlement, but unlike the Güell Park it was a success in its original conception. Commissioned from Francesc Berenguer i Mestres and built between 1898 and 1911 it contains one hundred good quality brick-built workers' houses on an axial plan, with a house for the manager, a school, social clubs and shops — a garden city in miniature. Gaudí's crypt is a wholly successful creation which still serves as the parish church, and has never felt the need for anything above it. At the same time, the bulk of the load-bearing columns gives some indication that Gaudí as ever was thinking big. With its mixture of original designs and modern copies for furniture, it retains the modest proportions of the arts-and-crafts rather than the gargantuan hubris with which Gaudí's name is more naturally associated. It is also interesting to see how the essential conservatism of the one man (Güell's paternalism) matched the essential conservatism of the other (Gaudí's Catholicism) despite the revolutionary trappings in which *Modernisme* dressed itself.

The other religious building, Gaudí's expiatory temple of the Sagrada Família (Holy Family), is still being built and may yet be completed. George Orwell hated it so much that he wished the anarchists had destroyed it in 1936. It is worth quoting the passage in full:

> For the first time since I had been in Barcelona I went to
> look at the cathedral — a modern cathedral, and one of
> the most hideous buildings in the world. It had four
> crenellated towers exactly the shape of hock bottles.
> Unlike most of the churches in Barcelona it was not dam-
> aged during the revolution — it was spared because of its
> 'artistic value', people said. I think the Anarchists showed
> bad taste in not blowing it up when they had the chance,
> though they did hang a red and black banner between its
> spires. (Orwell in Spain, p. 163)

At the time, Orwell was sleeping rough with two other
British volunteers, trying to avoid the round-up of POUM
supporters following the events of May 1937. No doubt a
little tourism was one sure way to keep out of trouble. The
comment is so Orwell, so public-school philistine — who
but an English public-school boy would have produced the
hock-bottles image? There are more serious criticisms to
be made of the project of the Expiatory Temple of the Holy
Family (it is not, as Orwell suggested, a cathedral). What
sins are the people of Barcelona expiating by contributing
to the costs of building? At one level, the sins of the Rose
of Fire — of violence, bomb outrages, ungodly anarchist
and socialist creeds. And there were plenty more to come
in the 1930s after Gaudí's death in 1926 under the wheels
of a Barcelona tram. There was desecration and burning of
churches, the public humiliation and murder of nuns and
priests dressed up as 'revolutionary violence'. More likely
now, perhaps, the sins of Barcelona are those of being a
rationalist, secular society with little interest in matters
religious or spiritual.

The ongoing construction work is being financed mainly
by the proceeds of international tourism, not least the
Japanese who have developed a very 'special relationship'
with Gaudí. Some of the work being done is good, in particular the completion of the nave vaulting, faithful to
Gaudí's concept of organic Gothic, and the way the trunks
of trees rise, divide into branches and shade the glades
beneath. But some is less good, most obviously the rather

grotesque crucifixion sculptures by Josep Maria Subirachs and the poor detailing of some of the newer towers, which do little to enhance the memory of a fine designer. Perversely, if it had not been for Franco, it is unlikely that the Sagrada Família project would have survived. The church became another symbol of a Catalan identity which was being trodden into the dust, and the slogan of those who promoted the cause (*Entre tots ho ferem tot* — We'll do everything between us all) carried an alternative message. Keeping 'everything' — the Sagrada Família — alive became another way of keeping memory alive, of keeping another 'everything' — Catalonia — alive. At the same time, as a symbol of the Catholic Spain his regime was supposed to represent, Franco could scarcely prevent work continuing. Masterpiece or folly? It remains an open question.

Cities have ways of absorbing architecture, of using it. Medieval churches find new purposes as concert venues or arts centres. Warehouses become luxury apartments. Barcelona has been very good at this. The national library is about to move from the medieval setting of the Hospital de la Santa Creu to the Victorian splendour of the Born market. Gaudí's Sagrada Família is more complex. In the first place it is simply architecture, in the second place a major tourist attraction in its own right, in third place a complex national icon. What it may be used for if ever it is completed is anybody's guess — except that for the moment it seems to be the question that no-one dares to ask.

It is a relief to take the bus up to the Güell Park, where Gaudí and Jujol had once begun a model, fantastic suburban housing development for their rich and sympathetic patron Eusebi Güell — industrialist, Catalanist and patron of the arts. Here they entered into a semi-rural setting where nothing was forbidden. Fantasy could and did run riot among the pines and Mediterranean scrub overlooking the city. It is a private world for children and those who have not yet lost the naivety of childhood. They will be enchanted by the colours and playfulness of the designs, the ceramic-encrusted towers of the various houses, the esplanade above what was intended as the market with its ceramic-encrusted balustrade and fine views, and footpaths which climb up the semi-wild hillside. In winter there is shelter from cold north winds, and in summer there is ice-cream to cool the visitor and beer to quench the thirst. Who cares that the original plan for an artistic little suburban development never happened? By design and by luck, a failed suburban housing estate has developed into one of the most attractive and surprising parks in Europe. Yet the failure of the Güell Park in its original conception, and the failure to complete the church at the Colònia Güell, conceal a point we shall take up more fully in the next chapter. Nineteenth century Barcelona was beginning to lose its impetus, was beginning to run itself into a design cul-de-sac. Few of the middle-classes wished or could afford to live as the Batlló, Güell or Milà families lived. *Modernisme* might be alright for concert halls or even hospitals, but did it give the right air of sobriety for a nation that prided itself on hard work and common sense?

The coming thing was *Noucentisme*, the spirit of the new century, the 1900s. Yet to the surprise and annoyance of those who had hoped for something truly modern, *Noucentisme* in architecture implied neo-classicism. Solid, impeccably Mediterranean, speaking of the past and of eternal values, it was a style for a nervous, cautious age that found its politics shifting increasingly towards the right. As Alan Yates suggests:

> (*Noucentisme*) called for obedience to an 'order' and service to the prospect of a culture, coordinated with a nationalist ideal and political programme, in which the interests of the artist and those of society would coincide. *Noucentisme* operated from the power-base of the most influential and assertive sectors of the Catalan middle classes, whose nationalism was massively stimulated by the failures and crises of the Spanish political system over

the turn of the century.
(in <u>Homage to Barcelona</u>, Arts Council exhibition catalogue, p. 253)

Chapter 8

Barcelona and the Twentieth Century

From *Modernisme* to Modernism

It is hard now to see in Catalan *Modernista* architecture a particular political statement. The politics move on, the buildings remain, largely detached from the particular social and economic circumstances that gave them their original sense and meaning. By and large it is the victors who live to tell the tale. As Colm Tóibín wrote:

> The Lliga lived to write history; the Anarchists' dreams came to dust. The class who built the *Eixample* came to be remembered for their Great Exhibition of 1888, for their *Modernista* buildings, for their patriotism. The fact that they paid less than subsistence wages to the workers who carted the stones which fulfilled their dream of a great new city did not become part of the myth, nor that they employed assassins to gun down trade union leaders, nor that they supplied both sides in the First World War, nor that they were prepared to support the dictatorship of Miguel Primo de Rivera. These men, as time went on, would be held high in the esteem of their compatriots. (Homage to Barcelona, p. 63)

Neither artistically nor politically could the high esteem in which *Modernisme* is now held have been predicted in 1920. *Modernisme* had substantially lost whatever sense of force and direction it may have had in 1900 during the first two decades of the century. By 1920 *Modernisme* was yesterday's style.

Yet the way was not yet open for Catalonia to plunge into what the rest of Europe meant by Modernism — the modern movement in architecture and design that emerged from the German Bauhaus and spread to most of the advanced industrialised world in the two decades between the two World Wars. Between *Modernisme* and Modernism came *Noucentisme*, the neo-classical style which placed Catalonia within the heritage of the Mediterranean and its civilisations. If, as suggested in chapter 1, *Noucentisme* produced interesting work in painting and sculpture, the same cannot be said for architecture. The two facts are not unconnected. The classical theme of figures in a landscape was treated as surface pattern and as nostalgia by the *noucentistes*, where it had been treated as deep ecology by Cézanne. The latter artist suggested a new manner of understanding the relationship between human beings and the rest of the natural world in a way that looked forward to the ecological concerns of our own times rather than back to the classical world. The more complex issue of buildings in landscape and of buildings in the complex urban tissue of a twentieth century city was beyond the wit of neo-classicism. It was Picasso in the 1910s, Fernand Léger in the 1920s and increasingly from 1930 the new art of film that explored these themes. With the chaos caused in Europe by fascism and war, many of the European Modern architects and designers settled in the United States of America, and the Modernism of steel and glass sky-scrapers became the hall-mark of global capitalism USA-style. It also influenced Europe in turn during the second half of the century, and this movement across the Atlantic and back is reflected in the career of the Catalan architect Josep Lluís Sert.

With a drawing in of the limits of art and design came political reaction. The dictatorship of Primo de Rivera in the 1920s marked a hiatus in every way for Catalonia. The bourgeoisie threw in its lot with reaction and the Lliga was never again to be a political force to be reckoned with. In

154

turn this was to open new political options for Catalanism during the period of the Republic (1931–39). This new Catalanism, like that of our own days, was socially more plural than the Lliga which had always been the party of the 'thirty families'. The 1920s were the years of the building of the National Palace on Montjuïc and the various buildings associated with the Great Exhibition of 1929. And the now decidedly tatty collection of buildings known as the Spanish Village (Pueblo Español). The Catalans have generally been embarrassed by this collection of traditional building styles from all over a country they reluctantly belong to, although tourists seem to like the place well enough.

Other buildings can be recycled: the stadium, for example, found new life as the 1992 Olympic Stadium, while the National Palace has long been home to the Catalan Art Museum, with its valuable collection of Romanesque murals from the Pyrenean churches. The Palace/Museum has acquired an impressive new interior modelling by Gae Aulenti, eventually completed in 1995, but it is difficult to mask the almost brutal classicism of this building. Ironically it was designed by Pere Domènech, who, as we have seen, had completed work on his father's elegant Hospital de Sant Pau. The transition between these two buildings marks the decadence of Catalan architecture and the contrast with the new style emerging elsewhere in Europe is best demonstrated by the physical proximity of that icon of twentieth century modernism, Mies van der Rohe's German Pavilion from the 1929 Exhibition, now happily rebuilt a stone's throw from both Spanish Village and National Palace.

Whatever arguments there may be about the exact relationship between art and politics, there is no doubt that architecture and politics are inextricably linked. For architecture embodies in itself our view of what the good life is, and who should enjoy it. It expresses, too, the balance or the imbalance between private and social goods, and between the comforts of the body and the aspirations of

155

the soul. So it was in Barcelona in the 1930s. Under the Republic, Barcelona saw a brief but intense flowering of social architecture under the guiding hand of GATCPAC, the Catalan affiliate of CIAM (the International Congress of Modern Architecture). In Catalonia, too, there was the important influence of the ADLAN group, the Friends of the New Art, who advocated an approach to design anchored in the present and the future, rather than the past. Modernism came to embody the finest aspirations and the most humane achievements of the Republic.

Modernism began in Barcelona, however, as a luxury style for the elite. If Modernism was an international movement for a mass age, that did not necessarily make it an architecture of the masses. Sixt Yllescas, perhaps better known as Josep Lluís Sert's assistant, designed the Casa Vilaró (1929) in the suburbs of Barcelona, while Primo de Rivera was still in power. As late as 1934, Sert was responsible for the destruction of the *Modernista* Café Torino at the Plaça de Catalunya end of the Passeig de Gràcia in order to create a new shop-front in International Modern style for Roca the jeweller's. Together with other radical young designers, Sert and Yllescas held their own shows in 1929 well away from the site of the 1929 Great Exhibition at Montjuïc. Between 1932 and 1934, GATC-PAC, together with Le Corbusier, drew up a plan for urban development (christened the Plan Macià after the President of the Generalitat) for those areas east of the old city and the Ciutadella Park which had either not been completed under the *Eixample* plans, or which involved the rebuilding of the industrial suburb of Poble Nou. There is little to show for this: by 1934 the Republic was in crisis and by 1936 at war. Yet the Olympic Village of 1992 and the even more recent plans related to the Universal Forum of Cultures of 2004 have both served to bring reality to the ambition of those 1930s modernists to complete the Barcelona *Eixample* to the sea and to the River Besós in the east.

Some house-building went on. Sert and Yllescas were

responsible for a corner block in Carrer Muntaner, with recessed balconies, duplex apartments and rendered surfaces. These were painted pale green and have now been restored to their original colour in contradiction to those who think of International Modern as always and only white. But the recently rescued flats in Sant Andreu, the Casa Bloc, give a clearer idea of the social democratic instincts of the group. The ground floor shops added during the second half of the twentieth century have been removed to restore views into the internal open areas created by the S-shaped design, one of which was used for a school, the other for a park. Characteristically, the duplex is the chosen house form, with living area and terrace below and bedrooms above.

The most important survival of this brief but determined attempt to transform society through rational architecture and enlightened social policies was the TB Clinic (Josep Lluís Sert, Josep Torres Clavé and Joan Subirana, 1934–38) at the corner of the Carrer de Torres i Amat and Passeig de Sant Bernat, close by the Plaça Universitat. Tuberculosis was the classic twentieth century disease of poverty. This is not a museum and is seldom mentioned in tourist literature. Nowadays, the four-storey, L-shaped building acts as a primary care Health Centre for this still deprived part of inner city Barcelona — the prostitutes, the African and Asian migrant workers, the poor who are always with us. The building itself is in excellent condition, the dark green tiles shining, the walls of glass tiles as striking as ever, the right angles still unrelenting. The entrance is through a patio in the crook of the L-shape, while the consulting-rooms are placed on the shady side of the building to resist the summer heat. It is humbling to think of this modest building being completed in the war years as the political project of Spanish and Catalan Republicans crumbled around it. It sums up, like the Peckham Health Centre in London, Ken Worpole's point that Modernism is the characteristic style of social democracy. It developed what he calls 'a civic aesthetic focussed on collective provision allied to modern design, and strongly predicated on a belief in the benefits of clean water, sunlight and fresh air. It was an aesthetic based primarily on public health and the reform of the stunted, malnourished bodies of the worker and his family' (Here Comes the Sun, p. 10) According to Tóibín, Le Corbusier said of Barcelona, 'At last on one living point of the earth modern times have found an asylum'. But modernity would have to wait.

* * *

Despite everything, the politics of Modernism lives on. Sert went into exile, to re-emerge as the Professor of Architecture at Harvard University. The physical presence of those few Modernist buildings in Barcelona (even if the Casa Bloc was used as military barracks), Sert's continuing personal contacts with Barcelona and eventually the building of his design for the Miró Foundation on Montjuïc in the 1970s were an inspiration to a much younger generation of Catalan architects. And to one English architect, David Mackay. Married to a Catalan, fluent in the language, he has lived and worked in Barcelona since 1959, since 1961 in partnership with Josep Martorell and Oriol Bohigas. In an interview with the present author, Mackay described the Casa Bloc development at Sant Andreu, with its community centre and central park as "a milestone in architecture, but nobody knew about it because of the Civil War and the Second World War. And therefore it never got into the history books, no-one realised it was built." If Bohigas has been the planner, ideologue and politician of the group, Mackay's own work has pursued a modest, understated modernism with environmentally friendly features, blending in well with the existing urban landscape rather than dominating it as tower blocks do, or clashing with it as 'English houses' do ('English houses' describes terraced houses with gardens, which are quite common now in the

Barcelona suburbs). His flats down in the old port district of Barceloneta are well worth a detour from the main tourist routes. They occupy the site of an old engineering factory and the monumental gateway has been cleaned and restored. There is the same idea of quiet interior space, private but shared, with little bow windows on the ground floor, but preserving the strict street-line of this eighteenth century district. People know their architecture here too: the barman at the local café, asked about the flats, confidently asserted: "these duplex flats are a different aesthetic. In Barcelona people live in flats, everything on the same level. Here they can be like the Americans and go upstairs to bed." They are, of course, the same duplex flats that Le Corbusier and the GATCPAC architects of the 30s had made one of their trade-marks.

Barcelona: during and after Franco

From 1950 onwards, immigration into Barcelona from other parts of Spain, especially Andalusia, resumed at a very high level. These 'New Catalans' had their characteristic building form as well — the shanties built by people themselves from whatever materials they could lay their hands on. Meanwhile, at the other end of the social scale the victors of the war were building flats and houses in their own image in the select new suburbs on the hills above the city. Although a start was made on social housing in the 1950s, it was not of the kind that GATCPAC or even the London County Council would have recognised. The quality of these blocks of working class flats was dire, and worse still there was little investment in such city infrastructure as roads, street lighting, schools or hospitals. Montalbán described the new housing for immigrants in the satellite communities of Sant Ildefons and Bellvitge as 'monuments to bad taste and bare-faced contempt for the popular classes.' (Barcelonas, p. 157) As fast as one shanty town was torn down and replaced by some more

159

blocks built by the town council, another would spring up. Much of Montjuïc was covered in shacks, although not immediately visible to the visitor to the National Palace or the Spanish Village.

Presiding over this unplanned urban squalor was Josep Maria de Porcioles, the Francoist mayor. He has a lot to answer for. The only positive aspect of the grim conditions in which so many inhabitants of the city lived during the 1950s and 60s was to provoke the rise of an active citizens' movement in the last years of the Franco regime. Soledad García traces its origins to 1969 and notes 1974 as a key date when the City Federation of Neighbourhood Associations was established to mediate between individual citizens, the various associations and the City Council. Between 1969 and 1975 the citizens' movement was involved in 83 documented urban conflicts, nearly all led by community associations and often accompanied by violence. These conflicts were over the bread-and-butter matters of urban politics — housing, education, health care, urban planning, city management. Issues taken up included the destruction of the Can Tunis shanty town to make way for port extensions, the 'improvements' on Montjuïc which evicted 1800 families of shanty-dwellers, the location of dangerous factories and rubbish tips next to housing estates. The citizens' movement became a force to be reckoned with in Barcelona before and during the Transition. And while the Associations are by no means as active now as they were in the 1970s and 1980s, partly because many of their leaders were absorbed into mainstream politics, their critical gaze has continued to follow the authorities into the brave new world of democracy. Soledad García has written of its success:

The urban social movement became an important political channel through which a large section of Barcelona's population was organized to oppose the authoritarian regime ... The success of the movement was due to its

160

capacity to co-ordinate and mobilize manual and non-manual workers, Catalans and immigrants, political activists and non-party members.' (<u>García</u>, p. 200)

The chaos of Francoist Barcelona meant that young architects were driven to be concerned with issues of urban design as well as individual building projects. The MBM partnership of Mackay, Bohigas, and Martorell had been actively involved in flat-building during the last fifteen years of the dictatorship, but the problems that had accumulated since 1940 could not be cured by isolated buildings, however good their quality. David Mackay expressed this very clearly speaking in 1990: "The individual architect or the individual building can't make a city." Or as Manuel Vázquez Montalbán put it in his novel *Southern Seas*, 'Each century builds its ruins, and the Franco regime built this century's quota.' There are different views on post-Franco Barcelona. On the one hand there is pleasure about the quantity and quality of new building in the city. On the other hand there is sadness about the negative impact that the logic of capitalism and property prices has continued to exercise over the city. If the social divisions revealed by architecture are nowhere near as great as they were thirty years ago, they still exist. It is not just a matter of some people living in larger flats and houses than others or the way the city is divided into desirable, less desirable and frankly undesirable suburbs. It is the pomp and showiness of corporate business compared with the modest gains achieved within the public sector — schools, hospitals, and parks. It is also the way that modestly priced social housing has been squeezed out of prestige developments such as the Olympic Village.

Still, Barcelona remains an exciting city to visit not least because there is always a new building to see, always a new scandal to share, always a new bar or restaurant or night-club that must be visited. There are many, many moments to enjoy what has happened, as well as moments in which to lament the shortcomings. If the planning and architectural initiative was centred on the MBM partnership, political leadership for the new Barcelona was provided by the mayor, Pasqual Maragall, middle-class, Catalanist and social democrat. Bohigas himself was on the town council for a time, just as Ildefons Cerdà had been over one hundred years before. There are three particular episodes worthy of comment. The first strand, and the least known by foreign visitors, includes a wide range of urban developments across both the heart and the suburbs of the city. The second episode relates to the building projects undertaken in relation to the 1992 Olympic Games, of which a British reader may know something. The third strand relates to developments since the Olympics, culminating in the Universal Forum of Cultures.

Urban Renewal — the Civic Model

Is Barcelona, then, to be just another world city? Part of the answer is to be found in the old town, that tangled web of streets and alleys and squares still sticking obstinately to its medieval street plan. Another part of the answer is to be found in the urban projects promoted by the City Council, but most especially in the working class suburbs. Peter Rowe uses the term 'civic realism' for this architecture that defines and expresses the meeting-point of the state (here the local state) and civil society (here most obviously the citizens' movement referred to above), contrasting the architecture of private enclaves and great palaces. 'It is along the politico-cultural division between civil society and the state,' he writes, 'that urban architecture of the public realm is best made, especially when the reach of both spheres extends simultaneously up to a civilisation's loftier aims and down to the needs and aims of its marginalized populations.' (Civic Realism, pp. 34/5) One of the most noteworthy features of the urban projects in Barcelona has been the successful attempt to spread such projects across the city. This is very much in accord with

Cerdà's principles of allocation — he wanted for example parks and gardens to be a feature of all parts of the *Eixample*, not just relegated to a single 'green' space. This is heady stuff, but what about the practice? Pasqual Maragall did not become mayor until 1983, and it was his predecessor Narcis Serra who initiated the urban programme. From 1980 a special division of the City Council, under the direction of an architect José Antonio Acebillo developed projects in all ten districts of the city, and by 1987 when attention became focused on the Olympic Games, one hundred had been completed. By 1997 there were 140. There is so much here to admire: hard *plaças* rehabilitated in decrepit parts of the city, soft flowery parks, a generous use of fountains and lakes, a wide-ranging programme of public open spaces and sculptures aggressively modern in tone, and yet often referring in subtle ways to Barcelona's past and industrial heritage. Many of these sculptures are by internationally acclaimed artists who worked for a fraction of their market price.

The 'rural' end of this continuum of projects is perhaps the Parc de la Creueta del Coll, developed from an old quarry high above the city. It includes a paddling lake for children and a vast sculpture by Chillida, a riot of trees and shrubs and flowers and an iron monolith by Ellsworth Kelly. The combination of abstract art and living nature is especially attractive. Somewhere in the centre of the continuum one might place the Parc de l'Espanya Industrial behind the main railway station at Sants, which plays quite deliberately with the duality of the romantic park of trees, lake and fountains, and the hard paved open space which is so much part of a Mediterranean open-air culture. Far from being hostile to children, such spaces encourage their fantasies, most obviously here in the metal dragon in which they can climb and play. The park exudes a remarkable sense of rest and tranquillity so close to a building (the railway station) that sums up everything that is restless and insecure about urban life, with its new arrivals from Africa and Latin America, its reputation for

163

petty crime, its noise and bustle. Beyond the park again is a softer area of gravel and plane-trees, an open-air café, a court for the playing of *pelota*, the Basque open-air version of squash. Somehow, the sociability is always there, whether we are talking rural or urban, hard or soft, medieval or modern, formal or informal. At the 'urban' end of the continuum comes the unrelenting Plaça dels Països Catalans, the area in front of the station, minimalist, metallic, an area to be crossed rather than a space in which to linger — a few benches, a little shade from the sun, and hard stone beneath the feet.

If the work around Sants station can often seem grandiose, there are many smaller projects to be found around the city. One such small project within easy walking distance of the Plaça Catalunya is the Pati de les Aigües at the corner of Roger de Llúria and Consell de Cent streets. This is a rare opportunity to see the inside of an *Eixample* block and to get some kind of feel for Cerdà's original intention of parks and gardens integrated into the dense urban texture. The park features a restored water tower rising above a paved square and a handful of trees. And in the old town a tiny area in the Carrer de la Palla has been laid with marble and protected by steel screens and canopy. There is a significant point to be made here about care, and the way both public agencies (including the town council) and private owners of flats and houses make their own smaller contributions to the overall feel of a city. The way Barcelona and London have slid past one another in opposite directions (Barcelona upwards, and London downwards) over the past quarter of a century in this all important sense of civic care and pride has been a feature much commented on by those whose lives include both of these great cities.

There are votes in urban projects too. Barcelona is the only major city in Spain where the socialists have been in power continuously since the transition, but they have had to work hard to maintain that majority. To their right are positioned the Catalan nationalists, as well as the Popular

Party, the Spanish conservative party. To the left are the ex-communists (now more properly described as an eco-socialist coalition of ex-communists and greens). In solidly working class Nou Barris, there are 150,000 votes to be had, divided mainly between socialists and eco-socialists. Nou Barris is densely urban, and there has been no attempt to introduce here the English conception of a park as the countryside in the city. The Plaça de Virrei Amat is easy to reach — it has a metro station — but very few tourists penetrate this far into working class Barcelona. The area used to be very run-down, choked with traffic, and the square has been transformed with fountains cascading down into a pond, a children's playground, a paved area, lamp-standards and sculpture. A whole block has been demolished to make way for these modest additions to the urban scene. Unlike the vast hotels and office-blocks that have been concomitant to Barcelona's increasing attractiveness as an investment centre, a place for meetings and congresses and the thrusting new world of global capitalism, these improvements are of real benefit to local people. It is here, not in the Olympic Village or the old port or the city centre, that people spend most of their lives, shopping, taking children to school, gossiping with friends, singing in choirs, organising politically, belonging to the many associations which mark out a vibrant civil society. The vibrancy of this civil society might well be over-estimated by the casual observer, impressed at the liveliness of Catalan street-life and the general sociability of its towns and cities. Many people still depend on the family for the kinds of practical support that in other countries have become regarded as the work of the state. They have little time or energy to spend on civic responsibilities and society is the poorer for this.

Improvements to the urban infrastructure like those in Nou Barris, developed in collaboration with local people, reject the notion that the benefits of global capitalism trickle down to less privileged groups in society. Political will alone can make that happen, and this applies as much to regulating the economy in order to ensure social inclusion of individuals, as much as regulating the city's infrastructure to ensure a decent level of public facilities spread across the whole fabric of the city.

The 1992 Olympic Games

We are fortunate in having an excellent book in English by John Hargreaves on the 1992 Olympics which dwells at length on the links between Catalan nationalism and the Games. Hargreaves is always better on how the nationalists (both Pujol at the Generalitat, and other more radical nationalist groups) attempted to use the Games for their purposes than how the mayor, Pasqual Maragall, or big business or property developers used the Games to promote theirs. The enormous amount of inward investment associated with the Games allowed many infrastructural projects to be fast-tracked, including road transport, extensions and improvements to the metro and telecommunications.

Barcelona has embraced roads, or more accurately has accepted them as an inevitable if not desirable aspect of modern life. On the inland side of Barcelona, the new ringroad makes extensive use of tunnels, passing unobtrusively, for example, very close to the back of the Hospital de Sant Pau. On the port side of the town, the Passeig de Colom has been re-arranged as an esplanade lined with palm-trees which also serves as an access road. Heavier traffic is largely confined to an underground tunnel and above this the roof of the tunnel serves as a broad walk-way. The pavilion at the north end is used as a restaurant and decorated with an enormous smiling lobster by the well-known contemporary designer Xavier Mariscal. The walk-way is linked in turn to the quayside by two red drawbridges. The whole project goes by the name of the Moll de la Fusta (the timber quay). People flow across the pedestrian Rambla del Mar, an extension of the *Rambla* opening Barcelona up to the port and the sea again, to the Mare Magnum complex of cinemas and restaurants and shops. There is now a pleasure palace where once there was simply water. A statute of the 1920s anarchist poet Joan Salvat Papasseit issues the stern warning 'You do not know/what it is like/to watch over timber on the quayside'. I suspect few people let this spoil their pleasure. And it certainly doesn't interfere with business at the vast International Trade Centre skyscraper which now dominates the port.

A mile or so up the coast, in the Poble Nou district, the Games allowed the City Council to clean up the mess and confusion of Barcelona's relationship with the sea. The shifting of the port to the area south of Montjuïc had left one hole. Another was the decline of heavy industries in the area lying between the main railway tracks and the sea. There are new marinas and new beaches, offices, shops and sporting facilities, while the Olympic Village has become a new area of housing looking straight out across the sea. The overall layout is by the Martorell, Bohigas, Mackay team while many other architects have contributed to the finished work. But inevitably there is something unsettling and triumphalist about urban development of this scale. The two skyscrapers of the Olympic area and the communications tower by Norman Foster above the city express this. That triumphalism is not just in the buildings either. There are controversial figures such as Mariscal, the lobster man, who also designed the popular little Cobi mascot for the Games. Writing several years before the Games, Tóibín saw Cobi as the apotheosis of the oppositional cultural figures of the 1970s, the writers and artists and singers who had 'hung out' at the Zeleste night-club: 'the people who were going to make money and reputations from the Barcelona Olympic Games in 1992, out of designing new buildings, out of the public relations, out of the vast organisation which would be required.' (Homage to Barcelona, p. 44) But like Sydney in 2000, Barcelona carried off the Olympics with style, panache and to the general benefit of the city and the particular benefit of its commercial sector.

167

In rather similar fashion to reservations about the Olympic Village, a number of buildings in the Olympic Ring at Montjuïc (in particular Isozaki's Sant Jordi sports hall, and Ricard Bofill's mockingly classical sports university) deal less than satisfactorily with the problem of fitting in with the 1920s classicism of the stadium itself and the National Palace. Christopher Woodward, whose survey of Barcelona buildings is an essential aid to the design-conscious traveller, is particularly scathing about Bofill, an architect whom people either love or hate. In the case of the Sant Jordi hall, there is not only the design question — just how do you make a sports hall look interesting from the outside? — but also the question of its future use. Since 1992, it has been underutilised, and in 2003 it even managed to acquire a temporary swimming pool for an international swimming championship. This is a new 'architecture of power', but the power is now the power of global capitalism and consumerism. Social democracy it is certainly not. If the Sant Jordi hall is not sure of its purpose, it is a relief to find way up on the hills above the city and right next to the romantic and unlikely labyrinth of Horta, the velodrome. This cycle track, finished as early as 1984 knows exactly what it is for — speed, dynamism, danger, all curves and angles and excitement that one never altogether feels around the Olympic site at Montjuïc.

Barcelona 2004
In 1979, well before he wrote his splendid *Barcelonas*, Manuel Vázquez Montalbán approached the same idea of cities within a city but from a different angle. In *Southern Seas* (published in English in 1999), Montalbán's detective Pepe Carvalho investigates the disappearance of a wealthy property developer Carlos Stuart Pedrell who is supposed to be spending twelve months travelling around the South Pacific. In fact Pedrell is taking evasion to its final consequence by spending a year living in a working class suburb

of Barcelona, on an estate he built himself. As Michael Eaude, an English writer who lives in Barcelona, pointed out in an article in the *Times Literary Supplement* in February 2001, daily life is ordinary for most people most of the time — in London, Tahiti and Barcelona. He writes:

> There is nothing exotic about daily life in Barcelona ...
> And, despite the tourists drawn to the city by its architectural glories, the beautiful climate, the sensuous life beside the sea, Barcelona cannot just be our dream of the South Seas — it is the poor growing old on bare arid hills, too.

The Universal Forum of Cultures, Barcelona 2004, was planned as an attempt to present precisely the ordinariness of the peoples and cultures of the world. Yet in order to justify a level of investment appropriate to such an ambitious aim, it was also obliged to present the whole world as a garish, globalised circus, the Olympic Games writ large. In July 2002, a big party was staged at the Olympic Stadium in Barcelona to celebrate the ten years since the Barcelona Olympics. In the official press briefing put out by the office of mayor Joan Clos, it was made quite clear that a major reason for holding the party was to promote the 'next great challenge' of the Forum. From then on, regular press briefings from the office relentlessly pressed the case for the Forum, with only occasional breaks to note the demonstration of 1.3 million people against war with Iraq (March 2003) or to celebrate the unrelated events of the re-election of Joan Clos as mayor at the head of a broad left coalition and 7,000 people assembled at Montjuïc to be photographed in the nude and en masse by the American performance artist Spencer Tunick (May 2003).

In the years between the Olympics and the Forum, there was a strong emphasis on completing some of the national cultural infrastructure of Catalonia. This includes the new national theatre, the new concert hall (the Auditori) and the beginning of work on the new national library at the old Born Market site. 2004, then, recast the net much wider, to attempt the impossible task of representing all the cultures of the world in one place over a period of five months. The aim was to include popular arts, food and crafts on display in the Forum Plaça, as well as a comprehensive series of performances of plays and concerts in a new auditorium overlooking the sea. Two major exhibitions on the site would focus on language and communication, and on sustainable cities, in both of which Barcelona has a particular interest. A series of internationally recognised United Nations days would be celebrated in the Plaça de les Convivències, ranging from Environment Day on June 5 to Peace Day on September 18. The Forum was based on the values and principles of multiculturalism — of respect for difference in culture, religion and language. Its themes were cultural diversity, sustainable development, and the conditions under which peace can flourish. Those themes matter enormously but only time will tell whether the Forum had positive outcomes other than still more tourists and still more business opportunities for the city.

The Olympics gave Barcelona an enormous nudge forward to complete in a short time a large programme of major urban improvements, fulfilling at least some of the hopes raised by the Modernist architects and planners of the 1930s. In the same way, the intention was that the 2004 Forum would complete the urban project begun with the 1992 Olympic Village of filling in the missing links in Barcelona's nineteenth century *Eixample*, and resolving the city's relationship with the sea. At last the Diagonal would meet the sea, and a properly regulated urban network would finally reach the River Besós. Yet the Neighbourhood Association at La Mina, representing 30,000 residents of a vertical slum built in the 1960s and 70s with minimal social infrastructure, did not agree. They felt the Forum would do nothing for one of Barcelona's poorest and most run-down areas, right beside the Forum site. New developments would include a con-

170

vention centre, the Forum buildings and Plaça themselves, a park, and new sea-front developments including a marina and a naturist beach. Little here for the working class. An agreement that local residents would receive preference in allocating temporary jobs created by the Forum only partially resolved local opposition. As ever, Barcelona continues to re-invent itself, but always manages to be controversial.

Images of the City

Barcelona exists not just for the resident and visitor but on the screen as well. Whit Stillman's *Barcelona* (1994) uses the backdrop of the International Trade Fair at Montjuïc and affairs between two US citizens and the girls who work there to reflect the cosmopolitan and commercial nature of the city. That is one image of Barcelona. Another very different one comes in Pedro Almodóvar's *All about my Mother* (1999). Barcelona is identified as the Barcelona of Gaudí with a flattering sequence of the Sagrada Família. But there is then a sudden change as Manuela goes to look for her ex-husband, a transvestite prostitute working under the name of Lola in an urban wasteland where cars circle nightly as their drivers search for satisfaction of the most lurid of sexual tastes. Perhaps the director sees the world of transvestites and street workers lurking behind Gaudí's flamboyant decoration. The contrast continues through the film. For example the parents of Sister Rosa, a nun working with the street workers, live in a smart middle-class block of flats with *Modernista* stained glass. But although the décor suggests their limited class-ridden world, Almodóvar also manages to assert the ability of any human being to transcend his or her background, the possibility of change, of an alternative way of doing things. It is the mother who accepts responsibility for her daughter's baby after Rosa dies in child-birth.

The director's overall point is that values — friendship, loyalty, family, kindness — exist independent of the bourgeois moral world in which some sexual practices are deemed respectable while others are condemned as perverted. There is an emphasis too on the kindness of complete strangers, a theme that runs through Almodóvar's work, and is symbolised in the act of donating organs which forms the opening scene of the film. The city, above all, is the place where we interact most commonly with complete strangers, and where complete strangers can become best friends. The modern here expresses itself as difference and tolerance, very different from the stern morality of the Barcelona middle-classes. And Gaudí, the fervent Catholic, is now ironically part of that world of difference. Jan Morris, who has written about Barcelona, saves for her last book, about Trieste, her discovery of a Fourth World in which people belong because of their personal qualities rather than their ascribed traits:

> There are people everywhere who form a Fourth World, or a diaspora of their own. They are the lordly ones. They come in all colours. They can be Christians or Hindus or Muslims or Jews or pagans or atheists. They can be young or old, men or women, soldiers or pacifists, rich or poor. They may be patriots but they are never chauvinists. They share with each other, across all the nations, common values of humour and understanding. When you are among them you know you will not be mocked or resented, because they will not care about your race, your faith, your sex or your nationality, and they suffer fools if not gladly, at least sympathetically. They laugh easily. They are easily grateful. They are never mean. They are not inhibited by fashion, public opinion or political correctness. They are exiles in their own communities, because they are always in a minority, but they form a mighty nation, if they only knew it.

There is a little of that in Almodóvar, a little in Barcelona too.

Chapter 9

Popular Culture

Culture and Politics

Some of the most recent and most controversial work on the Sagrada Família in Barcelona has been by the sculptor Josep Subirachs. Popular can come to mean kitsch and vulgar, the vulgarity of garden gnomes and Christmas decorations and advertising hoardings. Good fun as long as it's not taken too seriously and you don't have to look at it every day. Most English readers would probably want to define 'popular culture' as international 'pop' culture — the music of Radio 1, the TV of soap operas, the world of High Street fashion. It is essentially low key, ephemeral, soon forgotten. Those who hold on to it past its sell-by date become historical oddities — the people who go and listen to tribute bands or collect trivia related to particular actors or TV series, or those irritating friends who always know the answers in pub quizzes.

Popular culture in Catalonia has a very different sense. If Barcelona, that mesmerising agglomeration of the ancient and modern, the local and the international, finds its natural place at the heart of this book, then it is equally appropriate that an exposition of Catalan Popular Culture should lie alongside it. But this needs some explanation. First of all, the Catalan notion of popular culture has some affinities with the English notion of traditional culture or folklore. Except of course that English folklore is almost entirely something artificial, preserved by specialised groups, and having strong antiquarian and rather quirky overtones. There are signs of renewal, as English people

173

search for a post-colonial, post-devolution identity. Well-dressing is alive and well in Derbyshire, bonfire night celebrations are as popular as ever, in Somerset there are moves to re-introduce live music into the autumn carnival processions, and the wassailing of apple orchards has begun again in a small way. But, in most of England, there is little sense of a direct continuity with the pre-industrial past. Our popular culture is almost entirely the product of the past two centuries (spectator sports, TV and radio, and the popular press). This is not the case in Catalonia. Industrialisation came later. Large areas of the country were untouched by industrialisation until quite recently. People who migrated to the great cities were more likely to retain links with their native village and go back for local holidays and celebrations.

But it is more than just differences in the pace of economic and social change. A popular national culture survived, or in many cases was reinvented, precisely because of the turbulent history of the nation and the determined attempt to modernise (or Hispanise) it out of existence between 1715 and the mid-nineteenth century. From about 1850 a number of cultural forms emerged, or re-emerged, with specific nationalist meanings. These included forms as different as the *sardana*, the emblematic circle dance performed at almost all Catalan celebrations, the origins of which are lost in Mediterranean antiquity, and the *havanera* song and dance music imported into the coastal towns of Catalonia by colonial trade, music which fused Andalusian and African influences. The *sardana* became linked to a particular set of musical instruments — the *cobla* — most of which can be traced back to late medieval Europe: the *flabiol*, a kind of piccolo played one-handed, other woodwind and brass instruments, and the double bass and small drums. In the *sardana*, the band remains seated, but for any events requiring movement the key instruments are the *gralla* (shawm), the *flabiol* and the *tamborí* (small drum). These are ideal for use in processions, usually

174

played by small groups of musicians and are also the natural accompaniment for other popular events such as the parading of the *gegants* (larger than life figures carried on wooden frames) or performances by a group of *castellers* (human castle-builders). The *shawm* has always been an open air instrument and was played widely in Europe between the thirteenth and seventeenth centuries. These particular manifestations of popular culture have acquired a particular modern feel in the past one hundred years as an expression of cultural identity and continuity. In addition there are also a number of very specific cultural inheritances which seem to meld pre-Christian rites with Christian beliefs in rather complicated ways which can puzzle those of us who come from the north of Europe.

It is difficult to generalise about popular culture because of the fairly wide variations from one town or village to another. Popular culture is by definition local and specific. But there is also fusion, even within Catalonia: in the last thirty years, castle-building which was dominant in New Catalonia has spread north to other parts of the country while the *sardana*, the most typical event of Old Catalonia has spread in the opposite direction to the lands south of Barcelona. In the August celebrations in the Gràcia district of Barcelona, popular culture from all of Catalonia is represented, as well as more recent cultural arrivals from Africa, in a riot of colour and music and celebration which goes on night after night through the heat of a torrid Barcelona summer. There are people who will not leave Barcelona in August until the *festa* of Gràcia is complete. By and large the examples chosen in this chapter come from two fair-sized towns. Girona is the better known — a provincial capital with connexions into a rich hinterland stretching from the Costa Brava to the Pyrenees. Vilanova i la Geltrú, on the coast between Barcelona and Tarragona, manages to be fishing port, industrial centre (in particular Pirelli's fibre optics factory), commuter town and holiday resort. If Girona has all the cultural advantages with its Roman, Jewish and Gothic roots, as well as being much admired by foreign visitors, Vilanova has its own charms. It has a continuing tradition of popular celebrations which are public rather than private in character and usually take place in the open-air. In addition there is a well established international festival of folk music, much of which is of course folklore in the more English sense of the word. There is strong political support for popular culture, building on the base of a large number of voluntary associations in the town, and a number of local experts in the field. Their work feeds not just into learned journals but also into the way that contemporary festivities are celebrated.

Before we begin to describe some of the wild and magical events which take place under the heading of popular culture, there is further ground-clearing to be done. Popular culture does not exclude involvement in other kinds of culture. The same young people who take part in winter *carnaval* and summer *festa major* processions and dances also enjoy international pop music. Some of them may even enjoy classical music concerts as well. Many of them will also be fanatical supporters of Barcelona Football Club. In the 1970s the success of FC Barcelona was synonymous with the nationalist project, its successes on the football field seeming to mirror the progress of the statute of autonomy. Vilanova and Girona, like most Catalan towns, have their branches of the Supporters' Club, their premises decked out in the familiar blue and red colours. Anything less than total success is not tolerated, as Terry Venables found during his time as coach. A group of Vilanova *castellers* had to change its Friday evening meeting time because members did not want to miss a particularly popular TV quiz show. So the involvement of people in popular culture, especially in the case of young people, has to be seen as just one part of their lives, namely their desire to be actively involved in the cause of national identity.

It is as if the people of towns like Vilanova and Girona have seen even before the academics and the writers the double bind that lies at the heart of talk of globalisation. Globalisation lays before us all the riches and sorrows of the world, bringing together people and ideas and events that had previously existed in separate capsules of time and space. Its symbols are the communications media of TV, the mobile phone, the English language, the Internet and the icons of consumerism from Coca Cola through Hollywood to the latest pop idol. But globalisation brings too a sense of rootlessness and a loss of identity, both personal and collective. People turn to those local aspects of culture, language and identity which tie our lives to particular places and histories. At its worst this can lead us into the cul-de-sac of nationalism as racism and xenophobia, the world of ethnic cleansing, of refugees tramping the highways of the world. At its best it produces charismatic figures such as Vilanova's Sixte Moral.

When first interviewed by the author in 1990, Moral was the grandly titled Cultural Councillor of Vilanova, a handsome man in an open-necked shirt, his hair tied back in a neat pony-tail. By 2001, dark-suited and without the ponytail, he was the town's mayor, running a coalition of socialists (PSC), republican nationalists (ERC) and the eco-socialist alliance (Iniciativa per Catalunya/Els Verds). "Our intention," he said, "is to break with the idea of the individual consumer of culture sitting in front of a television set. What we are trying to do, on the contrary, is to encourage people to get together in public spaces as part of living together and taking part in society." Having fun with your friends, in other words. But behind the slogan *Vilanova és festa* are more important intentions. Carnival, in particular, is of economic significance to the city: a lot of money gets spent and almost all of it within the local economy (costumes, music, sweets and partying). Moral reckoned that even by 1990, between five and six thousand people were spending up to £350 each on Carnival. From a social point of view, popular culture is the chief agent of social cement, of social integration, whether we are thinking of new Catalans from other parts of Spain or more

177

recent arrivals from Latin America and Africa. Finally, popular culture provides Vilanova with a significant identity as a town in its own right rather than just another town 'close to Barcelona'. This last aspect had become more important between our two interviews, because communications had been much improved — a new motorway, and train times down to thirty minutes between the town and central Barcelona.

As with so many other aspects of Catalan life, the world of popular culture cannot be understood without reference to Franco. The cause of popular culture over the past 65 years has followed that of the language. An initial attempt by the Franco regime to clamp down on popular festivities was replaced gradually by an approach that might be described as folkloric, with a strong emphasis on picturesque regional costumes and customs. The policy was to keep the lid on cultural nationalism as a way of preventing the re-emergence of political nationalism, but some concessions were made. The main beneficiary of this was the *sardana*. Thus Barcelona in the 1960s seemed full of *sardanas*. Sunday evening in the Plaça Sant Jaume was always the grand event of the week. Nearby was the headquarters of the Catalanist 'excursionist' organisation. Reference has already been made in this book to the symbolic importance in national life of group excursions around the Catalan countryside and mountains. So returning to the city after a day out, Plaça Sant Jaume was the place to head for. Most often, the police, whose headquarters were also nearby, chose to stay away. Everyone knew the rules, even if they did not always stick to them: dancing would not lead to demonstration and riot, and the police would try not to provoke any disturbance to the weekly ritual. Compared with Sunday evening, Sunday lunchtime dancing in front of the Cathedral was a very low-key affair. People would drift down from the Palau after a Sunday morning concert and stop for a few minutes to watch on their way to drink beer in the Plaça Reial or stroll down to the port. Even during the state of emergency during the winter of 1968/9, when any meeting of more than three or four people was potentially an illegal act, *sardana* dancing went on. There was something powerful and strong and unspoken about it: the linked hands, always in a circle, the symbolic protest of a repressed people.

Other popular festivities fared less well. In Gràcia the *festa major* shrank and nearly disappeared. The decoration of its streets had always been an essential part of the celebrations, and at one point these decorations were replaced by old shirts, satirising the old guard of Spanish fascism — the so-called *camisas viejas* (old shirts). This was sailing too close to the wind. Religious ceremonies by and large continued under Franco, although with a strong emphasis on their religious elements and a playing down of their civil elements and roots in pre-Christian beliefs. Not all of these celebrations were Catalan in origin. In the working class suburbs of Barcelona, the workers who had moved up from the South continued to celebrate Holy Week with traditional processions and costumes, and the wailing, almost North African sound of the *saeta* — unaccompanied religious songs often sung from a balcony as the procession and its images passed underneath. The regime, always heavily dependent on the church for its shoe-string legitimacy, was always out to humour the ecclesiastics. *Carnaval* fared particularly badly, with its overtones of sexual intrigue, over-indulgence in food and drink and frank political satire. Its survival in places like Vilanova owed as much to business as to folklore. In similar fashion, commercial motives kept alive traditional markets such as the Christmas one in front of Barcelona Cathedral, which sells trees, decorations and candles, and especially the carved wooden figures for the crib which most Catalan families have in their homes over Christmas.

The Franco government attempted to trivialise and sentimentalise popular culture by turning it into a tourist attraction in which a few local people would perform for the benefit of an audience consisting largely of outsiders.

179

In a way this distinction has now become formalised. The Patum at Berga, a rowdy fire festival which Tóibín describes so vividly in his book *Homage to Barcelona*, has two versions. One is for the town-folk on the Thursday of Corpus Christi. They know the dances, the jumps and how to stay out of trouble. A rather more regulated version happens on the Sunday for visitors. There have, of course, always been participants and watchers: the difference is that whereas under Franco it was the spectacle, the watching, that was emphasised, it is now again the taking part that is valued. And in any case the significance of popular culture activities may be understood in different ways. It is perfectly possible to dance a *sardana* and think of it as dance, with no special political significance. In the same way, the mixing of the cult of Saint George the patron saint of Catalonia with the celebration of Spain's National Book Day led to a position under Franco where some couples were exchanging red roses and books as a courtship ritual while others were seeing this as symbolic of their Catalan identity and the oppression under which Catalan culture had suffered.

In a lengthy interview conducted some years ago by the present author with Josep Maria Ainaud de Lasarte, at the time a senior CiU (conservative nationalist) councillor in Barcelona and author of a number of books about Catalonia, he proudly claimed to have been the first to hang a Catalan flag in the Generalitat Palace during an April 23 celebration, when the whole place is extravagantly decorated with red roses (they usually manage to send a few over to the Town Hall as well, as a peace offering). Ainaud's view of Sant Jordi as the protector of the weak against the strong has a clear political resonance, even if it does play fast and loose with Catalonia's own imperial history. But even Ainaud de Lasarte accepted that this political aspect of traditional celebrations had been rapidly lost after the transition to democracy. As Sixte Moral said, "A display of *castellers* or *sardanas* or a *festa major* no longer embodies a spirit of protest, it's simply a playful, participatory, festive spectacle." The exchange of red roses and books on 23 April goes on, but the books change. Tóibín reports a joyous Sant Jordi exchange in which three boys give three girls red roses. The girls then go off and buy the boys three books about sex, including a sex manual and a pornographic novel in Spanish. Certainly Sant Jordi is a good day to visit Barcelona. Nowadays, many of the political groups outside the establishment politics of Catalan socialists (PSC) and Catalan nationalists (CiU) make a point of having street-stalls on that day. They include a wide variety of green, ultra-nationalist, gay and fringe leftist groups. The day usually ends with some ritualistic window-smashing and skirmishes with the police. This is, after all, still Barcelona, the *Rosa de Foc*.

The Cycle of the Seasons

Popular culture related first of all to rural life and the importance of the seasons in agriculture. It also related to pagan beliefs, and it is fascinating to read Sir James Frazer's classic *The Golden Bough* with Catalan popular culture in mind. There are so many parallels, so many resonances. Christmas and mid-winter festivals are more familiar to us in Northern Europe, but in Catalonia the tradition is that the Three Kings (Three Wise Men) bring the children presents on 6 January (Epiphany). In Barcelona they arrive each year from the sea in their splendid robes and proceed to take presents to children in hospitals and orphanages before settling down to a splendid feast. But in other rural areas there are popular celebrations that give priority to Christmas Day and the days of Saint Nicholas, Saint Catherine and Santa Llúcia, whose *festa* is celebrated by the Barcelona Christmas market. Christmas in Catalonia is in a state of flux. At the Santa Llúcia market, traditional wooden figures for the family crib are sold alongside cheap plastic ones and gaudy Christmas decorations. Christmas cards have put in an appearance, though fortunately it is not yet considered necessary to send a card to people you never see or actively dislike (or even both). The greatest effort, as with most Catalan celebrations, goes into the family meal, usually shared by different generations and different branches of the extended family, according to the limits of the family dining-table.

The Lent cycle of festivals can be broadly related to crop-sowing and to various beliefs about the driving out of evil spirits and the need for renewal. There is too the old belief that some sort of sacrifice is necessary in order to secure renewed fertility. A faint reflection of this may be seen in the celebration of *Els Tres Tombs* when animals are brought to church — but to be blessed rather than sacrificed. But it is *Carnaval* which is the major event. If a 'carnival' has in many countries become simply a generic term for any public merry-making involving processions and music and dancing, a Catalan *Carnaval* remains firmly anchored to the last few days in February or early March before Lent begins. It has been a long-standing cause of dispute between church and state, and civil society. It includes, for example, the character of the King of Fools, or Lord of Misrule, who preaches a 'sermon' to the people which usually consists of a satirical attack on local political leaders.

Carnaval in Vilanova involves a full week of activities from the last Thursday before Lent until Ash Wednesday. The King of Fools arrives on Friday to read his sermon. There are four complete days of masked dances and street processions that feature mock battles between revellers armed with sweets. These do less damage than the chunks of plaster used in the eighteenth century which were eventually banned because of the number of injuries. On Ash Wednesday the King of Fools is 'buried' in a mock funeral service; his 'will' is read, usually continuing the satirical note of the sermon. Frazer had much to say about the burying of Carnival which he equates with pagan rites of human sacrifice and scapegoating. He gives an example in

The Golden Bough based on the report of an English traveller to Lleida in 1877. It is worth quoting in full to see the continuities here:

> For three days the revelry ran high, and then at midnight on the last day of the Carnival the same procession again wound through the streets, but under a different aspect and for a different end. The triumphal car was exchanged for a hearse, in which reposed the effigy of his dead Grace: a troop of maskers, who in the first procession had played the part of Students of Folly with many a merry quip and jest, now, robed as priests and bishops, paced slowly along holding aloft huge lighted tapers and singing a dirge.

There was a twist in this, however. Once the funeral oration was pronounced and the lights extinguished, the devil and his angels appeared from the crowd and snatched the body, hotly pursued by the mob. 'Naturally,' concludes Frazer, 'the fiends were overtaken and dispersed; and the sham corpse, rescued from their clutches, was laid in a grave that had been made ready for its reception.'

Easter is of course a key time of rebirth and growth. Carnival and Lent have worked their magic; the world is green again. The greenery still accompanies the Christian Palm Sunday processions in Catalan towns, as everywhere in Catholic Europe. But this ceremony has very ancient roots, roots deeper than those of the Catholic Church. In Greece and Rome about this time there were festivals dedicated to the laurel and the olive. The olive and its oil were basic to the economy and therefore the culture of the Mediterranean world. The olive tree lived to an incredible age, by the measurement of a single human life. The laurel was much used in cooking in the form of bay leaves, and was reputed to have magic properties in warding off lightning, as well as being associated with the god Jupiter. The crown of laurels was the classical symbol of victory. The rich feasting which marked the end of Lent is continued in the form of the modern Easter egg, traditionally given to Catalan children by their godparents, a tradition that survives even in non-religious families.

After Easter comes the cycle of the tree and the rose, the ancient Roman Floral Games. This is reflected in Catalonia in a number of traditions. The rose of Sant Jordi is the most obvious one, but there are also maypole celebrations in various parts of Catalonia, while floral carpets are laid in Sitges and Girona. But the most vivid and popular celebrations are those that are related to — or rather have become attached to by the cultural glue of Christianity assimilating earlier activities — Corpus Christi. Corpus was an explicit attempt in medieval Europe, by Pope John XXII in 1320 to be precise, to provide a Christian alternative to pagan rituals associated with springtime. In Barcelona, Corpus was very big, very early. Hughes has a vivid description of these celebrations that were based on links betweens the church and the guilds that controlled much of the town's economy. He describes how the pavements of the streets would be strewn with 'flowering broom, thyme, rosemary, carnations, and rose petals' before the processions started. He refers to the processions of 1461 that included:

> The Creation of the world; hell, complete with four devils, Saint Michael and a dragon; a battle between twenty-four demons and twenty angels; Adam and Eve; Cain and Abel; Noah's ark, with animals; a dancing eagle with a man inside, symbol of St John the Evangelist, that brandished a huge book; and a dozen more scenes from the Old and New Testaments. (Barcelona, pp. 153–4)

And best of all the giants and giantesses, enormous twenty foot high figures elaborately dressed, the men bearded, tall and strong (Goliath meets Charlemagne) the women the acme of fashion. Corpus was the great civic event of the year, and it is already clear from the description above how many of the key players in the modern Corpus and *festa major* processions — *gegants*, devils, dragons — were already parading the streets and squares of Catalonia 550 years ago. Add a few mules and we are almost there. By contrast in England, to the best of this author's knowledge, the processional figures have all been corralled. Gog and Magog languish in London's Guildhall. But the saddest figures of all are The Giant and Hob Nob, the Salisbury processional figures immured in the Salisbury Museum in the Close. The Giant was the processional figure of the Tailors' Guild, and so his history is directly comparable to those of the medieval Catalan guild *gegants*. Hob Nob, with his mischievous ways and snappy teeth served the same role as the ill-tempered mules of Catalan popular processional culture. It was the reformation that put paid to almost all of England's giants, and the Salisbury Giant's increasingly infrequent outings became limited to great state occasions such as the 1953 Coronation. It is a reminder that public space does not belong to the people, but is the point at which state and civil society meet. It is an area of freedom but also an area of social control.

The *festa major* (or 'major festival') which takes place in nearly all Catalan communities during August and September and will therefore be familiar to many summer holiday visitors to Catalonia, has its origin in harvest festival. In some inland villages where the main crop is the olive, the *festa major* takes place in the winter when the olives are shaken down from the trees. There are two particular celebrations which reflect and symbolise the collective endeavour needed for a successful harvest. These are the *sardana* dance and the *castellers*, the human castle builders. Despite their roots, both of these activities came to the fore during the nineteenth century cultural revival, as previously noted. The *castellers* had their heyday in the coastal regions of New Catalonia, but the vigorous modern movement shows signs of spreading more widely. It involves people of all ages including the young children who scramble up on top of the men and women who form the lower levels of each tower. At the base of the tower is where the mass membership of the association gathers to lend their strength to the common effort. The *castellers* have been particularly successful in attracting the 'new' Catalans, immigrants from other parts of Spain and their children. Sixte Moral saw this integrative aspect of popular culture as very important in building the new, democratic nation. He pointed to the irony that few of the Vilanova children who performed the frightening task of climbing to the summit of the castle are from Catalan-speaking families. Whereas in 1990 he was talking about the children of families with their roots within Spain, by 2001 he was referring in like manner to more recent arrivals from Africa. But there is a lot more to the average *festa major* than the *sardana* and the *castellers*.

Summer in Vilanova

Vilanova i la Geltrú takes popular culture seriously, takes having fun seriously. It is something that people reflect about, especially during the quieter winter months. It is something that is being continually refined, and the most important groups have their own club houses in which to socialise and carry on these discussions. There is a strong research base to popular culture too, aimed not at an academic audience but at increasing the authenticity and popular appeal of popular culture. It was noticeable how many of the people interviewed by the present author came out with similar formulations about the importance of popular culture as a social and political statement during the Francoist period, the importance of public, participatory art forms, the human scale of street festivals. They are not always at one with the 'official' version of popular culture put out by the Generalitat in its publicity material. These local activists feel that all too often the Generalitat stresses the extraordinary and the unique (such as the Easter Week Dance of Death at Vergès near Girona or the Patum at Berga). And that there is insufficient stress on the importance of civil society appropriating public space for these festivities. Finally, they complain that all too often popular culture fails to address the interests of the new Catalans, both in sharing Catalan culture and in giving opportunity for public display of other cultures from other parts of Spain and other parts of the world.

Somehow the *sardana* seems to be at the centre of these concerns. Does the circle really express a solidarity that embraces all parts of the community or does it actively exclude the stranger and the newcomer? In theory anyone can join in a circle, but as the dancers get older and more set in their ways, it can feel like an exclusive club that is very difficult to break into. There are also more strictly musical complaints about the *sardana*. Xavier Orriols, a musicologist and popular culture activist in Vilanova, complained that the strict nature of the dance limited the potential of the band, the *cobla*. It does seem curious that these bands play no other music at all. All *sardanas* are different but all contain the same mixture of up-tempo (dancing with arms raised) and down-tempo (arms lowered) passages. Orriols was able to demonstrate that there has been evolution. Only the smallest pipe, the *flabiol*, retains its original form, while the wind instruments themselves were only a sixteenth century innovation, replacing the earlier bagpipes. His favourite instrument was the *gralla*, an authentic medieval instrument which has become the favourite throughout Catalonia for accompanying any kind of procession or spectacle.

It is the thin, clear notes of the *gralla* and *flabiol* that go on echoing through the head long after the smoke and noise and confusion of the *festa major* processions have passed. These processions usually take place in August, and it is always hot. By 6pm the groups of dancers and marchers are gathering, each with the distinctive costume of their particular club — *castellers*, stick-dance, dragon, devils. The heat hangs like an enormous awning over the town. By 7pm the crowd of strollers has thickened into a stream of well-dressed people in their Sunday best with

187

carefully groomed children anxious for balloons and ice-cream and excitement. Drum rolls and firecrackers announce the arrival of the procession. The pavement cafes in the *Rambla* are soon under attack from the little devils, their faces painted black, brandishing whirling sticks of fire, their multicoloured costumes decorated with red tails and horns. Dogs flee in terror and a few small children dissolve into tears. But the general reaction is one of boisterous enthusiasm. Blue-grey smoke drifts through the plane-trees in advance of the fire-spouting dragons, with their supporting cast of musicians, wearing the traditional white trousers and black sashes.

Such representations of semi-mythical beasts, already part of the late medieval Corpus processions, carried by one or more people, are ancient in conception and very modern in form. The most typical beast of Vilanova is the mule (*mulassa*) which comes later in the procession. Where dragons, the commonest processional beast in this part of Catalonia, represent the dark side of nature, the mule is nature tamed and domesticated but high-spirited and with a keen sense of mischief and comedy. It prances to and fro across the *Rambla*, charging the crowd, nosing into women's handbags, and taking the occasional crafty nip at the person leading it. This is first cousin to the Salisbury Hob Nob without a doubt, dancing to the traditional tunes of the bull-fighting festivals in far-off Pamplona and Navarre. It has the largest pipe and drum band, and the most fervent support from the home crowd. Vilanova certainly had a mule as early as 1629, which behaved more like a dragon, breathing fire and fire-crackers. It was banned in 1779, following a similar ban in Barcelona in 1771. These sober, hard-working, towns were already fighting their own little battles about what kind of country Catalonia might become. A century and a half later, Vilanova's *mulassa* was back, but found itself stranded at a Pueblo Español festival in Barcelona on the outbreak of war in July 1936, together with the Vilanova dragon and *gegants*. They all perished in the war, emphasising the point that the figures one sees today in procession are relatively modern.

Some of the noisiest characters in the Vilanova procession, dressed in knee britches, waistcoats and floppy Catalan berets, are the musketeers of the Ball d'en Serralonga (Serralonga's dance). This is a most curious historical relic which started life as a play and has ended up as a processional dance. It claims to tell the story of a group of Catalan bandits, led by Joan de Serralonga, who roamed the hills of Catalonia, more admired for their daring, chivalry and courage than condemned for their lawless existence. Does Robin Hood come immediately to mind? — he should. The dancers alternate between ear-splitting volleys from their antique muskets and a dance of extremely detailed choreography, pausing to recite some of the very rhetorical verses of the original drama. They enjoy all three activities, despite the noise and heat and dust.

As the tale of Serralonga, blood and thunder fades down towards the sea in a haze of fire and smoke, the local *gegants* have formed up opposite one another at the top of the *Rambla*. These enormous figures now perform a slow, stately dance which gradually moves down the avenue. *Gegants* usually go in pairs, as we noted in an earlier chapter at Tortosa. Here in Vilanova there are three couples: one aristocratic, one in peasant dress, and the final pair in regal turbans. The district of La Geltrú, the smaller but older half of this twin town, celebrates its own *festa major* but its giants take part in this procession too. Whatever their origin, the giants seem to represent a certain formality and gentility after the excesses of dragons and mules, of devils and musketeers. The Vilanova ones are fortunate in being able to make a dignified entrance into the Town Hall foyer, where they live and can be visited. At Mataró, an industrial town up the coast from Barcelona, the end of the *festa major* is signified by an intricate ceremony called putting the giants to bed, since they can only be got in and out by lowering them onto their backs. But at least they are spared the prison of Salisbury Museum.

Musically the procession is very varied. The traditional dances and figures are accompanied by small groups of *gralla* players and drummers. But there is also the town brass band and children's band, much as you might find at an English carnival, plus the band from Vilarreal, Vilanova's twin town in Valencia. But definitely no pop music — that will come later. Other musicians take the opportunity to show off traditional instruments. There are numerous groups of children dancing with hoops and sticks, and the crowd from time to time breaks rank to form up around a particular group, parting again to allow them to continue on down the *Rambla*. By nightfall, the heat and noise will have taken their toll and some of the dancers, the children especially, will look quite exhausted. But the *festa major* lasts for several days, and all of these groups will be out again in the morning for a further procession around the town. In addition, the small pipe and drum groups will be going around the town from eight o'clock to remind the inhabitants that it is *festa* time — a fact hard to miss or ignore. At sunset the *castellers* will perform in the Plaça de la Vila, the topmost child level with the balcony on which the official party will stand applauding, very much as in the photograph on the cover of this book. By 11 o'clock conditions will be perfect for the night-time firework display which attracts enormous crowds to the harbour. And still the party will go on, with all-night dancing in the park by the beach. The red moon will sink into the sea and the red sun rise out of it, and sleep seems still far away.

Autumn in Girona

The Fires de Sant Narcís are the patronal festival and fair of Girona, and take place at the beginning of November, coinciding with the celebrations for All Saints Day. Even by the standards of the Catalans, a people wedded by both tradition and impulse to partying, this is a large-scale affair. A main site is the Devesa, the pleasant, shady parkland which extends from the railway line and the main road (from France to Barcelona) to the banks of the River Ter. Here there is the major trade fair, reflecting the continuing importance of agriculture in the economy of Girona province, which includes not just the Costa Brava and a solid chunk of the Pyrenees but also much rich farming land between. There is also a funfair, in the English sense, of roundabouts and side-shows and pop music where young people from the town and its surroundings villages can dance the night away.

Back in the town itself, the narrow streets of both the old town and some of the newer town on the west bank of the Rover Onyar, especially the Plaça de l'Independència (Independence Square), are full of stalls selling all manner of goods. Catalonia has taken to the Farmers' Market model for the simple reason that there has never been the divide between consumers and producers that has developed in other parts of Europe. Market shopping is still, for many people, part of the daily routine. During the fair, there are many opportunities to sample the traditional products of the region — honey, sausages, cheeses, wine, medicinal herbs, chocolates and sweets. Consumption here is not just about human need (food, clothes, shelter) but also about taste and choice and life-style and preference. There is also a vast art and craft display all along the river banks and through the narrow streets of the old town, including demonstrations of lace-making, embroidery and other traditional crafts.

Sant Narcís provides a wide range of free entertainment for locals and visitors alike, including guided street walks around the medieval city and its Jewish ghetto. Choral music is still popular in Girona and the Mercè church, converted into an Arts Centre provides a good setting for the Cor Maragall to perform to an attentive and appreciative audience at a free lunchtime concert which mixes old music and new music, religious and secular music, ending

191

with a rendering of Duke Ellington's 'Freedom' which is then repeated as an encore. To see a traditional Catalan choir fronted by jazz piano and double bass is to experience tradition as a powerful link to the present and future. Yet the men, young to middle-aged, in buttoned up shirts, tieless, bear a striking resemblance to Santiago Rusiñol's nineteenth century painting of Enric Morera conducting a workers' choir in Barcelona. Choral singing, as in so many European countries, is still a living tradition and marks a clear point of intersection between the local and the international.

On the Sunday morning the town is full of *gegants*, not just the Girona ones but those from all over the province, come here to show off and make merry, with their accompanying bands and supporters. It is an unusual and slightly disconcerting sight, these huge figures forming up in front of the church of Sant Feliu and then parading through the old town, twisting and dancing, dodging the odd bit of building work en route. Kings and queens, peasants and landlords, each *gegant* tells a story about the traditions of the village; each represents the voluntary work of dozens of people meeting together to design and make costumes, to learn and rehearse the music, to raise the money required. Most of these giants are relatively new, even where the tradition is ancient. They float impassive, expressionless above the heads of the crowd, along the river bank and over the bridge to the new town. The air is full of music, of that haunting harmony of *flabiol*, *tenora*, *gralla* and drums. Anthony Baines, an English writer of folk music, wrote half a century ago that 'a European town in the sixteenth century must have sounded like present-day Barcelona or Girona on a Sunday morning'. Even he would have found it hard to credit the extent to which this music, this culture, continues to fill the streets of Girona every year.

World Cultures and Local Cultures

If every locality has its own culture, then there is also a world market-place of culture. Nowhere is this clearer than in 'world music' with its contrasting emphases on the particularities of music and culture but also the idea of fusion, of the ways in which cultures overlap and intermingle. Popular culture in Catalonia has never seen itself as an isolated phenomenon. A good example of this comes in the International Folk Festival at Vilanova, where every year musicians and singers gather from all over Europe and beyond to make music and enjoy themselves beneath the palm-trees and the chattering parrots. Both jazz and the blues are played in Catalonia and are the subject of annual festivals.

Popular music, especially, tries to keep step with changing conceptions of Catalonia. There is a strong tradition of inviting bands to play in Catalonia from the other Catalan lands — Valencia, the Balearic Islands and French Catalonia. But more recently there has also been a determined effort made to invite artists from North Africa or even Sub Saharan Africa, reflecting the new communities that have now come to live in Catalonia. Those communities have begun to establish themselves musically too. For example the Sora group in Barcelona consists of musicians from a number of different countries who have coalesced around the figure of Djiby Cissokho, a Senegalese musician who has lived in Barcelona since 1994. Their music is traditional African music, influenced by Black American music, and even what Cissokho's promoters call 'Latin rhythms and Mediterranean sensuality'. There is also Catalan rock music with a large following and a strong Catalanist flavour.

What is no longer possible in Catalonia is the purist view of Catalan culture as expressed by that formidable (and racist) nineteenth century cleric Josep Torras i Bagès. Hughes remarks how much he derided the music of Castile and of Andalusia, with its sexual passion: 'Nothing could be more antithetical to the Catalan character, or be more damaging to the severity and restraint of our race' (in <u>Barcelona</u>, p. 321). Catalans, he thought, should stick to the *sardana*. It is even harder, of course, to tell that particular message to the many Catalans whose roots lie precisely in other parts of Spain, and in particular in the south, with its flamenco and its *duende* (the spirit of flamenco). With Andalusian arrivals came Andalusian culture and in particular musicians and dancers. This brings us to the curious story of Carmen, Barcelona-style. Carmen Amaya was an international flamenco dance star through the middle of the twentieth century, 'often billed,' according to James Woodall, 'as hailing from Sacromonte, the holy ground of flamenco dance'. 'In fact,' continues Woodall, 'she was from Somorrostro on the Barcelona outskirts. It was a *barrio* famous for gypsy dwellers and Carmen was gypsy in everything she did in life, from her *baile* (dancing) downwards.' (<u>In Search of the Firedance</u>, p. 242)

By excluding flamenco and Romany culture from its notion of 'Catalan' culture, has Catalonia replaced a mono-cultural Spain by a mono-cultural Catalonia? In confronting the different cultures of more recent arrivals in the country (African, Muslim, Latin American) Catalonia may first have to confront older cultures of difference (Romany, Andalusian). Edging towards a more plural and inclusive view of culture may be part of the work still to be done in Catalonia, even after the Universal Forum of Cultures.

Chapter 10

Tourism in Catalonia

The British Tourist and the Costa Brava

> Of all noxious animals, too, the most noxious is a tourist.
> And of all tourists the most vulgar, ill-bred, offensive and
> loathsome is the British tourist. (Francis Kilvert, English
> clergyman and diarist, 1870)

Generally speaking, Catalonia has accepted tourism, not
least because it has provided jobs and prosperity. Seaside
towns such as Blanes and Salou have been ceded to international package tour operators. Some parts of the Costa
Brava have been retained as Catalan holiday enclaves. As
Tóibín writes:

> But the old world still exists beside the new world of dis-
> cos, high rise apartments and package tours. The old,
> solid sedate world. The Catalans have repossessed the
> hills a few miles inland from the Costa Brava, made them
> their own, built houses, sheltered by the pine trees. It is,
> to an extent, a secret world, untouched by the mass
> tourism of the Costa Brava; it is a stable, traditional soci-
> ety. It pays no attention to what is going on a few miles
> away. (Homage to Barcelona, p.168)

John Langdon-Davies, who himself contributed to the
British taste for Catalonia, running a modest hotel at Sant
Feliu de Guíxols for some years, also wrote about the
impact of tourism. One of his final books was simply entitled *Spain*, published in 1971. In it he weighed in the
balance the positive and negative impact of mass tourism

and came to some pretty sensible conclusions. Conclusions that make it possible to distinguish between serious concerns about the impact of tourism and the snobbery of people who simply don't like big, brash holiday resorts, whether at home or abroad. He pointed out that tourism had brought some advantages to Spain. For example it had created an increased market for agricultural goods (and in retrospect therefore paved the way for Spain's entry into the European Union). It had provided employment not just in hotels and restaurants and theme parks, but in the construction industry too. It had been a boost to Spain's consumer durables industry (washing-machines and television sets, for example). Langdon-Davies also pointed to the *context* in which tourism had grown — and this is perhaps his most important insider's contribution to the debate:

> For example, there was the period of the Black Market which followed the wars, and which seems at first sight to have been nothing but a calamity. Nevertheless, without the Black Market there would have been no commerce of any sort whatsoever; it gave an opportunity for enterprising young men to learn the tricks of the trade and to become the first of a nouveau-riche generation which has taken the place of the older, and possibly worthier, stock, and has changed Spain as much as tourism.
> (Spain, p. 207)

So Spanish and Catalan tourism owe as much to the wiles of native sons and daughters, and inadequate government controls, as to 'offensive and loathsome' British tourists. The decline of the cork industry in Girona province, and the availability of cheap labour in the form of migrant workers from the south of Spain were other factors which changed the face of Catalonia in the 1960s.

Spanish and Catalan tourists enjoy the Catalan coastal resorts too. Although foreign visitors are everywhere, in most beach resorts the Catalans and Spanish will outnumber the overseas visitors. In the unfashionable resorts between Barcelona and the Costa Brava, where the beaches are separated from the towns and villages by not just a busy road, but also the coastal railway, or in some of the beach resorts between Vilanova and Tarragona, it is still as unusual to see a foreign tourist as it is to see one in Clacton or Weston-super-Mare. It was not inevitable that the Catalan and Spanish *costas* should have developed in the way that they did. Spain in the 1960s was a centralised autocratic state. And at the centre stood Manuel Fraga Iribarne, Minister of Information and Tourism from 1962 to 1969. This is the man who has since reinvented himself as a democratic, conservative politician. Even the name is different — Manuel Fraga *tout court* — and to add to the irony he is also the President of the Galician *Xunta*, part of the process of national and regional autonomy in Spain. He has deserted the crowded beaches of the Mediterranean for the unspoilt Atlantic beaches of the north-west, unspoilt that is apart from the occasional massive oil spill from some careless super-tanker. In a 1990 press interview in Majorca, looking back already a quarter of a century, Fraga claimed to have no regrets about the development of tourism. It had been a source of immediate wealth in a poor country, but also a strategic factor, as Langdon-Davies had written twenty years before. It had permitted, said Fraga, other forms of economic development as well as widening mental horizons and getting 'our country' better known in Europe. Fraga refused to acknowledge the extent to which the uncontrolled capitalism practiced by the young tigers of Opus Dei and their supporters inside government had precipitated a process which has spoilt visually much of the Catalan coastline, created large numbers of low skill, low wage, seasonal jobs and produced serious environmental problems in relation to water supply and sewage disposal. If all political careers end in failure, Fraga is certainly not admitting it yet.

There is some evidence, too, that the type of tourism that has developed along the coast of Catalonia is very susceptible to the uncertainties of economic life. After some years of growth in the 1980s, the number of package holidays sold in Britain declined from twelve million to eight million in just two years between 1988 and 1990, almost as if people sensed the coming of the early 90s depression before it arrived. In only one year (1989–1990) the proportion of those holidays taken at Spanish resorts (mainland Spain, Catalonia, Balearics and Canary islands) declined from 45% to 34%. There was further tourist growth through the 1990s, but the new century has brought further uncertainties. Even before the attack on the World Trade Center in New York City (on Catalan national day) there were signs of world recession. United States travellers have certainly been less in evidence, but by and large European tourists, more used to the occasional terrorist outrage, have gone on holiday-making — so far. Another major war in the Middle East or further terrorist incidents in Spain could change all that. Most observers of the impact of tourism on Catalonia have observed that it tends not to spread much beyond the sea. Langdon-Davies (Spain, p. 205) claimed that 'As little as 400 yards beyond the sea-shore you will find, unspoiled and unaltered, much of the original Spain. There are places behind the popular resorts which are absolutely as they were 200–300 years ago. They are sometimes visited but are seldom altered by tourists.' Looking back on this statement thirty years later, it is hard to resist the conclusion that so many of the changes have come not from foreign tourism but from within Spanish and Catalan society — more contact between town and country, the influence of the mass media in even the most remote villages, the decline of the Catholic religion and even the family in the face of doubt, uncertainty and the sexual revolution. If Catalonia is more Catalan, it is also more networked into the North American inspired global economy and culture than before.

At the same time as Langdon-Davies was preparing his final book, the present author (as a very young man) was embarking on a cold, wet, early spring walking tour of the

Costa Brava with two books in his rucksack, both written in the middle of the last century. What both Rose Macaulay (*Fabled Shore*) and Josep Pla (*Costa Brava*) reported was a genuinely wild and rugged landscape of cliffs and tiny silver beaches (*cales*) dotted with fishermen's huts that can now only be imagined by the visitor from the odd remnant of unspoilt coast that survives. Even by 1969 the collections of fishermen's huts had developed into hotel and apartment block resorts. At Canyelles Petites, beyond Roses, a single fishing hut noted by Pla had developed into what was then the latest urbanisation on the coast, a messy complex of half-built breeze-block villas and wild maquis scrub. The kindly owner of the local bar-restaurant, one of the first permanent houses to be built there, would show visitors photos of only a very few years before showing three or four houses. Yet even in 1970, beyond Canyelles were the flowery cliffs towards Punta Falconera and Cap de Norfeu dipping towards the smooth, turquoise sea. In more recent years this whole peninsula has been declared a protected site, and it is unlikely that further mass developments will take place along these cliffs, much as National Trust stewardship has now safeguarded the future of much of Britain's remaining coastline.

Pla and Macaulay were alert to both natural beauty and endearing meetings with local characters. Both Pla (the local boy) and Macaulay (playing the eccentric Englishwoman) appeared to enjoy them equally. But it is also the case that, unlike so many travel writers, both gave honest reports of poverty and backwardness as well as of the picturesque. Isolated from major transport routes, this part of the coast did not share in the prosperity of Catalonia in pre-war years. At the same time it shared fully in the tragedy of the Spanish War and its aftermath, cut off from Europe, cut off from North American aid, and despised by other Spaniards for what was perceived as its clannish sense of national identity. In Cadaqués, now the trendy haunt of artists and artistic tourists as it had been

199

in the 1920s, Macaulay met a waiter who had worked for ten years in New York. She remembered reading (perhaps in Pla?) that many Cadaqués men had emigrated because 'life in Cadaqués is hard'. Potentially, then, tourism brought a useful diversification of economic activity. But also, given the almost total lack of planning controls that Franco, Fraga and their business supporters insisted on, tower blocks, urbanisations and other tourist amenities were all placed to take maximum advantage of the splendid coastal views and to ruin those views in the process.

Even so, it is still a subjective issue as to how bad the results are. An interesting case-study is Tossa de Mar, for Macaulay's the 'most interesting and beautiful of the Costa Brava towns'. She admitted that it had been a 'picturesque resort of English writers and artists' before the war, but declared herself satisfied with a town that 'has everything', adding (in parenthesis) 'except those smart amenities believed to attract tourists'. Well, Tossa is full of amenities now. It is also an exceptionally well-ordered resort and it would be hard to find fault with modern Tossa unless you were looking for solitude. The beach, one of a number on this coast boasting European blue flag status, is busy and jolly and convivial, but not uncomfortably crowded even in mid-August. The walled precinct of the Old Town that guards the sheltered bay adds calm and gravity to the animated scene. Beneath the Old Town are older white-washed houses along the shore, giving way to modest hotels and apartment blocks rising to no higher than five storeys at the other end of the double crescent of sand. Anything bigger is tucked away out of sight, and the line of pine-clad hills rising behind the town remains unbroken. All day people clamber up the steep paths above the Old Town to the lighthouse above. The light changes as it has always changed at Tossa — deep-green morning sea and deepest blue sky modulating to deepest azure sea and pale blue evening sky with golden highlights as the sun dips towards the hills. In the little cobbled streets of the Old Town, cats hold court amid the flower-pots, and from the lighthouse there are miles and miles of Costa Brava scenery spreading in both directions, south towards Lloret and north towards Sant Feliu. There is a pleasant little museum and several art galleries and the scent of pine hangs in the air. Towards nightfall the last rays of the sun light up other ancient walls in a straw-coloured light like pale, dry sherry. The near sea sparkles green and silver, the far sea is deepest purple. It is hard to object to all this, to feel anger at the passing of poverty and obscurantism. Tossa proudly flies the flags of Catalonia, Spain and Europe. Something in the pine-scented breeze suggests that Tossa may have got the modern world about right.

If Tossa represents a municipal solution to the future of this coast, other places represent the failure of public authorities to control private greed. For example, the much praised little *cala* at Cala Gelida (frozen inlet) turns out to be just another urbanisation, with terraced houses and villas smothering the hillside above the (admittedly) picturesque little rocky coves. One senses that somehow neither the modest municipalism of Tossa nor the private enterprise solutions of Cala Gelida can offer solutions to the big resorts like Blanes and Lloret at the southern, more accessible, end of the Costa Brava. They cater for large-scale foreign tourism with large-scale facilities. Everything seems out of scale here — the massive hotels and apartment blocks on a rather flat and undistinguished bit of coast, the restaurants serving their own synthetic brand of local cuisine.

And yet even closer to Barcelona is another town that suggests that all is not lost along the string of more or less continuous resorts (the Maresme) stretching down to Barcelona from the dry estuary of the Tordera at the southern end of the Costa Brava. It is a matter of looking just a little below the surface, although there are some things that it is impossible to ignore. There is, for example, the railway. There is also the coastal road keeping it company, always slow-moving, always liable to jams, or, as the Catalans call them, 'collapses'. Like many towns on the coast, Arenys is really two linked towns, one 'de Mar' on the coast (and road and railway) the other 'de Dalt' or 'de Munt' further up the hillside. In the case of Arenys, the two are joined by an exquisite sandy and shaded *rambla*, lined with busy local shops which become less and less touristy as you move up from Arenys de Mar to Arenys de Munt. The beach is tiny and the showers a necessary precaution, but there are impressive modern sporting facilities, and the fishing port is still one of the largest in Catalonia. Sardines, lobster and red mullet are the basis of the catch which is immediately auctioned at the fishing co-op on the quayside. The co-op has a small, beautifully furnished bar with bright, twisty lamps and bentwood furniture, enabling it to double as a popular local nightspot. Chairs and tables are laid out where earlier in the day fish has been auctioned in a richly incomprehensible Catalan decorated with knowing glances exchanged across wooden boxes of ice and still-twitching fish by market-stall holders in their traditional white smocks.

For the young people of the town, there are limited opportunities and the bright lights of Barcelona call. There are seductive jobs in night-clubs and discos in more fashionable resorts. Yet, like the Vilanova we described in the previous chapter, Arenys is attractive because it seems like a real place — a place to visit and explore and get to know people rather than just a vehicle for sea and sun and sex. The family at the beach café, the fishermen and the market women at the fish auction, the old people on the benches in the *rambla*, they all have their tale to tell and time to tell it. And Arenys is a microcosm of Catalan society and the external influences on it, a town that did well from the Americas trade in the nineteenth century, that in the first half of the twentieth century attracted holiday-makers from Barcelona and in the second half commuters. That has seen in the last fifty years a richer mix of people with the arrival of migrants from the South and from North Africa. Yet its character, its feel, so difficult to pin down in mere words, is still defined by the sea and seafaring and trade and fishing. And the calm, which its favourite son, the poet Salvador Espriu, defined in a 1946 poem as:

... l'ombra	... the passing
viatgera d'un núvol	shadow of a cloud
i el lent record dels dies	and slow memory of the days
que són passats per sempre	which are gone forever

If Catalonia for Espriu was a mythical country, Arenys was its sentimental heart.

A Tale of Two Books

Paul Scott is a very fine writer. The four novels that make up *The Raj Quartet* — about the last days of British rule in India — deserved their popular acclaim as both books and television serial. But in *The Corrida at San Feliu*, published in 1964, he got Catalonia badly wrong. What the novel does is to sum up the incongruities of tourism. Beautifully crafted around the metaphor of human life and taurine death, it begs one very important question which is central to the perverse impact of mass tourism on Catalonia: why a *corrida*, a bull-fight, at San Feliu, or to give it back its correct Catalan name, Sant Feliu? The rituals of blood, gore and death are of little interest to the Catalans. In Barcelona there is still some enthusiasm for the bulls, shared equally between Andalusian *aficionados* and foreign tourists. But on the Costa Brava, the bull-fight is an import, a specially contrived entertainment for foreigners, part of the packaged experience of 'Spain'. Yet Paul Scott was an educated man, and his narrator, also a writer and therefore by definition an educated man, showed no perceptible embarrassment at placing such an obviously alien symbol in a Catalan setting ... He might usefully have visited Langdon-Davies, by this time a well-established resident of Sant Feliu de Guíxols. Perhaps Langdon-Davies was thinking of Scott but anxious not to offend the younger man when he wrote, a few years later:

> If you go to San Feliu de Guixols, capital of the Costa Brava, you will find a bullring, but only since the town became a tourist centre. The spectators will mostly be French, English or German, and those Castilians who have migrated from the south to make a good thing out of the tourist trade. (Spain, p. 38)

Patrice Chaplin wrote about Catalonia in a novel, *Having it Away* (1977) and an autobiography, *Albany Park* (1986). Both books reflected Chaplin's own gradual awareness of the difference of Catalonia. It is cleverly done. In *Having it Away*, a small group of English tourists scandalise the locals in a village on the Costa Brava, who in turn try to turn them over to the authorities as a health hazard. Their holiday home is variously referred to by the locals as the 'house of flies' and the 'lesbian brothel'. Throughout the English characters refer to 'Spain' and the 'Spaniards'. Catalonia only appears in the penultimate chapter:

> The first meeting of the association of Catalan artists was held in Olot, a village north of Gerona. Luis sat at the top of the table and proposed plans to protect Catalan style, the Catalan language, from the plebeian influence of the rest of Spain. Elsewhere in the province a group of people were discussing plans to protect Catalan money, which the rest of Spain was far more concerned about. Luis had already approached several international artists to become 'friends of Catalonia'. (Having it Away, p.113)

It is so subtly done that the inattentive reader might miss it altogether . . .

Albany Park may be an autobiography, but it is written like a racy, comic novel, with lots of black humour around drugs, sex and prostitution. But there is a serious underlying theme about politics, Catalan identity and opposition to Franco. And the growing realisation of two young English girls, Patrice and her travelling companion Beryl, of what their 'Spanish adventure' is really about. Yet the Catalan is only very gradually revealed to Patrice, which is how it happened for most of us who first went to Catalonia in the 1960s. Gerona keeps the Castilian version of its name, as does José (the local writer they meet). Thus the deceptive opening line: 'I first saw José Tarres on the stairs of the Hotel Residencia Internacional in Gerona, Spain.' Only in the last third of the book, from the meeting with the real-life Salvador Espriu in Arenys de Mar do politics and Catalanism become apparent:

> We walked down the road to Arenys de Mar and met a writer he knew, Salvador Espriu, who'd been born there. I'd been reborn there so that was something we had in common. He said it was a magical place. I knew that too but didn't have the words to define exactly what I meant. You needed subtlety to express a mystical requirement. But José spoke with him about the state of the world — he really meant Catalonia — and promised the older man that the great things would return. Espriu had written a book of poems about Arenys de Mar, the happiness he'd found there. *Cementiri de Sinera* it was called. For him the resort was Paradise. But just one foot outside it was Paradise Lost. (Albany Park, p.139)

'The state of the world — he really meant Catalonia': it is lean but exact. José says: 'But this is a difficult country. It could have been something once. The Civil War wounded it and it healed up wrong.' They are still trying to put it right.

Could it be Different?
It could be different, and, to some extent, it is already different. But until recently, no effort was made to promote the uniqueness of Catalonia. The message was that 'Spain is different' but in a bizarrely undifferentiated way. The Spanish tourist industry has been a tourism of exclusions, glossing over difference and marketing a standardized product which can be enjoyed equally well on the Costa

Brava, Majorca or the Canary Islands. Despite the efforts of a few recent English language writers, popular assumptions about what goes on south of the Pyrenees are only just beginning to change. Paul Richardson in his *Our Lady of the Sewers and Other Adventures in Deep Spain* discovers a hilarious world of cultural diversity in settings as varied as the Basque Country, rural Andalusia and Castile, and the Canary Islands. Yet there is still a tendency for the Spanish National Tourist Office in London to put out advertising material which lumps together the different regions and nationalities into one amorphous mass. The distinctiveness only appears at local tourist offices within Catalonia, which are increasingly acquiring a strong, local flavour. One of the best without a doubt is in Girona, at the epicentre of a province which includes not just the Costa Brava but a lot of the Pyrenees and a large expanse of little known countryside between the two. The success of tourism in Catalonia over the next ten years will be measured not by what happens to the coast but by the success or otherwise of local and regional government in attracting tourists inland. To attract them, that is, away from the cosmopolitan life-style of the coast to the more authentic settings of Catalan life. To attract them in subtle ways, a little as Patrice Chaplin was gradually seduced by the particularities of Catalonia.

Cadaqués has for many years shown the way. It lies a little off the beaten track, which is perhaps why things have happened differently here, but also why until recently it seems not to have had much impact on what happened elsewhere. Cadaqués turns its back on Catalonia and looks out to sea. Is it town or village? Perhaps a little of both. From here it is only a few miles to France, yet the railway and roads pass well inland, leaving the rocky hills and high, steep cliffs of Cap de Creus alone. It has long been the haunt of writers and artists, not exactly upmarket, but different, certainly. The Catalans come here, as do the French, and a scattering of other nationalities. It is popular with naturists too: the secluded rocky coves and the scarcity of visitors have long made swimming costumes seem rather redundant, except on the busy main town beaches. Most important, Cadaqués has retained its profile. It can be easily recognized from old photos — the church immediately above the sheltered little harbour, the little alleyways scurrying hither and thither between white-washed houses, all eventually falling to a number of coves fronted and linked by porticoed houses. Additional villas and apartments there are, but well back from the old centre, while good car-parking on the outskirts and efficient traffic management have managed to save Cadaqués from turning into just another car-ravished beach resort.

There is no doubt too that the presence of Salvador Dalí, whatever one thinks about him, has been a positive thing for Cadaqués. Dalí lived for many years in the old fishing quarter of Port Lligat, about half-a-mile from the centre round a rocky headland. There has been some development here, but again it is modest, low impact stuff in general. The shock of Port Lligat and what brings visitors back again and again is how instantly recognisable it is. And this is another reason for a more scrupulous than usual attitude to development hereabouts. For the scenery of Port Lligat is the scenery of Dalí's paintings. If the images are surreal the background might better be called hyper-real. The rocks, worn into fantastic shapes by wind and waves are the rocks of the 'Christ of Saint John of the Cross' in the Kelvingrove Art Gallery in Glasgow, and of countless other well-known paintings. If there is a beach and sea and rocks, then it is Port Lligat. In the 1920s the poet Lorca came here too, Lorca who hoped he might be an Andalusian bridge between Castile and Catalonia. One suspects that the gay Lorca fancied Dalí. Dalí certainly thought as much. It is also probable that Dalí's sister fancied Lorca. She wrote vividly of him, recalling boat trips, naps in shady coves, and the harsh heat and light of this unique landscape. Cadaqués and its environs remain a wonderland of ambiguity and difference where Catalan fishermen wave greetings to Scandinavian mermaids at the rocky entrance to the harbour, where naked walnut brown swimmers strike out from one headland to the next through the blue Mediterranean water. Cadaqués is strikingly, well, different.

It is not compulsory to prefer the eccentricities of Cadaqués to the more predictable pleasures of (say) Arenys or Tossa. It is more a matter, perhaps, of taking the country as it comes, of being able to embrace both kinds of experience, the familiar and expected, and the new and challenging. In recent years Dalí's theatre-museum at inland Figueres has become a focus for holidaymakers who want something a *little* different. And get it in the strange atmosphere of this theatre turned interactive art gallery.

Just inland from the Costa Brava lies Peratallada, an excellent example of what 'restoration', sensitively approached, can achieve. The first message is a crucial one — this is not just for tourists, people are living here. A drift of wood smoke from a chimney, a face at a window, a supermarket and a post office in the arcaded Plaça de les Voltes. Everything is stone. Stone houses line the streets with massive doorways and lintels. There is a Romanesque and Gothic church just across the road from open fields on the outskirts of the village, with a straggling old farmhouse next door. Peratallada is old, but it is alive. There are of course countless examples between the Mediterranean and the distant peaks of the Pyrenees of exactly this kind of harmony between people living local lives and tourists in search of the keys that will unlock the doors of local distinctiveness. The village of Durro, mentioned in chapter 2, is not easy to find, tucked away in the Boí valley in the National Park of Sant Maurici i Aigües Tortes. It must be very quiet in winter but in summer its gardens are alive with apples, marrows and flowers. It has the inevitable Romanesque church, farms and holiday homes. Sunday lunchtime the village bar is as crowded and animated as an English country local would be at a similar time, with no single group dominant, and a relaxed

208

intermingling of local and not so local: farmers who live and work around the village, people born and brought up in the valley who have come back to spend their summer holiday, and other people renting houses in Durro for the summer or dropping by for a break before heading off to their next Romanesque belfry. It is a fragile balance but one worth striving for.

Elsewhere in Lleida province there is real enthusiasm for tourism development. It is traditionally the least visited of the four Catalan provinces. Yet it has always had more specialised visitors who come back year after year for winter sports, mountaineering, cross-country trekking and Romanesque churches. The tourist service of the Generalitat makes a point of producing leaflets about each of the traditional local government areas — the *comarques* — which emphasise the local distinctiveness, including food and drink, local festivities and wildlife. They also produce excellent guides for visitors who want to follow particular themes such as Romanesque art across a relatively wide area of the country. The newspaper style *Discovering Romanesque Art in Catalonia* has background articles and information about museum collections, as well as six detailed recommended routes, two of which are mainly in the Lleida province. But there are also schemes afoot to attract visitors to the less immediately obvious areas such as the dry lands south and east of the provincial capital. The provincial tourist office, with support from the Generalitat, has produced a leaflet for the 'Route of the Olive Oil', outlining the special charms of these ancient towns and villages, with their castles, churches and monasteries, Jewish and Muslim quarters, wind and water mills. But a gap remains, a gap between this carefully produced local information with its sense of local distinctiveness and local histories, and the large-scale advertising of Spain (including Catalonia) in the press and television of other European countries.

In a number of important ways, Langdon-Davies was wrong when he saw the increasing cosmopolitanism of the

209

Spanish *costas* as sounding the death knell of local distinctiveness. He wrote on the last page of his final book:

> What has happened in Spain has happened the whole world over, and we have realized since the last war, I think, that nationalism is doomed, and that cosmopolitanism has come to stay. There is not a beach in Europe which is not overcrowded, and there is not a town in Europe that does not sell the same sort of goods as other towns. Soon there will be no telling the difference between some of the Costa Brava resorts and Blackpool or any other English pleasure town. (Spain, p. 209)

Well, nationalism is clearly not doomed. On the negative side, we have the bloody breaking apart of the old Yugoslavia, the decision of Czechs and Slovaks to go their own way (but within the European Union), the continuing conflict in the Basque Country and vicious attacks on migrants and refugees and asylum seekers. Everywhere minority languages are in decline except where governments have taken positive steps to support them as in Catalonia. Even then, they may find themselves swimming against the tide, as in Ireland. But on the positive side, interest grows year by year in local distinctiveness, whether this is a question of music, popular culture, food and drink or sports. Spain with its new, decentralized, democratic constitution has led the way in this. 'Deep Spain' is on the march.

The reasons for the emphasis on local distinctiveness are not just cultural, but also ecological and environmental. The impact of mass tourism has not only been negative in cultural terms, but in the destruction of local landscapes and habitats. Encouraging tourists to consume local food and drink products has implications for the urgent need to re-localise the way we eat and drink. In the long run, the shifting of bulk foodstuffs around the world is not sustainable, and increasingly their processing is seen as a threat to people's health and well-being. Green tourism is already thriving in Catalonia, with tourists staying on farms, getting to know the wildlife of the region, eating home-grown food and generally learning to make their footprints across Catalonia a little less deep and obvious. In a country where rural depopulation has been an issue over the last fifty years, this is also serving to put new life into declining rural communities. As in Britain, closed railway lines are finding new life as 'green ways', providing long-distance routes for cyclists and walkers. Girona used to be linked with Olot, in the volcanic area of la Garrotxa, and Tossa, on the Costa Brava, by two narrow-gauge steam railways. These towns are now linked by carefully maintained green ways. A similar route links Ripoll and Sant Joan de les Abadesses. Places to stay and eat, and hire cycles are growing up around these new tourist routes. There is reason for cautious optimism.

Not all the problems of tourism in Catalonia can be laid at the door of the Spanish government or insensitive foreign tourists. There have been serious questions asked in recent years about the effectiveness of sanitary regulations, with well documented outbreaks of illnesses such as typhoid and food-poisoning in popular resorts. There are also public health issues about the cleanliness of beaches, the disposal of sewage and the custodianship of the national parks, a subject considered further in chapter 14. There may also be an attitude problem. The people who work in the tourist industry are the human faces who link the industry and its customers. The most noticeable fact, and one which is true of many countries, is that the majority of staff are young, badly paid, temporary workers. Sometimes minimum wage regulations are flouted. Where the holiday has been booked and paid for outside of the country, as is the case with most package holidays, most of the profits will remain outside the country too. It is not surprising, then, that stories of poor service and inflated prices abound. But a culture has developed in which foreign tourists, with their inability to speak Spanish or Catalan, or understand local customs, their nervous 'please' and 'thank you' (neither of which are much used by locals), have acquired a low status in the eyes of many service industry workers.

There is an overall assumption the that tourism is simply a means to an end — earning a living, making money — rather than an end in itself, something that can enrich people's lives as well as contribute to the local economy. If tourism is merely a product, merely the connecting link between seller and buyer, then it is probably not worth bothering over. Ultimately, tourism, as we are told, is about money. It is an industry, so they say. Thus the bitter last few lines of Goytisolo's novel *Marks of Identity*, copying the notice on the coin-operated telescopes of the Mirador at Montjuïc in Barcelona:

INTRODUZCA LA MONEDA
INTRODUISEZ LA MONNAIE
INTRODUCE THE COIN
GELDSTUCK EINWARFEN

Chapter 11

National and International: some twentieth century artists and musicians

Introduction: The Two Pauls

> I would like to think that when our ancient melody, 'El Cant dels Ocells', now reaches you, it will give voice to the love we bear Catalonia. That sentiment, which makes us proud of being her sons and binds us all together, must now make us work as one, as brothers united in a single faith, for a tomorrow of peace when Catalonia will again be Catalonia.
> (Pau Casals broadcasting on the BBC World Service, 1945)

This chapter tries to deal with some sensitivity with 'Catalan' art and 'Catalan' music, recognising, inevitably, that these are charged terms. Pablo Picasso and Pau Casals exemplify these difficulties in their life and work — Pablo and Pau, the Spanish and Catalan versions of Paul. Casals was often referred to as Pablo, whereas Picasso was never referred to as Pau: Castilian Spanish is always the norm from which Catalan is considered a diversion.

Picasso, born in Málaga, was not a Catalan. Casals, born in El Vendrell, was. Picasso's claim to being treated as a Catalan artist rests on the fact that he grew to manhood in Barcelona. It was there that he learned the painter's art, developed that extraordinary ability to draw, to make a line do things, express things, that no other twentieth century artists ever equalled. He was part of that *Modernista* world that drank at Els Quatre Gats in Barcelona, attended artistic get-togethers at the Cau Ferrat in Sitges and watched the raising of great buildings such as the Palace of Catalan Music.

Even his departure for Paris was a conventional career move for young Catalan artists of the first decade of the century. Yet in Paris he drew inspiration not just from what French artists were creating (Cézanne, Matisse, Braque come to mind at once), but from African masks, from the work of the Russian Kandinsky and (later, maybe) the Swiss Klee. His politics, too — Communist, internationalist — link him with trends far wider than Catalonia or even France. When he painted 'Guernica', that great work of anger and mourning over the Spanish War, he chose a Basque theme not because he wanted to be a Basque painter, but because it was Guernica in the Basque Country which had been chosen by the German Nazis to trial the effects of *blitzkrieg*, of mass bombing. The subject found the artist. Had it been Catalonia which offered up the subject, that would not have made him a Catalan painter. The evil that Picasso recognised in 'Guernica' has no borders. Picasso is present in Barcelona, as we shall see. No book on Catalonia and its cultures can ignore him, but nothing can make this most international of painters a Catalan artist.

On the other hand, Casals spent the first half of his life working not just for the cause of classical music, that is to say, European music, but working at it in a very particular, very Catalan, way. His ambition was to do for orchestral music what others in Catalonia had done for choral music: to make it a popular movement, as open to the working class as it was to the middle classes who patronised concerts in Barcelona, as available in the villages and market towns of rural Catalonia as it was in the great cities. The greatest cellist of his age, he scarcely played the cello in public in the decades before the Spanish War, and was known as a concert promoter and conductor, the public face of music.

From 1939, this most Catalan of Catalans did not set foot in Spanish Catalonia. If music was a universal language, it did not encompass what Franco was, what Franco had done, and what Franco stood for — a denial of everything in the human soul and in human society which strives for love, co-operation and harmony. After 1939, he played his cello once more, played to shore up civilisation against the barbarians who remained in power in Barcelona and Madrid, Seville and Bilbao. He played his cello above all for peace, and against the new threat of nuclear war, the threat of those men of whatever nationality who were willing to trade the future of humanity against their own insecurity and ambitions. And in each concert he played a simple little tune called *El Cant dels Ocells*, the Song of the Birds, a Catalan folk tune that sums up the mystery of how one place can become the world. How all the sadness and joy of our world can only be experienced in the time and the place that we inhabit, and for which we are ultimately responsible.

The presence of Picasso and Miró in Barcelona

Picasso's presence in Barcelona remains a very public affair. His murals of scenes from Catalan popular culture decorate the outside of the College of Architects. There are murals inside too, one portraying a port scene and the traditional Barcelona landmark of the three factory chimneys outlined against Montjuïc, the other *sardana* dancers against a stylised background of hills and mountains. The designs are picked out in dark grey pebbles on rendered walls. Els Quatre Gats, the café where Picasso and his Catalan friends met and drank and talked art and literature, has been re-opened not far away. Modelled on the 1890s Chat Noir in Montmartre, it was both café and exhibition space and concert venue. Picasso's first one-man show was staged there in February 1900; Isaac Albéniz and Enric Granados performed there.

The Paris–Barcelona axis is central to the artistic history of this period. Most of the Catalan *Modernista* painters spent time in Paris. At 6 rue Cortot, in 1891, Santiago Rusiñol painted Erik Satie as 'The Bohemian'. Ramon Casas also painted him. For a short time in 1893, Miquel Utrillo and Erik Satie shared a lover, Suzanne Valadon, an artist's model and later a fine painter in her own right. Only Joaquim Mir never visited Paris. Paris was life-style, but Paris was also Impressionism (and eventually post-Impressionism). As a result, atmosphere rather than anecdote became the subject-matter of Catalan painting. But whereas Picasso was to go on to become a leader of the Parisian avant-garde, the Catalan painters of his Barcelona circle remained rather local figures. It is instructive to compare Picasso's early work (in the Picasso Museum in Montcada street) with the work of Catalan contemporaries in the Modern Art Museum (part of the Catalan Parliament complex in the Ciutadella Park). There is a generalised sadness in this turn-of-the-century art, but only Nonell, in his pictures of hunched figures in dark tones, achieves any real depth of feeling, a sense of the closeness of death and tragedy. It was Picasso who explored further this darker side of life. The suicide in 1901 of his close friend, the painter and writer Carlos Casagemas, with whom he had shared studios in both Paris and Barcelona, influenced him profoundly. Death and suffering dominate the paintings of the Blue Period (1901–04), the period immediately following his closest contact with Barcelona, and recur at other times in his long life. Poverty, disappointment in love, illness and premature death are the other faces of the high-spirited Bohemianism which characterised turn-of-the-century Paris and found its reflection at Els Quatre Gats.

Picasso has been lucky with his Barcelona Museum, installed in two adjacent Gothic palaces. It has never set out to give a comprehensive view of Picasso's development, and there is a heavy emphasis on the formative years of 1895-1901 when Picasso was most obviously a

Barcelona artist. The initial gift was of the collection of his friend and secretary Jaume Sabartés, to which have been added further gifts by the artist himself and some pictures from the Modern Art Museum. There is also the set of 44 paintings done in 1957 on the subject of Velázquez's 'Las Meninas' which draw out the latent grotesqueness and human frailty implicit in the artist's painting of the Spanish Royal Family. Spain remained an issue in Picasso's art for the rest of his life. Not just in the obvious pictures like 'Guernica' (now in Madrid) but in his attention to the bullfight as subject-matter, well represented in Barcelona. In the College of Architects murals, in which a young girl leads a bull, bullfighting is not just about male chauvinism and striving but also about how the female principle of harmony can triumph over it, and civilisation live on despite the violence and tragedy of Picasso's century.

After the end of the Spanish War, Joan Miró kept away from Barcelona. Through most of the Franco period he lived in relative seclusion in Majorca. He had after all designed the famous Republican 'Aidez l'Espagne' poster during the War and it suited him to keep his head down. He kept in touch though. Across the Atlantic was the architect Josep-Lluís Sert, and as Miró's work became better known, it was Sert he commissioned to design his island studio. From the mid-1960s he was more often in Barcelona, designing for avant garde political theatre groups like Els Joglars. The repressed anger of so much of Miró's work becomes less repressed, more overt. His role in shaping what was to become the contemporary Catalan theatre, physical, intense, often political, always spectacular, cannot be underestimated. But it was not until 1979, towards the end of his life, that Miró really arrived in Barcelona. In that year, the Miró Foundation, designed by Sert, opened its doors on Montjuïc, overlooking the city that had never quite taken the artist to its heart. Unlike the rather traditional Picasso Museum in the city, or the entertaining but scarcely serious Dalí Theatre-Museum in Figueres, the Foundation

217

is a living cultural and educational centre, with temporary exhibition space, library and lecture rooms. Music recitals, often first performances of contemporary music, are given there. In the first flush of democracy in the late 1970s, there was a unique inaugural exhibition which attempted to span the whole of Catalan cultural heritage.

Following Miró's death on Christmas Day 1983, a decision was taken by the trustees to enlarge the Foundation to incorporate a permanent exhibition of the artist's own work. Space was also required for the beginnings of a permanent collection of contemporary art in memory of Miró. This exploits Miró's own longevity to represent the modern movement from Léger and Max Ernst through Roland Penrose and Anthony Caro to a younger Catalan contemporary — Antoni Tàpies. There is also an excellent small exhibition of Sert's own work, which clarifies the various stage of his career: his International Style buildings in Barcelona in the 1930s (the Casa Bloc and TB clinic); his North American work (especially the new buildings at Harvard, where Sert was Dean of Architecture from 1953 in succession to Walter Gropius); his later European work (Miró's studio on Majorca, the Maeght Foundation at St Paul de Vence in Provence, and the Miró Foundation).

The images of Catalan rural life which appear in the early farmyard paintings stayed with Miró, and reappear in the late sculptures, with their direct use of familiar tools such as the three-pronged pitchfork made from a single tree branch. The 'Pagès Català' (Catalan peasant) of 1968 is both a celebration of human life lived in harmony with the natural world, but also a criticism of the inhumanities of modern urban industrial life, as played out in both the public and private arenas. Another such figure, holding the emblematic pitchfork, presides over the terrace and pond in front of the Foundation building and so, thanks to the clever placing of the building on the hillside, over the city, reminding it of its rural roots, just as the three factory chimneys left standing below make a statement about its industrial past and present.

218

After the War was over . . .

Miró created a world. By allowing the free play of the sub-conscious to create form in his paintings, he was able to create an artistic replica of the real world that was both intensely private, but also contained a rawness of emotion that remains intense, powerful and haunting. It is this sort of personal, symbolic mode of expression that made him quietly useful to the younger artists who, in the 1950s, were to set about exploring the limitations and possibility of art under Franco. Thus despite the War, despite everything that might have created discontinuity, there is a thin line flowing through Miró to the work of the younger artists who belonged to the Dau al Set group in the late 1940s and 1950s. Two names stand out, those of Joan Brossa and Antoni Tàpies.

Did Brossa perhaps spread himself too thinly? He was a poet, a sculptural (concrete) poet whose work can be seen near the velodrome at Horta in Barcelona, and a visual artist. He dabbled in film. Both as a poet and a visual artist he set out to intrigue and amuse and question the viewer and reader. His subject-matter is the ambiguous relationship that exists between apparently unrelated objects, the objects that he, the artist, chooses to place within the picture frame, scatter across the hillside, or place on the page of a book. There are always fresh interpretations possible, always new questions to ask. Only one thing is certain: there is no truth to find. Brossa refused to take either himself or life very seriously. In Girona, the Film Museum is announced in the square outside by a classical column surmounted by the letter A. The first letter of the alphabet for film, which Brossa regarded as both the most recent and the greatest of art forms.

Tàpies on the other hand took himself extremely seriously. Though some people continue to see his work as obscure and difficult, he has been hugely successful. He has his own Foundation in Barcelona, just a block away from the Passeig de Gràcia, in an important building in its own right: Domènech i Muntaner's design for the

219

Montaner i Simón publishing house. Born in 1923, his early work was influenced by Klee and Miró, but by the 1950s he had moved towards Informalism (or Informal Art). Natural materials like straw and sand found their way onto the canvas and there was some use of collage. In the 1970s his work acquired a political cutting edge which placed him at the head of those artists demanding radical social and political change. Both Tàpies and Miró took part in the 1970 protest at Montserrat when intellectuals and artists locked themselves in the monastery in protest against the show trials of Basque nationalists in Burgos. This in turn led to the setting up of the Catalan Assembly in 1971 which succeeded in uniting different ideological tendencies behind a simple programme in support of Catalan self-government. But Tàpies worked through this political phase, thrust upon him by the difficulties of artistic life in Franco's Spain, and emerged with broader and very personal ambitions. He has made it clear in his prolific writings about art that he supports a broadly Marxist analysis of society, but that this does not exclude a philosophical quest inspired by Eastern ideas from Taoism or Zen. The artist is a voice (*veu*) rather than a spokesperson (*portaveu*) for a particular political party. He has also proved that a difficult artist can also be successful. Tàpies is less well known internationally than Picasso, Dalí or Miró, and his images have not passed into the popular imagination in quite the same way. Yet he has collaborated successfully with poets, musicians and graphic artists to produce record sleeves, posters and book covers.

The picture gallery of the Fundació Tàpies could not be more different from the Fundació Miró. Two floors of the building have been knocked out to create a space well suited to the large dimensions of so many of Tàpies' works. There is a small raised external patio, dominated at one end by a large black-on-indigo painting. On a second side are 45 degree mirrors reflecting the sky and on a third side, more 45 degree mirrors, this time reflecting the spectator and the picture. This is puzzlement on the grand scale, and there seem to be issues here about the relationship between the real world beyond the gallery and the processes of artistic imagination and creation. Tàpies is a highly cerebral painter. The original *Dau al Set* had been both a group of practising artists and a literary and critical magazine. Tàpies's writings on art and culture through the 50s and 60s began to be collected and published in book form from 1970. In this way, either positively or negatively, he has remained highly influential in the field of Catalan non-figurative art. He considers that the viewer of a painting requires initially a degree of spontaneity in response to the work of art, but that in order to understand the artist's reasons for creating a particular image in a particular way, some apparatus of art criticism is required. Yet the gallery eschews the didactic approach that the Miró Foundation is so good at. It can be quite hard to get beyond an initial spontaneous reaction which is exclusive to the individual viewer.

Tàpies stressed the importance of originality in art and criticised the concept of high culture which merely distracted people from the essential problems of their existence and the world about them. Such views can be understood from within a Western intellectual framework. But a visit to the library/study area reveals the depth of Tàpies' interest in Eastern art and philosophy. One of the purposes of the Foundation is to act as a launch-pad for the study of non-Western art. His view of the whole created world as an art-form, the rejection of the humanity-nature dualism and the notion of creating beauty in everyday life and action, require a more Eastern set of mental tools. Such ideas can help the viewer to understand why the artist's palette has changed so little over the years, with white, cream, ochre and grey often representing his full range. Colour is an event in his paintings and is used to stress the cryptic symbols (including mathematical symbols, letters and numbers) which punctuate his personal pictorial world.

Yet meaning can also be startlingly direct in Tàpies, as in 'Earth on Canvas' (1970) where soil is attached to the canvas, nearly obliterating it, rather as earth begins to cover a coffin in a freshly dug grave. Another example is 'Concert' (1985) in which the artist applies black and white paint to newsprint stuck onto the canvas, in such a way that only a few stories are readable. These include 'The Sky in September', the television and radio programmes, the stock exchange, and a page which reports a court case being brought in Burgos against the mime group Els Joglars for blasphemy. The exact relationship between these stories is left for the viewer to work out . . . The same suppressed anger burgeons forth in his monument to Picasso in the Passeig de Picasso, often decried as a pile of old rubbish. Which is, of course, exactly what it is, a satire on modern, material Catalan society. The words are by Picasso: 'No, painting is not made to decorate apartments but is a weapon of war, offensive and defensive, against the enemy.'

The Sad Story of Salvador Dalí
In the summer of 1910, Picasso was at Cadaqués. He had reached the stark, geometrical flatness of Analytical Cubism which confirmed the emptiness he had already visited in the Blue Period. Cadaqués was disenchantment, and Picasso was to spend much of the rest of his life trying to find re-enchantment in the world and in art. That other Catalan figure whose name is so closely linked to Cadaqués, Salvador Dalí, retreated inwards in search of enchantment to the fantastic images of his subconscious, re-inventing himself and his relationships as the subject-matter of his work. Yet he located them more often than not in the hyper-real scenery of the Cap de Creus peninsula, with its cliffs and strange rock formations and scraggy maquis.

Dalí is an important painter. He is also popular, as the enormous crowds of tourists at the Theatre-Museum in

Figueres, and the more modest knots of visitors at his house in Port Lligat, testify. It is not the purpose of this chapter to give an account of his life and times, which can be found in any book about surrealism. Rather it is to see how Dalí dealt with the two important themes at issue in this part of the book: the relationship between a culture and the local places in which it emerges, and the relationship between culture and its political and social environment. Dalí and Picasso had radically different views on the second of these two issues:

> What do you think an artist is? An imbecile who has nothing but eyes if he is a painter or ears if he is a musician, or a lyre at every level of his heart if he is a poet? Quite the contrary, he is at the same time a political being, constantly aware of what is going on in the world, whether it be harrowing, bitter or sweet, and he cannot help being shaped by it.
> (Picasso, quoted by Nadine Gordimer in *The Guardian*, 15 June 2002)

> I was decidedly not a man of history. On the contrary, I felt deep down inside antihistorical and apolitical. I was either too far ahead of my time or too far behind it, but I was never the contemporary of the ping-pong players.
> (Dalí)

The ping-pong players were those he saw and heard as he escaped from Catalonia in 1934. The feuding between the newly elected right-wing government in Madrid and the leftist Companys, newly installed as President of the Generalitat, was getting out of hand. Companys had declared the existence of a separate Catalan State within the Spanish Republic. Dalí feared the revolutionary mood in the streets and did not wait to see Companys thrown into prison. The ping-pong players became for Dalí a symbol of the political game, a presentiment of the Spanish War which he later described as a 'great armed cannibalism'. Orwell too noted Dalí's fastidiousness about conflict, his flight to Italy during the Spanish War, and from

France back to Spain and then the USA during the Second World War. Yet to describe Dalí as apolitical would be a grave error. He set himself on Franco's side, which meant on the side of privilege and tradition. He set himself on the side of Spain against Catalonia. His views on the Franco regime are clear:

> In our times of mediocrity, everything great, important and authentic has been carried out in extraordinary ways, often completely against the tide. Before Franco, politicians and governments increased confusion, disorder and lies. Franco broke openly with that false tradition, reimposing clarity, truth and order throughout the country at its moment of greatest anarchy. (author's translation)

'Clarity, truth and order', then, provided it did not interfere with Salvador Dalí living his own life, playing out in reality his own perverse sexual fantasies, and above all making lots of money. Franco, who had an enormous capacity to be flattered, seems to have been alternately delighted and embarrassed by the attention paid to him by the painter. At least he had one friend in Catalonia. There is little indication that Dalí's art had any significance impact on post-war Catalan art. In a defeated country, Dalí had placed himself on the side of the victors. Yet it is hard not to think, as one watches the crowds queuing outside the Theatre-Museum in Figueres, that Dalí, the consummate joker, has had the last laugh. If the Catalans would not love him, at least the tourists would.

The story of how the Theatre-Museum came to be set up is bizarre, as one might expect, and spans the years from 1961 to 1974. The actors included Dalí himself, General Franco, various government ministers, including Manuel Fraga Iribarne (who is infiltrating himself assiduously into this book), and local municipal figures in Figueres. Dalí gave three reasons for wanting the old, ruined theatre, bombed in 1939, as a museum. First, because he saw himself as a theatrical painter; second, because the theatre is opposite the church where he was baptised;

third, because his first painting exhibition had been in the theatre foyer. It was Fraga who got it right, recognising that such a development would be complementary to the development of the Costa Brava as a tourist area. After several face-to-face meetings, and much flattery, Franco agreed.

The actual funding of the conversion and reconstruction of the bombed theatre was through the Ministry of Housing, using money set aside for post-war reconstruction in Figueres but never spent. This in turn aroused furious criticism in Catalonia. One Barcelona paper asked why Dalí, a dollar millionaire, was being given nine million pesetas (some £60,000 at 1960 prices) to build himself a 'home' for when he was dead. Nine million pesetas at that time was the going price for a single Dalí painting. As a museum, it is definitely wanting. It is dangerously crowded, for a start, and since many of the paintings are unlabelled, it is almost impossible to know which ones are originals and which ones are copies. This is more theme park than museum: the Dalí experience, complete with games, visual punning, and a 'Gaia looking out to sea' which transmogrifies into Abe Lincoln at the correct distance. At least, that is what is supposed to happen ... The Museum pokes fun successfully at the stuffy atmosphere of so many museums, but finally it also seems to poke fun at its own visitors: this is your world, your culture, your hideous commercialism, you gullible people who have been stupid enough to queue and pay to come in here. But queue and pay we do, and most of us seem to enjoy it. Catalan by birth, Dalí is the artist turned international entrepreneur. Where Miró shattered the mirrors, and Tàpies theorised about them, Dalí placed them so that they just reflected one another ad infinitum.

A Little Light Music

We have seen that the notion of a 'Catalan artist' is a complex one. Tàpies, Miró, Picasso and Dalí all relate differently to Catalonia. All four can be claimed as international artists. Much the same applies to the musicians, with the added complication of Spain. Spain in music was almost entirely a foreign, not to say French, invention — Bizet, Chabrier, Debussy, Lalo, Ravel — with a little help from Russians like Glinka and Rimsky-Korsakov. As James Woodall makes clear, 'Like the poets in their writings, these late-Romantic composers were intent on evoking an idea of Spain, of Andalusia above all, which had literary and painterly correspondences, but few to reality.' (In Search of the Firedance, p.153) And unsurprisingly, in looking south they missed Catalonia entirely, despite the fact that Felip Pedrell, the most important Spanish musicologist, was a Catalan.

Woodall describes Pedrell's influence on Albéniz and Granados, both Catalans, and later on Falla. In particular, he asserts that Pedrell's *Cancionero*, a collection of folk tunes from all corners of the peninsula was a direct influence on the structure of Albéniz's suite for piano and orchestra *Iberia* (1909) and Granados's *Goyescas* (1911). But there are complications here. Albéniz was only Catalan because he spent a short period in his youth at Camprodon in the Pyrenees, where his father was a customs official. But Albéniz's youth was short indeed and his adventures included stowing away on a boat to South America and being hailed as a child prodigy in the USA before he was old enough to be hailed as a teenage prodigy. He studied and worked across Europe, but Paris was his base. Granados was more obviously a son of Catalonia, developing slowly while earning his living as a music teacher in Barcelona, achieving fame with the *Goyescas* in 1911 but then drowned in the English Channel when his ship was sunk by a German torpedo in 1916. But both the *Goyescas* and *Iberia* draw on a wide range of Spanish folk music, especially Andalusian. That was what the concert-going public expected, and to a large extent still expect, from 'Spanish' composers.

The most important Catalan musical tradition was that of choral singing. From 1860, under the influence of Josep Anselm Clavé, choral singing had been an integral part of the Catalan *Renaixença*. Such was his influence that the male voice choirs that sprang up in all the major Catalan towns were referred to as the *cors de Clavé*. Folksongs were revived and new songs written. From 1892, with the establishment of the Orfeó Català by Lluís Millet and Amadeu Vives, the choral tradition developed rapidly. The Orfeó extended Clavé's work in at least three ways: first, by introducing women's and children's voices; second, by extending the repertoire to include church music; and third, by extending the range of music to include choral works from the wider European tradition. By 1895 there were 145 branches of the Orfeó in Catalonia. It was left to Enric Morera and his Catalunya Nova choirs to continue the tradition of working class male voice choirs into the twentieth century.

What Clavé, Vives, Millet and Morera did for choral singing, Casals tried to do for orchestral music. As noted above, he spent more time before the War organising and conducting than playing his cello. He was both famous and popular. As early as 1927 a street was named after him in his home town, El Vendrell; this event was celebrated by an open-air concert with an enthusiastic working class audience. The spirit of Catalan music at this period (its rootedness and its internationalism) was demonstrated at an official Generalitat concert at Montjuïc in 1932. The first part was devoted to *sardanas* played by a traditional *cobla* band. In the second part, local choirs joined forces for Beethoven's Ninth Symphony with its choral finale. And in the third part the Orfeó Català performed songs, including their conductor Millet's setting of 'El Cant dels Ocells', the song with which Casals' exile, first at Prades in French Catalonia and later in Puerto Rico, is inextricably linked.

Beethoven's Ninth Symphony was to recur in the musical history of Barcelona. Casals was asked to conduct it again, as part of the celebration of the alternative Olympics of 1936 at Montjuïc, in celebration of world peace. He was rehearsing it at the Palau de la Música on 18 July 1936 when news of the military rebellion came through. Colm Tóibín picks up the story:

> Casals and his orchestra were advised to go home as quickly as they could. They had completed the first three movements of the symphony, and Casals asked the musicians and singers if they would finish it. They agreed. . . . Within a month Lorca would be murdered in Granada; over the next twelve months the city of Barcelona would tear itself apart; over the next two years a dark shadow would move across Spain. The choir began to sing the choral section of the Ninth Symphony:
>
> > By this magic is united
> > What the harsh past held apart
> > All mankind are sworn brothers
> > Where the gentle wings abide.
>
> It was the afternoon before the Civil War. (<u>Homage to Barcelona</u>, pp. 105/6)

'It was the afternoon before the Civil War' — it is more than a rhetorical trick. When Helen Watts and Gerald English, the Coral Sant Jordi, the Cor Madrigal, the Orfeó de Sants and the Coral Cantiga performed the Ninth Symphony in the Palau on 5 June 1970, there was a shiver of anticipation as the Barcelona Orchestra struck up the first bars of the final movement. It was an 'I was there' moment.

The Casals museum at El Vendrell is located in the coastal suburb of Sant Salvador where a neat row of period houses gives straight onto the beach. Some of these houses date back to the nineteenth century when Sant Salvador was an important port for the export of wine to America. The Casals family home is surrounded by a garden heady with the scent of pines and the sighing of the sea-breeze in the palms. When the author visited the house for the first time ten years ago, the friendly curator compounded the confusion about Catalan and Spanish music by putting on Rodrigo's *Concierto de Aranjuez* as a token of welcome. Art and nature, life and art, land and sea, culture and politics, this little museum makes the links in the most effective way possible, drawing these themes around the life of an artist of international standing who remained faithful to his humble roots on the coast of Catalonia.

In the sitting-room of the house there is a glass cabinet containing a collection of locally carved figures for the crib, that distinctive Catalan tradition still kept up in most Catalan families in the weeks preceding Christmas. Here is the inspiration for Casals' great peace anthem, the oratorio *El Pessebre* (The Crib). This was performed all over the world after 1960, including Berlin, London and the United Nations in New York, as part of the celebrations of the fifteenth anniversary of the Universal Declaration of Human Rights. In a message to the United Nations in 1958 Casals said: 'I used music and my voice to draw attention to the suffering which afflicts mankind because of the great and perhaps mortal danger of nuclear weapons threatening us. Music, that universal language which is understood by everyone, should be a source of communication among men.' Casals died — in exile — at the age of ninety-six, and in 1979 his remains were brought home to Catalonia.

Another Catalan composer who took the road to exile in 1939 was Robert Gerhard. But his musical journey is rather different to that of Casals. Born in Valls, Catalonia, in 1896, he was the son of a Swiss father and a Catalan mother. Between 1923 and 1929 he studied with Schönberg in Vienna and Berlin. Returning to Catalonia in 1929 he became closely identified with the most modernising tendencies in Catalan art which, as we have seen, ran parallel to the modernising and secularising political project of the Republic. Alban Berg's Violin Concerto, possibly the only twelve-tone piece still in the regular concert repertoire by the beginning of the twenty-first century, was especially written for the International Society for Contemporary Music festival in Barcelona in April 1936. That such a festival was taking place in Barcelona owed much to Gerhard. Also in Barcelona in 1936 were the young English composers Lennox Berkeley and Benjamin Britten. It was their first meeting. They became close, and worked together on a suite called *Mont Juic*, which uses folk-tunes they had heard at a folklore display on Montjuïc. The second movement, a Lament, represents Britten's own pacifist horror at the Spanish War. The piece is subtitled 'Barcelona, July 1936'.

In exile in Cambridge, Gerhard earned a living by writing music for films (including Lindsay Anderson's *This Sporting Life*), theatre, television and radio. It appears to have been at this time that he adopted the ambiguous 'o' at the end of 'Robert' (a traditional Catalan name). Perhaps his English friends advised him that it might be easier to market his music as Spanish Roberto than Swiss-Alsatian-Catalan-English Robert. In his opera *The Duenna* (broadcast by the BBC in 1949 and revived by Opera North in 1992) Gerhard found a ready-made English libretto on a Spanish theme in Sheridan's 1775 box-office success of the same name. The music weaves austere passages in the style of Webern, Schönberg and Berg with music owing much more to the Spanish light opera tradition of *zarzuela*. Add a central character who happens to be an old, mean Portuguese Jew attempting to marry a beautiful young woman, and there are reasons enough to be anxious about the work. Yet in other works, such as the *Concerto for Orchestra* (1964), Gerhard manages to weave in *sardana* references within a taut and innovative single-movement framework. This concerto was one of only four Catalan works played at the London Proms 2002 season devoted to Spain and Spanish-inspired music. Just four out of thirty-eight works, although nearly half the total were written by composers from other countries seeking inspiration in Spanish and Latin American music. When the National Orchestra of Catalonia (the old

Barcelona Symphony in its new guise) played the *Concerto for Orchestra* at the 2002 Proms, they also played Xavier Montsalvatge's *Cinco Canciones Negras* (1940). These Five Negro Songs link poems by a Central American poet with music inspired by sources as various as Poulenc, traditional Spanish melodies and Caribbean rhythms. If the piece by Gerhard showed an international composer pining for his Catalan roots, then the Montsalvatge songs suggested the complex ways in which globalism gathers up the music of the world and redistributes it along the routes of trade and cultural interchange.

Part 3:

Catalonia Today

Chapter 12

On Being a Nation

The Global and the Local

Building on the rich tapestry of Catalan national history, the measure of autonomy within the Spanish state achieved by the end of the twentieth century goes some way (but by no means all the way) to meet the competing demands of those who recognise a Catalan nation, a Catalan identity and a Catalan dimension to their lives. We must also, of course, give some attention to those who prefer to think of themselves as Spanish, or Europeans or human beings. *'Som i serem'* (We are, and we shall be), is a slogan often repeated in Catalonia, especially by nationalist politicians and supporters. The slogan bears a resonance and a truth, but also by its very insistence hints at uncertainties and insecurities as to what the future of Catalonia will be. The simple fact that so many Catalans feel the need to worry the bone of national identity so often and so insistently says something important about them. Castilian identity is not a subject that keeps people awake in Madrid or the other cities of Castile — Segovia, Toledo, Salamanca. This present book is both an attempt to communicate something of the vitality of Catalonia's past and present and to point up some of the unanswered questions that keep the thoughtful Catalan awake at night. 'What constitutes the core of this "we"?'; 'What shall "we" become?'; 'Who counts in this "we"?' 'Who is excluded from this "we"?'

Daniel Conversi, in writing about the Basques and the Catalans, has referred to the 'fallacy' of globalisation —

'the fallacy that the advent of a global culture could inspire peace, prosperity and a general lessening of conflict.' It is hard to recognise, in any case, such a 'global culture'. What is easier to spot is the massive advance of the language, values and material culture of the United States of America, in the face of which almost all national identities squirm with discomfort. It is true that there are multinational companies based in countries other than the USA, and that some local cultures are integrated into the global culture, as in the curiously named phenomenon of 'world music'. But any homogenisation that may exist is almost entirely dependent on the Coca Cola dream of the world being 'one' in its patterns of consumption. Thus globalisation is a very different animal from internationalism — the more risky, but more rooted cause of respect for national traditions and languages, and the complex task of working out political solutions for who counts as 'a nation', how each nation wants to rule itself or be ruled, and inter-national relations and how they are to be ordered. What we have at the moment is a reaction to globalisation in which national groups (and sometimes religious groups too) assert their difference from the USA model, but at the same time suppress the identities of smaller groups within their midst. There is, too, a pressure to take sides which may cut across people's intuitive grasp that it is possible to have a floating identity, and to participate in different ways in different cultural formations. Helen Drysdale's *Mother Tongues* is a moving account of the persistence of local languages and cultures within Europe. But one of her persistent chagrins as she travelled around Europe seems to have been the many people she met who had a weak national identity and seemed rather happy about that state of affairs.

Globalisation, in the form of the hegemony of the USA, cannot be ignored. One of the features that kept Franco in power for so long was the deal by which the USA got use of Spanish bases for its Cold War nuclear arsenal, and in return pumped millions of dollars into the Spanish economy. In recent years, USA-based companies have made many inroads into the Catalan economy. There is nothing to be gained by replacing the all-powerful state by the all-powerful corporation. While some academics, noticeably David Held at the London School of Economics, have argued that globalisation incorporates a growing number of international regulatory bodies, the evidence for this is extremely weak. The World Bank and International Monetary Fund have never really emerged from the shadow of the USA government and financial institutions; the United Nations continues to be rather ineffectual at peace-keeping, aid distribution and the promotion of human health. The most effective international organisation is probably the World Trade Organisation which sets out to assert the rights and powers of multinational corporations as against those of national governments. The USA and UK governments showed their contempt for the UN in their decision to go to war against Iraq in 2003 without seeking UN backing. International agreements on the environment are made and then flouted. The USA has not yet recognised the World Court. Even the European Union, in many ways the success story of internationalism in the second half of the twentieth century, seems likely to continue as an economic club, its social and political ambitions relegated to a withered appendix.

Catalonia and the Basque Country

The advantage of the wide perspective suggested here is that it enables us to see Catalonia as a special case of a common phenomenon in the modern world, a nation struggling for identity but never quite sure of the basis for that identity. To set another paradox: a nation struggling for identity but also people struggling for identity, unconvinced that what is on offer suits them. Some further purchase may be obtained on the issue by comparing the contrasting fortunes of Catalan and Basque nationalism in modern Spain. Let us avoid for a moment the question of nation, and ask first the question of what sort of place Catalonia is. And then ask the same question of the Basque Country.

For those Spaniards who speak a different language, who recognise a different nation, dealing with the Francoist past is also a matter of dealing with the violence done to those languages, those cultures, those nations. Already in 1938, Franco had announced: 'The character of each region will be respected, whenever it does not threaten national unity, which we want absolute, with only one language, Castilian, and only one personality, Spanish.' In the Basque Country in the latter years of the Franco regime, violence was increasingly met with violence. The assassination in late 1973 of Admiral Carrero Blanco by members of the Basque military organisation ETA coincided with a show trial of ten leaders of the clandestine trade union movement *Comisiones Obreras* (Workers' Commissions). Sadly, democracy has not seen an end to this particular violence. In Catalonia, there have been sporadic outbreaks of violence, using the sort of Molotov cocktail device which can be manufactured in anyone's kitchen, but the response has been in the main political and cultural, as it has been in Galicia, in northwest Spain.

It is important to consider Catalonia in the context of widening horizons and changing patterns of population. Since the late nineteenth century, Catalonia has been a major destination for emigration from the poor rural areas of Spain, first of all from Murcia, later from other parts of Andalusia and from the remoter parts of Extremadura and Galicia. Much of the labour that went to build the huge hydro-electric schemes in the Catalan Pyrenees came from outside of Catalonia, and José Camilo Cela, the Spanish Nobel Prize-winner, wrote of this with both humour and affection in his *Viaje al Pirineo de Lérida*. But go further back, and we find that Catalonia has always been a place of passage, of transit, for both people and ideas. Benedict Anderson has a fascinating discussion of the massacre of the Albigensian heretics in the south of France in the thirteenth century. He points out that most of those slaughtered would have spoken Provençal or Catalan rather than French. Far from being a cosy little 'French' affair, this was an attack inspired by religious bigotry that pitted Europeans from a number of places against those who lived in that particular place and time. While nationalist historians write and speak of their thousand-year old nation, the medieval Catalan empire was a multilingual and multinational affair that took the name of Castilian-speaking Aragon. Contemporary Catalonia contains many features that place a large question-mark against the idea of nationhood. Not least, the large number of people for whom Catalan is not the customary everyday language and the many Catalan-speakers outside Catalonia who show no desire at all to be part of a Catalan nation. To add a final paradox, then, we have a people whose claim to nationhood has coincided with the arrival in their midst of large numbers of people from other parts of Spain and Europe, but also from Latin America and North Africa).

If we turn now to the Basque Country, we find a zone distinguished not by passage but by isolation, a people whose language is so ancient that no-one knows where it came from, a people who remained unconquered by Romans and Muslims. While non-native-speakers of Catalan who speak (say) Castilian or French, can rub along quite easily with Catalan speakers, the same is not true of the Basque Country. Despite the strong hold of Catholicism in the Basque Country, the Basques remained loyal to the Spanish Republic in the 1930s and suffered similar humiliation in consequence to that of the Catalans. Like Catalonia, the Basque Country has experienced large-scale industrialisation and immigration from other parts of Spain, with the result that Basque speakers are now a minority. Whereas Catalonia has been able to integrate non-Catalans through its language normalisation policies (the regular use of Catalan in the mass media, and

239

for road-signs, education, business and public life), this option has not been open to the Basques. Yet rather than isolating Basque and non-Basque populations, the effect has been to radicalise Basque nationalism. The political nationalist movement that developed in the later years of the Franco regime soon turned to violence, including high profile assassinations. It stressed action, participation and armed struggle: it was not essential to know the language to be a good Basque, but it was necessary to be committed to action. What matters are not cultural signs (use of language) but political signs — in particular the willingness to be involved in the direct action politics of demonstrations, civil disobedience, bombings, kidnappings and extortion rackets. State repression, both under Franco and since, has exacerbated the turn to violence in Basque politics.

Events before and during the democratic transition of the 1970s have had a strong influence on subsequent nationalist mobilisation in the two areas, as Conversi makes clear. The Catalans were able to call on the energy generated by a broad cultural movement in the final decade of the dictatorship in Catalonia, as cultural nationalism evolved to political nationalism through various political parties achieving a common platform in support of autonomy. These groups included nationalists, communists, socialists, Catholics and even some anarchists. But in the Basque Country, political nationalism fragmented, eventually producing military nationalism. The Christian Democrat style conservative party, the Basque National Party (PNV), was unable to keep a rein on its younger, militant members who organised the armed movement known as ETA and its political wing Herri Batasuna (HB; Popular Unity). Conversi described HB as 'one of the most unorthodox, unconventional and *sui generis* parties in Europe' (The Basques, the Catalans and Spain, p. 150), including as it does in its ranks Marxists, environmentalists, punks, gay rights activists, feminists, priests, small-town businessmen and peasants. Yet there is no shared culture on which either PNV or HB can call in asserting Basque identity, no Basque equivalent of that heady Catalan cultural mixture of *sardanas*, human-castle-builders, singers and football. The common stem from which political difference and debate can grow and flourish in a democratic and peaceful way.

In the meantime, for many years ETA has received not only the voluntary support of many Basques, but also financial support from racketeering and extortion. At the time of writing, the new Spanish government has continued the ban on HB, a move which is likely to perpetuate the current stalemate in Basque society. With or without HB the Basque Country will remain a land of fear. If Catalonia suggests a positive outcome for national sentiment in the modern world, events in the Basque Country prefigure a different kind of end-game, with the aim of asserting national rights demanding and justifying violence.

Can Spain survive?

If the total lack of interest of the average Catalan in the fortunes and misfortunes of Spain in recent football World Cups is anything to go by, the answer is probably not. As one of Europe's most intelligent footballers, Pat Nevin, remarked, Spanish clubs do well in European club competitions but Spanish national sides seldom deliver the goods in major tournaments. A few years back he was heard to wonder aloud on prime-time television if Spain actually existed. He echoed the views of an academic commentator, Michael Keating, who complained that 'The Spanish state has historically been conspicuously unsuccessful in building a unitary nation.' What is curiously lacking from the Catalonia-Spain amalgam is that characteristic English schizophrenia which finds it quite simple when abroad or at moments of national crisis (in wartime, for example) to assert a British identity, while living for most of the time in a cosy, mythical Little Englander mindset. In a sense this brings us to the crux of the 'Catalan problem'. They

241

are not an oppressed minority, although they have been in the not too distant past. Their language, their economy, their culture — all flourish. And yet there is still that uncertainty summed up in the hidden questions behind '*som i serem*'. The Catalans want clarity and certainty, not fudge and compromise.

For Keating, it is all very simple, a matter of stepping back in history 'to an era of overlapping authority, multiple identity and complexity, before the rise of the modern state'. The Scots seem to be managing it quite well, with the help of a hugely over-budget multi-million pound parliament building designed by a Catalan, Enric Miralles, which perhaps explains Nevin's smugness as a Scot himself. The Welsh are not so sure, divided as they remain between the industrialised English-speaking south and the rural Welsh-speaking areas of north and west. The English have not really got started on this one yet. The Catalans are living it intensely but not quite understanding the processes they are undergoing. Usefully, Keating contrasted the 'ambitious' rhetoric of the nationalist (CiU) alliance with the limited opportunities available in practice to express national identity in other than a cultural sense. He pointed out that the Catalans in opinion polls felt both more Spanish and more European than the Basques. At least three identities, then, are open to them, although in practice many prefer to turn their back on public life in preference for a private, family sphere, or to enjoy the global Coca Cola culture. Meanwhile the Galicians are in the curious position of being ruled by an ex-Francoist minister elected under the standard of the Spanish Conservative Party. So despite the Catalan/Galician/Basque Declaration of Barcelona (1998; later of Santiago and Vitoria too) with its demand for a plurinational and confederal state, there is little sign of a common position emerging. One suspects that any discussion of what a plurinational and confederal state might look like in practice would rapidly descend into chaos.

As the years stretch away from the heroic 1970s, it becomes more and more obvious that whatever political solutions are reached will have to recognise that culture is not just a question of 'national culture'. Within Catalonia, there are now many different cultural identities available. They are part of the fabric of Catalonia as a nation, as they are part of all European nations. In choosing their lifestyle, often in resistance to the imposition of a homogenised global culture, Catalans do not want to be restricted by a limited notion of a 'Catalan' culture any more than they want to be limited by a 'Spanish' culture. In rejecting the hegemony of globalisation USA-style, it is important not to allow the world to be carved up once more between intolerant nation states, or even nations without a state.

The Case of the 1992 Olympic Games

How, then, does it all work out in practice? If we turn now to the powers of the Generalitat, the Catalan government, we will find that it possesses complete control over language and culture, health, education and social policy. The contrast with centralised France, where there is rigid central control over the key cultural areas of language and education, could not be more apparent. Who cares about law and order, or economic development (Spanish state powers) when the hand that rocks the cradle is so clearly a Catalan hand? What are the implications for the public life of Catalonia? What does cultural politics look like, exactly? How does the daily grind of politics fit into the broader trends of national life in Catalonia and Spain?

There is an excellent, relatively recent case-study by John Hargreaves of the events leading up to and surrounding the holding of the 1992 Olympic Games in Barcelona. Hargreaves has shown how the Games highlighted the supreme political skill (or political trickery, depending on one's point of view) of the then ruling Catalan party, the CiU, and its now retired leader, Jordi

Pujol. Pujol was long an exponent of what Hargreaves describes as 'civic nationalism'. This contends that all those who live and work in Catalonia are part of the Catalan project of nation-building. In particular, Pujol denied that his brand of Catalan nationalism was based around ethnicity, which would have excluded migrants from other territories. In reality, Hargreaves claims, Catalan nationalism is more complex, less civic and more ethnic than Pujol claimed:

> The Catalan government vigorously promotes Catalan culture in every shape and form. That ethnic nationalism predominates over civic nationalism is evidenced by the many public statements that Pujol has made concerning the centrality of the language to being Catalan and, above all, by the government's policy of 'linguistic normalisation', whereby Castilian native speakers are compelled in a number of ways to become culturally Catalan. Most importantly, the school curriculum is taught in Catalan and proficiency in the language is a condition of employment in much of the public sector. The Catalan government has succeeded in some ways in Catalanising the mass media, especially the popular government-controlled Catalan-language TV channel TV3.
> (Hargreaves, <u>Freedom for Catalonia</u>, p. 34)

But this is to assume that the confident Hargreaves has got it right. For example, his use of the language issue is by no means clear-cut. We might notice, for example, the importance of language in the 'civic nationalism' of the USA. A basic knowledge of English, and of the constitution, is regarded there as a prerequisite for citizenship. It also helps to look at the reality of the language issue as well as the way it comes over in law. As we have already seen in the contrast with the Basque Country, the inescapable fact is that Catalan is very closely related to Castilian. It is not unusual to hear conversations being carried on between Catalan and Castilian speakers in which speakers will happily use their own first language. Hargreaves himself notes that there is considerable overlap between Catalan and Castilian-speaking communities in Catalonia, with intermarriage, job mobility, shared schools, churches and community associations being just some of the features that contribute to largely harmonious relations. We are not dealing with two sects that do not communicate with one another. To find a pure Catalan is about as difficult as finding a pure English person. As the Catalan writer Juan Marsé has suggested, we are all *xarnegos* (an abusive term for newcomers to Catalonia) now.

Of course, such cultural blurring is itself no guarantee of peaceful relations. The experience of ex-Yugoslavia shows how very quickly neighbours can become deadly enemies, can be forced to choose after spending most of their lives preferring not to choose. Under Serb bombardment, it was hard for the citizens of Sarajevo to maintain a sophisticated indifference to the issue of ethnicity. Hargreaves makes much use of social survey material which asks people whether they feel 'only Catalan', 'only Spanish', 'more Catalan than Spanish' and vice-versa. Clearly, those brought up in 'ethnic' Catalan families, where Catalan is the daily linguistic reality, are more likely to have a strong Catalan identification. However, the most interesting point here is the overlap with social class: those with a 'Catalan' background are more likely to belong to the middle class, as well as having the strong Catalan identification. This also leads to the observation that well-educated middle-class people from Catalan-speaking households predominate in all the major political parties. The political debate, as has often been noted, can be a family affair, with family connections cutting across political barriers. As with most family quarrels, the debate about national identity in Catalonia acquires a particular edge because it is precisely a quarrel between those who share in the mainstream Catalan culture.

The key constraint on Pujol in the run-up to 1992 was that the Games are allocated to a city, not a nation. Neither Catalonia nor Spain could claim the Olympics.

The man who could and did so was Pasqual Maragall, the socialist mayor of Barcelona and therefore a constant opponent of Pujol. While at one level, Maragall had to take note of the multicultural nature of his city, at another, psychologically crucial, level he shared in the 'family' devotion to Catalan culture. It is the conundrum he has been attempting to resolve all through his political life. As so often in Catalonia, it was best expressed in music. Hargreaves described the Closing Ceremony, in which 'the soprano Victòria de los Ángeles . . . accompanied by Lluís Claret on the cello, sang the beautiful Catalan folk song the Cant dels Ocells . . . made popular by the cellist Pau Casals, in a version by the composer Xavier Montsalvatge.' (Freedom for Catalonia, p. 104) But of course, the world telespectators would have seen something rather different — the joy of the athletes, the recorded highlights of their performances, the fireworks, the colourful costumes. But every Catalan would have noticed 'our little tune'.

In sporting terms, the Barcelona Olympics can best be described as a scoring draw, with both Pujol and Maragall scoring goals for their particular brand of Catalanism. Maragall was able to achieve the renewal of the infrastructure of a great city, making it in the process the preferred destination of global capital and international tourism alike. Pujol was able to portray the Games as a triumph for national identity, with the key cultural features of nationalism (the flag and the *sardana*, above all) on very public display. Perhaps neither man was prepared to push the debate too far towards the edge, where stood the warning figure of Juan Antonio Samaranch, a Catalan, president of the International Olympic Committee (IOC), and a reconstructed Francoist politician. His presence alone must have regularly reminded Pujol and Maragall of what they had in common as democratic politicians.

There were less attractive aspects of the Olympics. In particular, there was the role of Acció Olímpica, the nationalist front organisation, in putting pressure on the IOC and the Town Council to 'Catalanise the

Games'. Pujol managed to balance public rejection of their activities with private support. His own son was photographed running alongside the Olympic torch as it was carried through Catalonia, bearing a 'Freedom for Catalonia' banner. He also used the junior partner in the CiU coalition to support the *call* of Acció Olímpica for only the Catalan flag to be flown from balconies during the Games (as opposed to the Spanish flag, or the quartered Barcelona flag which bears the familiar red cross of St George in two corners and the red bars on yellow background of the Catalan flag on the remaining two quarters). As for the Town Hall socialists, the extraordinary investment in central Barcelona and the port area once again threw into relief the high unemployment and relative poverty of the working class suburbs and small towns with their declining manufacturing industries in the Barcelona hinterland. In at least two of these, Terrassa and Mataró, there has been racist conflict in recent years, in which African immigrants have been the victims. The scapegoating of these recent arrivals has thrown into relief the cultural and political poverty of the manoeuvrings which Hargreaves describes in such compelling detail.

And if the games highlighted rather than resolved the tensions and contradictions within Catalonia, they also failed to resolve the tensions within Spain itself. While 84% of people in Catalonia evaluated the use of the Catalan language in the Games as good or very good, 58% in rest of Spain thought it was average, bad or very bad. Whereas half the people surveyed within Catalonia thought the Games had improved the image of Catalonia in the rest of Spain and relations with Spain, only one third agreed with this in the rest of country. Spain failed in both the 1492-1992 celebrations in Seville and the 1992 Barcelona Olympics to come to terms with its own history.

Let the People Decide!

Pujol is the politician who never lost an election, elected and re-elected as President of the Generalitat since the first elections in 1980. His retirement at the end of 2003 marked a watershed in Catalan politics. It is hard to imagine any other politician continuing to sit on the fence as successfully as Pujol and the CiU did. Not least he was an accomplished manipulator of Spanish politics, his party having at different times kept both socialist and conservative governments in office in Madrid. The nationalist position is inherently ambiguous: if a congruence between nation and state does not exist, is that the fault of Spain? How federal does Spain have to be to satisfy nationalist opinion? Does Europe make the powers of the nation-state redundant in any case? In this emergency room of unanswered questions, nationalism both thrives and festers. Even the position of the *independentista* (pro-independence) groups is not clear. While the largest group (ERC, the Catalan Republican Left) supports the independence line, it does not argue for withdrawal from Europe. It seems therefore to follow that rather than sharing sovereignty with Spain, an independent Catalonia would share power with the European Union (EU) much as Slovakia and the Czech Republic are now resuming relations as new members of the EU. So *independentista* and *catalanista* groups occupy spaces which look increasingly similar.

The clearest division remains that between the *catalanista* and *españolista* positions — those who recognise Catalonia as a distinct place and a distinct identity, and those who prefer to think of themselves as part of a uniform Spanish nation. This distorts politics in Catalonia. The Spanish conservative party (PP) gets few votes in Catalonia because it requires supporters to be both conservative and *españolista*. On the other hand the *catalanista* socialists (PSC) led by Maragall have always found it very difficult to get a high level of electoral turnout in Generalitat elections among their traditional working class and Spanish-speaking supporters, many of whom would have *españolista* feelings. There is still the feeling among the older members of such communities in Catalonia that the Generalitat is somehow none of their business. A further handicap for the Catalan socialists is that they are (like the conservatives) part of a larger Spanish political grouping. In general, then, identity politics continues to be a major force in Catalonia, interacting in often unpredictable ways with other political ideologies.

It always seemed likely that the 2003 Generalitat elections would see a major change in Catalan politics. With Pujol retiring, and his replacement as leader (Artur Mas) struggling to emerge from the shadow of his predecessor, the stage seemed set for Maragall and the socialists to finally take control of the Catalan government. They appeared to run a good campaign, setting up a parallel organisation to the socialist party called *Ciutadans pel Canvi* (Citizens for Change) to create a bridge between what was seen as conventional politics and politicians and the many voluntary and professional groups active in Catalonia. Earlier in the year, there had been large demonstrations in Catalonia against the Iraq War, encouraged by the open support given by the conservative Spanish government to the USA-led coalition. Both Maragall and Carod, the republican leader, had staked out positions more radical than that of the CiU in demanding a new federal constitution for Spain which recognised the rights of the historic nations to self-government rather than the concessions of autonomy allowed to the seventeen nations and regions under the 1978 constitution. Supporters of a new constitutional settlement pointed out that circumstances both within Spain and within the European Union had changed since 1978 and it was time for review and renewal.

Those who supported change had various choices. The winners of both the anti-government feeling generated by the Iraq War and the sense that it was time for a change in Catalonia were not the socialists but the republicans of ERC, led by Josep Lluís Carod. The socialist vote stayed much the same as in the 1999 election, the CiU support fell to just beneath that of the socialists, and that of ERC doubled to 16%. Given the complicated system that gives greater weight to the votes of the three more rural provinces as opposed to those cast in Barcelona province, this meant 46 parliamentary seats for CiU, 42 for the socialists, 23 for the republicans, 15 for the PP (Spanish conservative party) and 9 for the eco-socialists (IC/Verds). It was a difficult position. While CiU had worked with PP in national government, its nationalist position would scarcely allow it to do so in Catalonia; while the socialists worked with the republicans in local government, it was hard to see how they would bridge the gap between the republican preference for independence and the socialist option for federalism. In political Right/Left terms, the Centre Left had emerged victorious but it was not a victory that pointed to an obvious ruling coalition. A minority CiU government, supported by conservative and socialist groups abstaining, was not out of the question, as a way of keeping the republicans out of power.

What emerged from the lengthy negotiations was a triple alliance between PSC, IC/Verds and ERC with Maragall as President. In the investiture debate, Maragall paid handsome tribute to the role of all three parties in the democratic history of modern Catalonia. In particular, he acknowledged that PSUC (the communists before they changed both their name to ICV and their politics to eco-socialism) had '. . . contributed perhaps more than any other (party) to the recovery of our democracy, our liberties and our national rights.' The new government would be based on a written agreement between the three parties. Its success would depend not just on the internal tensions between those three groups, but on the result of the 2004 Spanish general election. A socialist government in Madrid would be much more likely than a conservative one to accede to a renegotiation of the Catalan Statute. The situation was complicated still further by continuing unrest in the Basque Country where a quite different set of conservative nationalist politicians (the Basque

250

National Party) were also demanding a review of Spain's federal arrangements. Thus the unexpected victory of the socialists in the March 2004 general election has created a unique opportunity for political advance in Catalonia.

Conclusion

Benedict Anderson's phrase 'imagined community' is so useful because if does remind us that we create and recreate our identities in our minds. A rethinking of the Catalan national project now seems more probable than possible. It might or might not include the acceptance of the complexity of identity and community within Catalonia. Yet the thing that holds Catalonia together, and will probably continue to hold it together rather against the odds, is that deep-down feeling that there is a point in solidarity, both between social classes and between groups with differing understandings of ethnic and national identity. Catalonia has been, within living memory, to the brink and beyond of purity in politics. Manuel Castells who, despite his global reach as a scholar and writer, remains a good Catalan at heart, has described how Catalonia is uniquely well placed to find its place in the modern, global world in which cultural identity and state-power have become divorced, and where a network of power-sharing institutions is the characteristic shape of government:

> By not searching for a new state but fighting to preserve their nation, Catalans may have come full circle to their origins as people of borderless trade, cultural/linguistic identity, and flexible government institutions, all features that seem to characterize the information age.
> (Castells, The Global Age, vol. II, p. 50)

Chapter 13

Mind your Language

Europe of the Languages

The identification of one state with one national language is rather like monogamy — much praised as an ideal but as often ignored in practice. The language question turns on the key question of the desirability of bi- or multilingualism. Growing up speaking a number of languages can be an antidote to the kind of linguistic imperialism that insists on Spanish in Spain — or English globally. It is also a useful counter to a certain sort of linguistic particularism: this is my language and I intend to use it and no other — full stop, end of story. It is still frustrating how often one comes upon claims about the dominance of monolingualism in the world, to the obvious counter-evidence of the hundreds of millions of people who naturally speak at least two languages on a regular basis.

As Helena Drysdale makes clear in *Mother Tongues*, multilingualism is the rule in most countries in Europe, whether we are looking at 'big' groups (Flemish and Walloons in Belgium; French and German in Switzerland) or the many linguistic minorities with which she is most concerned. Though anecdotal, she does manage to get across a number of strong points. For example, dialect and language are social rather than scientific terms, and languages can be invented as well as disappear. Drysdale is especially strong on the Byzantine tale of how Bulgarian, Slovene and Serbo-Croat (now itself splitting into Serbian and Croatian) emerged as 'languages' from the mass of Southern Slav dialects, and how as late as the second half of the twentieth century, the Macedonian language claimed a separate identity from Bulgarian to support Macedonia's status as one of the Yugoslav Republics, and now an independent state.

The linguistic situation in one country, let alone its political ramifications, does not necessarily help to explain the situation in any other country. For example, in the UK, the Welsh language is rather closely connected to nationalist politics, and the Welsh Language Society has taken the lead when it comes to direct action politics. But in Scotland, the persistence of Gaelic in the far north-west and the offshore islands is rather detached from the nationalist cause, which has a powerful hold in contexts as different as the rural north-east and the industrial heart-land of central Scotland. At the 2001 census, the figure of Gaelic users had fallen below 60,000. Scots is barely recog-nised as a separate language. Yet despite the apparent linguistic weakness of Scotland, it has been able to retain many separate institutions through the period of union, and to claim a greater degree of autonomy in the new devolved UK than has Wales, where a nationalist Welsh-speaking north and west often finds itself at odds with Labourist, English-speaking South Wales. The persistence of Welsh has not strengthened the nationalist cause, gen-erating a backlash both from English incomers who do not wish their children to learn what they see as an archaic language and from militant nationalists who identify the claims of the language with their own political claims. Neither Welsh nor Gaelic, of course, can make the claim of mutual intelligibility which exists between Catalan and Spanish, whatever those who have good reason for deny-ing this claim may insist.

One key to the continuing success of the Catalan nation-alists in the Generalitat has been the recognition that a radical and initially controversial language policy in schools has been carried through without major disasters. It is the envy of many other minority languages in Europe. Children in Catalonia begin schooling in Catalan, with

Castilian (even though it may be the child's first language at home) introduced as a second language in primary school. This means that for young Catalans, there is no language problem, just a continual and often unconscious mental juggling of when one language is appropriate and when the other.

Catalan — a 'Normal' Language?

The enormous increase in the use of Catalan as an administrative, educational and cultural language was one of the main contrasts facing any visitor to Catalonia during the years after the establishment of the Catalan autonomous government. By 1990 there were newspapers and magazines in Catalan, a thriving Catalan publishing industry, radio and television in Catalan, *EastEnders* in Catalan (for some reason often held up as a sign that Catalan had arrived as a world language). By European standards, Catalan is a big language. Exactly how big no-one quite knows. In the 1980s Alistair Boyd arrived at a figure of some ten million, deducting two million from a total Catalan population of six million on the basis of limited fluency in the language, but adding in the Catalan-speaking populations of the Balearic Islands, Valencia, Andorra and French Catalonia (*Catalunya Nord*). At about the same time, the newly recreated Generalitat arrived at a rather unlikely figure of 20 million. A few years later (1990-92) they adjusted these figures to a rather cautious six-and-a-half million speakers and nine millions who claimed a passive knowledge of the language. For Catalonia itself, over five million of a population of six million understood the language, but less than four million could speak it, and less than two million could write it. These figures have undoubtedly increased as the policy of linguistic normalisation has taken root and flourished. Most teenagers completing initial school education have a good knowledge of Catalan, though one only has to listen to children from schools in the industrial belt around

Barcelona to realise that Castilian Spanish is still the language of many playgrounds, in itself a reversal of the previous situation where Catalan was the language of the playground and Castilian the language in school.

The present position of Catalan has not been achieved without a struggle. This makes Drysdale's optimism concerning Catalonia and its language even more surprising. She writes:

> Castilian (speaking) immigrants have always learned Catalan with ease, and quickly become Catalans themselves, unlike the Castilian immigrants into the Basque Country who find themselves faced with a language unlike any they have ever encountered. And unlike the Basques, who traditionally feared that their language, their race — and their morals — would be corrupted by incomers, the Catalans have embraced immigrant workers and turned them into fellow Catalans.
> (Mother Tongues, p. 221)

This would seem to underestimate both the ease with which you can slough off one cultural skin and acquire another, and the ingrained feeling against the outsider of some Catalans. For children, it is easy. For adults, even where there is the will, the means may be lacking. Until recently there were few mechanisms for teaching and learning the language. Older adults would have had the experience of a monolingual press and mass media up until 1975. On a daily basis, Catalan, as Kathryn Woolard explains, was the marked language, Castilian the unmarked. This meant that the assumption in shops and offices, in bars and in social situations, was that a stranger would not use Catalan until they were sure of the Catalan identity of the other person. Thus even an attempt to speak Catalan with a obviously foreign accent would be met by a reply in Castilian, unless the speaker made a point that s/he was trying to learn the language.

Given this hidden position of the language, the Scottish-French poet Kenneth White, on a visit to Barcelona, in the early 1960s, managed not to mention Catalan in an evocative prose piece he called 'Night in Barcelona'. A man with an extraordinary sensitivity to language, his contacts with drunks, prostitutes and other people of the night were conducted exclusively in Spanish. Except, except ... that he noticed too the irresistible rise of English, with advertisements for films such as *El Hijo de Jesse James* and *El Regreso de Fu Manchu*. Eventually he met drunken USA sailors (presumably the Sixth Fleet was in town — one of the fruits of Franco's accommodation with the USA) emerging from bars with names such as San Francisco, Texas and Moby Dick. At first their words are limited to the 'infantile cry of triumph' 'Yoop-yoop!' but eventually a few lines of a song emerge ('I got a girl her eyes are green/ She goes down like a submarine') followed by more primitive cries of 'Yoo! Yah! Yee!' No doubt readers who ventured out after dark in the port area of Barcelona in the 1960s will remember the curiosities of its globalised night-life, 'the syphilitic end of the overhuman bloody world' as White puts it.

It was an abnormal situation, and one that the autonomous government has sought to change. Language is about power and power is about politics. Catalan is now the high language, the language of power within Catalonia. That has not always been the case. Back in the nineteenth century, Catalan was the low language of the peasantry, Castilian the high language of government and commerce. It was the Industrial Revolution that gave the Catalan bourgeoisie an identity distinct from that of the Spanish-speaking oligarchy locked into a backward, rural economy, and it was the cultural *Renaixença* promoted by that class which brought Catalan back into a position of respect. The key event in the recent history of Catalan is without doubt the 1983 Law of Linguistic Normalisation. This recognised that Catalan and Spanish are both official languages of Catalonia, and that citizens in their dealings with the state have the right to use which language they prefer. Yet the bulk of the law is concerned with establishing the circumstances under which Catalan might once again become the normal language of administration, commerce, education and civil society. For example, Article Two states that:

> Catalan is Catalonia's own language. All its citizens have the right to know the language and express themselves in it, both verbally and in writing, in their everyday lives and in public acts, both official and unofficial. This right implies, above all, being able to address Government bodies, public organisations, and public and private enterprises in Catalan either verbally or in writing; express oneself in Catalan at all meetings; carry out professional, labour, political, and trade union activities and receive schooling in Catalan.

The law also protected the right of the people of the Vall d'Aran in the Pyrenees to use their local language, Aranese, another Romance language similar to Catalan.

In practice, of course, change did not happen overnight. As the Law had envisaged, for example, an extensive programme of teacher-training was required in order to familiarise all teachers in Catalonia with the language. In secondary, further and higher education, it has taken a considerable time for suitable text-books to appear or to be translated into Catalan. For many years, road-signs were normally written in both languages, and it was only towards the end of the century that the Generalitat finally allowed monolingual (Catalan) road-signs. Despite dire warnings by the opponents of normalisation, there was no dramatic upsurge in either road accidents or travellers getting lost in remote rural areas. Given the comparatively low figure of about one-third of Catalans writing Catalan at the time of the new law, it has been necessary to provide an extensive linguistic advice service for firms and for public agencies, advising them of correct translations and terminology. Catalan publishers have normally employed, in addition to the usual copy-editors and proof-readers, an additional linguistic specialist who would vet the text for correct grammar and terminology. Thus even while Catalan was being extolled as the normal language of use, its proponents were still honing it to be fit for the purpose.

Despite linguistic normalisation, Catalan remains the marked language in many places, most noticeably in central Barcelona and the industrial belt around Barcelona. In other words, still not the language of normal, everyday use. For Kathryn Woolard, researching in and around Barcelona in the early years of the fledgling democracy, the task was complex. Everywhere she found people's perception of what actually existed — the way they used language on a day-to-day basis — overlaid by political ideology, a sense of what should be the case. She recognised too, in those that she interviewed, how difficult it was to simply treat language as happenstance, as an accident of birth or upbringing, and to relate freely across the barrier of Catalan mother tongue/Castilian mother tongue. In particular she pointed out how difficult it was for individual people that the symbol of Spanish political domination over Catalonia (the language) was the same symbol which differentiated the two broad communities in Catalonia. For a Catalan, then, Castilian was not just your friendly neighbour's language, but also the language of the Spanish state that within living memory had tried to obliterate all traces of your own language. And yet it was also the case that support for the use of Catalan in schools was extremely high among parents whose first language was Castilian. Here at last was a way to access the socially more elevated world of the Catalan speakers, the language of distinction, the high language. Thus Woolard's broad point, that the use of the language symbol to differentiate Catalonia from Spain was unduly complicating the process of building a national identity within the country, seems to bear less force now than it did in 1980 when she was conducting field-work. As more people, especially young people, have access to Catalan, it becomes less and less the internal barrier that it was for Woolard. She noticed that her teenage respondents used their own sense of identity to determine the language they used, a state of affairs which she called the 'bilingual norm'. Over the past quarter of a century this has become increasingly the case, as the impact of education in Catalan has spread upwards through the population.

It is clear that the outcome of the present linguistic shift in Catalonia is that Castilian is now acquiring the status that Catalan has abandoned — a language of in-group talk and use. Yet in the process it has reinforced a tendency that was latent even in Franco's time: Catalan is now clearly the language of power and privilege. Woolard pointed out that both Castilian and Catalan speakers recognised Catalan as the higher status language. She quoted Consuelo, a factory worker, as saying that "Catalans not only *sound* more cultivated and refined; they *are*." Woolard concluded that 'it is the greater economic power of Catalans that is the basis for the assignment of linguistic prestige; it is who speaks a language rather than where it is spoken that gives it its force.' (Double Talk, pp. 121/2)

The Language of Books and Literature
One of the ways in which the power and prestige of Catalan is reflected is in publishing. During the early years of the Franco period, very few books appeared at all — Alistair Boyd gives a figure of only 12 in 1946, for example. By 1968 this figure had risen to over 500, and to 600 by the year of the dictator's death (1975). By 1990 the figure had reached 4,500 titles, and now the annual output of new books in Catalan is 8,000. A fair number of them will certainly appear on St George's Day and the buoyancy of the Catalan publishing industry depends in part on what happens on that single day of the year. It is not only Sant Jordi, and a public holiday throughout Catalonia, but also of course the birthday of both Cervantes and Shakespeare. In recent years Sant Jordi has also become an enormous marketing event for the Catalan publishing industry, with

open-air book-stalls in most towns. Every bookshop will have its readings by local authors, its book launches and its parties.

One of the ironies of the publishing business in Barcelona is that it is best known for its Castilian books. Not only Spanish writers but also Latin American authors look to Barcelona publishing houses to publish their work. Thus in 2000, 17,000 books were published in Spanish in Catalonia, but only 8,000 in Catalan — some 30% of the total. Publishing in Catalan is itself a minority business even within Barcelona. The economics of publishing for a potential reading group of about five million are not easy, especially when it comes to more specialised texts. The Generalitat influences publishing in several ways. Firstly, the increasing use of Catalan within the education system has generated a lot of text-book production. Secondly, the library services of the Generalitat will purchase 200-300 copies of every book appearing in Catalan, which is a sub-stantial public investment in a small country. In addition, some of the 8,000 annual new books will be published directly by the Generalitat. Their publishing efforts amounted to 1,000 titles in the decade 1980-90, and this rhythm of general publishing has remained constant since. The aim of this official publishing activity is to fill a gap in commercial publishing, mainly the sorts of books which sell between 1,500 and 3,000 copies, and will never make a publisher rich. The Generalitat catalogue follows the alphabetical list of government departments, so Agriculture, Livestock and Fishing is rather curiously fol-lowed by Art, and then Bibliography, Libraries and Museums. Titles range from Guide to Weed Control (Agriculture) to Trans Sexual Express (Art) and The Frederic Travé Library of Classical Mythology (Bibliography). These titles are typical of the list, but there are a few items of more general interest. *Idees* is a thoughtful social science magazine which the present author has used to focus his own ideas on themes such as national identity and language. The tourist section includes some relatively popular books such as the annual guides to hotels, camp-sites and rural holiday homes, in an interesting range of languages including all four 'Spanish' languages (Basque, Castilian, Catalan and Galician) as well as English, French and German, and pictorial tourist guides which sell well in versions in the main European languages (here Basque and Galician are excluded).

Kathryn Crameri has made an important contribution to our knowledge of Catalan literature with her book *Language, the Novelist and National Identity in Post-Franco Catalonia*, published in 2000. Most important, she does not attempt to draw rigid lines about who counts as a Catalan writer. The overall thrust of her book is how difficult and controversial is the writer's choice of language. Or rather, how intuitive, how easy such a choice might be but how continually complicated by political considerations. She has taken a particular interest in the position of Juan Marsé (born in 1933), who writes in Castilian, observing that although he is thought of in Spain as a whole as a Catalan, he has been disowned by the Catalan literary establishment. Marsé was adopted as a child by a couple from Barcelona, and spent his youth in the Barcelona district of Gràcia, which, as we have already seen, is one of the most 'Catalan' areas of Barcelona. Educated in Castilian, although bilingual of speech, he has chosen to write in Castilian. Crameri points to the contrasting career of Montserrat Roig who chose to write novels in Catalan but to do journalism in Castilian, a neat way of paying the bills. Yet both writers have championed the cause of the Barcelona working class, both have been members of Communist parties. They both write in great detail about the city and its people.

Crameri has an especially interesting discussion of Marsé's *El amante bilingüe* (The Bilingual Lover). Precisely because it takes account of the use of both Catalan and Castilian in the daily life of Barcelona, Crameri sees this as a true reflection of the city, taking into account 'the bilingual nature of its society and the mixture of cultures which influence its people.' The wife of the central character is no less than a sociolinguist working on the Language Normalisation programme, and Crameri draws a wide but plausible significance from that fact:

> Marsé is indicating that Catalonia itself is dependent on the input of immigrants, that they have formed an important part of its past and must therefore also be part of its present and future. To deny their influence on Catalonia is to deny a major part of its history, personality and soul. Norma (the sociolinguist) needs immigrants for sexual reasons, but Catalonia, Marsé implies, needs them because they are an integral part of its national identity.'
> (Language, the Novelist and National Identity, p.185)

Literature, concludes Crameri, is sandwiched between choice of language, in a situation of linguistic diversity, and Catalanism as an expression of an assumed but often unproven national identity. And as the selection of his work from the 1980s in Sobrer's *Catalonia: a Self-Portrait* reveals, even Quim Monzó, who has written both journalism and novels in Catalan, is as conscious as any of the pressures of Catalan literary orthodoxy, of a political correctness that can make it hard to describe the somewhat confusing reality of Catalonia today.

A further example of how very simple, but far-ranging, linguistic choice can be, comes in the work of Javier Cercas, who has lived most of his life in Girona. In a sense, language has only become an issue because of the enormous success of his novel *Soldados de Salamina (Soldiers of Salamis)*, set in Catalonia, but written in Castilian. Interviewed by the author in Girona in 2002, Cercas explained that the choice of language had been very straightforward:

> JP: But you're not Catalan? You're from Extremadura, aren't you? — right over on the Portuguese border, a long way from here.
> JC: Yes, but as you know jolly well, lots of people from

the South, from Andalusia, from Extremadura, came to Catalonia, because of the higher standard of living. People came here to make a living, to get on in life. That's what happened to me. My parents brought me here when I was four years old. So I've lived here a long time, Girona's my city ... although my link to Extremadura is very important, and that's perhaps why I write in Spanish rather than in Catalan.

JP: But was that a difficult decision for you, to write in Spanish or in Catalan?

JC: Not at all. I don't think you choose your language — the language chooses you. I write in Castilian because it's the language of my parents, it's the language we speak at home — well, of course I speak Catalan to my wife. But it's not been a difficulty for me, rather a spontaneous choice to write in Spanish. I mean, it's like me asking you if you found it difficult to decide to write in English. It's your language. It's the same thing! There was no decision there for me to take. It was my language.

It is not, of course, the same thing, because English writers rarely have an alternative, but the point is well made. Yet Cercas shares in the bilingualism of Catalonia: his name appears on his university office door as Xavier, and twice during the interview he was interrupted by students who spoke to him in Catalan. His novel has now been translated into Catalan and English.

The Press and the Media

Books are not the only cultural fruit. One particular area in which there has been a steady advance of the use of Catalan in recent years is the press. For those of us who remember the Franco years, it seems little short of miraculous that Barcelona news-stands can now offer a choice of newspapers and magazines in Catalan. Yet it has proved difficult to wean readers accustomed to the daily press in Castilian on to the Catalan language press. Newspapers depend on forming habits among readers: particular layouts, journalists, cartoonists; a particular balance of the urgent and the background; a particular balance of the serious and not-so-serious. In 1992, Marc Leprêtre's official Generalitat publication *The Catalan Language Today* put the figure for Catalan language newspaper sales at 12% of the total within Catalonia. By 1997 this had risen to 15%. The spectacular breakthrough came towards the end of 1997 when the popular daily *El Periódico* made the rather rash decision to produce a Catalan language edition in addition to its Castilian edition. The following year it already accounted for 50% of total sales in Catalan, and had pushed the percentage of paper sales in Catalan up to the 25% mark. Serious papers such as *El País* also publish cultural and artistic supplements in Catalan. Outside of Barcelona, there are lively local papers in Catalan as well, noticeably *El Punt*, the Girona daily, which has not only managed to steadily increase its sales over the years, but has also spawned editions in other Catalan towns such as Tortosa. The local press in Catalonia is dominated by the Catalan language. In Vilanova i la Geltrú the local paper, already over one hundred years old, has achieved with very little difficulty the change-over from one language to another, from the *Diario* to the *Diari*.

All of this is encouraging for supporters of the Catalan language, but the Catalans have never been as avid readers of the press as, say, the British. Even *El Periódico* does not begin to approach the determinedly down-market populism of *The Sun* or *Daily Mirror*, a market which in Catalonia is shared out between the daily sports papers and the weekly magazines with their news of goings-on among pop celebrities, TV stars, assorted royals and the dross of the late unlamented European aristocracy. In many ways what happens on television is much more important. In Catalan-speaking families, the presence of radio and television has always introduced the bilingual nature of the public space into the monolingual family environment. For Spanish-speaking families, then, radio and television in Catalan can achieve the same effect, challenging the supremacy of their own daily, domestic use of

Castilian. There is no doubt that, in their day the dubbing of programmes such as *EastEnders* and *Dallas* into Catalan broke down psychological barriers and encouraged the idea that Catalan could be both popular and fun, rather than the language of endless minority cultural programmes. Yet ironically, that effect has been diminished by the steady growth of independent commercial stations using cable, digital and satellite. There is more choice and consequently it matters less whether certain dominant stations transmit in one language or the other. In this Benetton world of contemporary media, the mass has been replaced by the niche, and it is relatively easy to exclude either Castilian or Catalan from your household. It is also easier to include English, especially the United States version of it, in the form of channels such as CNN. There is a certain history behind this: for many years during the Cold War, Radio Free Europe broadcast USA propaganda from its base beneath the pine trees on the Costa Brava. If CNN reflects a slightly less simplistic view of the world than Radio Free Europe, it is nevertheless a useful reminder that Castilian Spanish is not the only rival of Catalan.

Catalan beyond Catalonia

So far, this chapter has concentrated exclusively on the use of Catalan within Catalonia itself. But there is, of course, the wider question of the Catalan language beyond Catalonia, in what cultural nationalists call the *Països Catalans* (Catalan lands) — Andorra, *Catalunya Nord,* l'Alguer in Sardinia, the border strip of Aragon, Valencia and the Balearic Islands. Catalan became, by conquest, an international language. It remains the main language of Catalonia, Valencia and the Balearic Islands. This idea of the *Països Catalans*, of a historic homeland of the Catalan-speaking people, is still very much alive in nationalist circles. Yet within a federal Spain, the Valencians and the islanders have their statutes of autonomy which are valued as highly as that of Catalonia itself. There is considerable cultural contact, such as town-twinning and the success of the Valencia weekly magazine *El Temps*, widely read in Catalonia and in the Balearic Islands. There is little evidence, however, that Valencia wants to be drawn into a Catalan federation that would certainly be dominated by Catalonia in general and Barcelona in particular. Barcelona-Valencia football matches are as sharply contested nowadays as those between Barcelona and Real Madrid. While most Catalans welcome linguistic and cultural links, the economic argument for Catalan autonomy tends to outweigh the emotional appeal of a Greater Catalonia. There are votes to be won by speaking of the *Països Catalans* but probably not in doing anything about it.

Progress towards normalisation of the language in Valencia had been much slower than in Catalonia. In 1991, the Anglo-Catalan Society published a booklet by Jude Webber and Miquel Strubell called *The Catalan Language: Progress towards Normalisation*. This placed progress towards normalisation within Catalonia very firmly within the context of the wider debate about Catalan. The authors are guarded in their remarks, aware no doubt that their booklet is not in any case intended to be about the *Països Catalans*. They refer in their conclusion, however, to 'those Catalan-speaking areas which lag behind the Principality in terms of institutions and the application of language policies.' They also refer to the problem that 'In Valencia and the Balearic islands some ultra-Conservative groups maintain that Catalan is being "imposed" on them in school and official circles.'

It is not exclusively, of course, conservative speakers of Castilian who have views about language policies. In the early days of television broadcasting in Catalan, there were quite reasonable complaints from Valencia about the domination of Barcelona voices, speaking the Eastern variant of Catalan, as opposed to its Western variant spoken in Lleida province and right down through Valencia as far as Alicant (Alicante). It is perhaps such considerations that lead Webber and Strubell to show some interest in what they call the 'artificiality of "regional" linguistic divisions within the *Països Catalans*' and the possibility of 'a "standard" oral variety of the language.' Yet British experience here would suggest the marked advantages of moving beyond the domination of the media by a single received pronunciation version of English to the present situation where a variety of regional English accents, together with Welsh, Scottish and Irish voices, are seen as essential for a national broadcasting service. While the attempt by the Franco regime to destroy the language and with it Catalan national identity was a crime, the Catalans of Catalonia do need to approach their relations with other Catalan-speaking territories with some sensitivity.

A further cause of disagreement in relation to Catalan has been the European Union. The EU has always maintained a Bureau for Lesser-Used Languages, but its budget is tiny and its influence less, given that language policy is clearly a national state issue. In any case, the situation of a big minority language such as Catalan is very different to that of small languages such as Scottish Gaelic or Sami, always hovering on the edge of extinction. The situation of Catalan, certainly in Catalonia itself, is in no way comparable to these languages. The Generalitat has long maintained an office in Brussels and argued the case for Catalan as a European language. But although some advances have been achieved, such as the publication of the fundamental treaties of the EU in Catalan, there has been no progress in seeking acknowledgement as an official European Union language. The reasons are not hard to find: with a further ten countries now in the EU, several of them with substantial linguistic minorities (for example the Romanians in Hungary), the linguistic basis of the EU looks set for simplification rather than a move to accommodate ever more languages. The argument that there are as many regular users of Catalan as there are of Danish has cut little ice.

Still an Issue

Catalan remains an issue, both within and outside of Catalonia. The survival of the Catalan language has not been inevitable. It is a cause for celebration, a small victory for the cause of diversity in a world where large cultures and languages increasingly downgrade the value of local cultures and vernaculars. Biodiversity would appear to be a worthy cause for human beings as well as animals, insects and plants. Yet ironically, one of the strengths of Catalan within the borders of the Spanish state is that the bilingualism, deplored by some of the language's most outspoken supporters, can seem to an outsider one of its virtues. To possess a language which asserts the importance of the local, the internal solidarity of a people and its history, is important. But it is equally important to share in a second language, Spanish, which is one of the great world languages, and gives access not only to the culture of other parts of Spain, but to much of South and Central America too. And in one of those ironies that is always turning up with languages, while English (in its North American, Coca Cola-ised version) is becoming increasingly spoken of as the world language, Spanish is rapidly gaining ground as the second language of the USA, spoken on a daily basis by several million inhabitants and recognised in public policy from New York to California.

Chapter 14

Green Catalonia

Another Green and Pleasant Land

Flying south across Catalonia towards Barcelona airport, the country appears a fertile, green, rather spacious land of mountains, forests and river valleys. But as in all the advanced industrialised countries, nature is under attack, from industry and the growth of towns and cities and from what people do to the countryside. That includes both those who live and work there, and those town-dwellers set on becoming country-dwellers or otherwise using the countryside for their own recreational purposes. In Catalonia, all this is complicated by tourism, which often seems set on cooking and eating the hen that laid the golden egg of prosperity where people once scratched a living from the soil or fought with the changing moods of the sea. Catalonia is, perhaps, a naturally a 'green' country, much in the way that England is. It seems there is nothing like a good dose of heavy, polluting industry, of which there is plenty within spitting distance of Barcelona airport, to focus people's attention on what they have lost and what they still have but may be on the verge of losing. Just as in England there is still that strong, vibrant myth of England's 'green and pleasant land', so in Catalonia there is that strong tradition of going to the hills in search of physical and spiritual renewal and reassertion of national identity. Except of course that in England this produces unreal scenarios in which planning permission is often refused for a local person wanting to set up a clean cottage industry in their back-yard, while no-one objects if four farm labourers' cottages are sold as a single rural hideaway for rich Londoners. In the same way, there is a split personality in Catalonia which loves the Pyrenean tarns but can't be bothered with the details of nuclear power, which loves the secret coves of the Costa Brava but can somehow ignore the untidy coast forty miles either side of Barcelona, littered with apartment blocks, theme parks and 500-bed hotels.

Some of the greenest corners of Catalonia are to be found in Barcelona itself: environmentally friendly open spaces like the Parc de la Creueta del Coll, and new low energy buildings. Green Catalonia is not just about National Parks and Natural Parks, admirable as those are as places where visitors can encounter a nature not yet spoilt by human hands. It is about how every aspect of life can be made more pleasant and more humane, by thinking just a little more carefully about how we live, and how much we consume, and whether all our lives might be just as happy if we scaled them down a little. Most of the big single issue campaigns in Catalonia — the nuclear industry, the River Ebro — are reflected in the day-to-day decisions that people make about their own life-style. Every single Catalan, like every single British person, contributes to the mess and the pollution, and there is no single issue on which the sum total of millions of individual decisions could not make a difference. Having said that, there will also be issues in this chapter in which the Generalitat or the Spanish state might make a difference, and also issues about which only concerted international action can change things. One good example which we shall not go into in detail is the level of pollution in the whole Mediterranean, a sea that, lacking tides, is especially vulnerable to the rubbish tipped into it by citizens of many nations.

The Rain in Spain

> Water is not a commercial product like any other but, rather, a heritage which must be protected, defended and treated as such.
> (*EU directive establishing a framework for community action in the field of water policy*)

The avocet raises its head, stands motionless, perfectly balanced on pencil thin legs, decides the British visitor is too far away to be a danger, and lowers its beak back into the water in search of tiny snails and other crustaceans. In Britain this would be a rarity — not for nothing is the avocet the symbol of the Royal Society for the Protection of Birds. In the paddy-fields of the delta of the River Ebro, it is a common sight. Four hundred nesting pairs live here year round, and the winter population reaches maybe 1,500. Besides avocets, there are large populations of egrets and herons, ducks and grebes, owls and bitterns and marsh-harriers. Over 300 separate species have been seen here, between residents and winter visitors, and 60% of the total number of bird species recorded in Europe.

Despite its Natural Park status, there is very little natural about the Ebro delta, if we take natural to mean unspoilt nature. But if by natural we imply a desire for a sustainable and harmonious relationship between people and their environment, then the delta matters a lot. It also has to be said that it is not always the prettiest place in Catalonia, as flat as a pancake, and often lashed by strong winds funnelled down the tight steep gorges of the Ebro north of Tortosa. The geometric fields divided by drainage channels and criss-crossed by equally geometric roads and tracks have a mournful quality to them like the East Anglian fens. The eye is pulled back in search of horizons and meets only the bare mountains that fringe the delta. By rail and road, people speed across the new Ebro bridges on their journeys. A few days exploring the delta with the *vent de dalt* blowing can make even the most hardened traveller want to move on to a more sheltered landscape.

The first recorded attempt to grow rice in the delta was by enterprising Cistercian monks in 1607. But the most significant developments date only from the middle of the nineteenth century with projects to canalise the Ebro up past Tortosa. While these canals have not prevented the decline of Tortosa as a port, they have provided a good source of fresh water for irrigation and created the right blends of fresh and salt water for rice production (paddy fields now occupy three-fifths of the cultivated land) and for a wide variety of wildlife. It is interesting to simply list the variety of landscape that occupies the other two-fifths: freshwater ponds, river, salt marsh, sand dunes and beach, lagoons, orchards and salt pans. Fruit and vegetables grow close to the main channel of the river where water is freshest; further away, rice predominates, more tolerant of salt than most other crops.

The human population of the delta has increased alongside that of birds and rice, from only 5,000 in 1850 to 50,000 today. Malaria was endemic here until well into the twentieth century. People moved from the olive-groves sprawling across the parched mountains inland to a landscape that must have seemed at first sight strangely green and flat, but which has become their home. Poble Nou del Delta is a nondescript village already upon its second name, having been christened Villafranco del Delta (Franco Town) in 1947. The most extensive town, Deltebre, is a recent creation combining older settlements of Jesús i Maria and La Cava. Most of the towns only received the status of municipalities with the surge of democratic enthusiasm in the late 1970s. The present mouth of the river is the result of floods as recent as 1937. Previous to this, there were two outlets, one to the east and one to the south, which explains the two curious lobules of sand-dunes at Punta de la Banya and Punta del Fangar. The river itself is a wide brown stream between luxuriant fields and gardens, crossed by raft-ferries that prove very popular with visiting school-children who hire cycles from one of the Natural Park centres. It is a strange and special landscape. At times it seems more like equatorial Africa or tropical Central America than Catalonia or Spain. Palms and eucalyptus both grow well here and add to the sense of the exotic. And where river and sea finally merge, the green-brown water of the river gives reluctant way to the deep blues and turquoises of the Mediterranean.

This area is under attack. The previous Spanish government planned to spend European Union money on a massive scale to transfer waters from the River Ebro to the dry lands of south eastern Spain, from Valencia through Murcia to Almería. To spend money on 69 new golf courses to attract foreign visitors to new holiday villages. To spend money on yet more unsustainable agricultural schemes that will turn the parched and arid lands of Alicante, Murcia and Almería into — not orchards, meadows and gardens — but a wilderness of plastic greenhouses, bags of fertiliser and drums of insecticides. Over the last few years, speculators have been buying up arid land in south east Spain in the expectation of rich profits if the plan to divert the Ebro waters is approved. But the campaigners are well organised and very experienced. In August and September 2001 they organised the Blue March from the Delta up the Ebro valley into Aragon and eventually to Brussels to protest against the combination of greed and cynicism that was driving these plans. They were rewarded by a resounding vote in the European Parliament on 28 February 2002, which declared itself

> ... deeply worried about the precedent set by proposals for the development of unsustainable water management schemes across Europe, and calls on the European Commission for these reasons not to provide any EU funding for these water transfer projects.

The emblem of the marchers is the knotted pipe, their inspiration the image of *Lo Riu*, (the river), in the local dialect of Catalan. So much of the history of Spain is the history of water, of how men and women have learned to use it, or not learned to use it from the times of the Romans onwards. There are mighty Roman aqueducts at Tarragona, at Segovia in Castile and at Mérida in Extremadura. The Muslims understood water too — not just to create the gardens and the fountains and ponds of the Alhambra in Granada, but to put scarce resources to maximum use for both domestic purposes and irrigation, not least in the areas around Lleida and Tortosa. Much of this knowledge was lost in later centuries, but some remained. The demonstrators understood too that this is not just a protest about something abstract called 'The Environment', not just about unique landscapes and birds and plants and flowers. It was also about jobs and livelihood, not least the livelihood of the rice-farmers of the delta who make a living from the delicate balance of salt and fresh water, and the availability of sufficient water to flood the fields through the hot Spanish summer to support the growing rice. Further up the river are villages in the hills of Aragon which will be flooded by new dams and lakes, traditional farming communities dependent on the regular use and re-use of the nearly 1,000 mile River Ebro.

The old conservative Spanish government, led by José María Aznar, drove the National Water Plan through parliament, despite massive protests from the people of the autonomous communities that live on either side of the river. For the River Ebro and its tributaries, the Plan will involve the building of nearly one hundred new reservoirs and a massive 1,000 kilometre infrastructure of pipelines to carry the water from northern Spain to the south-east. The government tried to exploit regional feelings for their political purposes, always a dangerous game in Spain. Communities that reject the water plan were accused of being 'separatist', of putting local and regional feelings before solidarity between the various nations and regions. Behind the Spanish conservatives lay the shadowy figures of their allies in big agro-business and tourism. Two junior ministers attracted the attention of the State Prosecutors for appearing to have one foot in the political camp and the other firmly planted in the business camp.

The figures are complicated, but the case for the transfer of the Ebro waters is based on the assumption that climate and rainfall are constants. This we know they are not. As Joan Sabaté, the Mayor of Tortosa, the ancient city just inland from the Delta pointed out, northern Spain is becoming drier. So the average river flow for the past ten years is far below the average flow over the whole twentieth century, the figure on which the Spanish government plans are based,. As Julian Pettifer found when he did a BBC Radio 4 programme on the National Water Plan in 2002, opposition is massive. 400,000 attended a rally in Barcelona, 200,000 in Madrid. Saragossa and Brussels have also witnessed large demonstrations. The Platform in Defence of the Ebro is a powerful coalition of organisations from towns and villages up and down the river, typical of the new politics that surrounds green issues, in drawing in people who would not normally want to be associated with party politics. The *Radio Times* referred to 'one of the greatest public displays of anti-government sentiment Spain has seen since the days of the Franco dictatorship.'

Despite the fact that party politics were not at the heart of the protests, two sets of political careers were at stake, according to Joan Sabaté. Most obviously the Conservative government in Madrid. But also the nationalists who ran the Catalan regional government in Barcelona. The Conservatives ruled alone in Madrid but in the Generalitat, the nationalists depended on a very few Conservative votes to keep them in power. They were therefore in the position of having to give grudging support to the conservative national policies for their own backyard, policies which were far from popular in Catalonia. The issue of the Ebro waters played an important part in the 2003 Generalitat elections. All three Centre Left parties — socialists, eco-socialists (IC/Verds)

277

and republicans — claimed the issue as their own. The resulting victory for these three parties reopened many questions, not least the future of the National Water Plan. The new President, Pasqual Maragall, stated that he supported the Plan, but not the Ebro transfer — a major element within it.

It is not just the Spanish government but the European Union that is being asked questions here. The EU framework directive on water resources, which was approved some time before the National Water Plan, outlaws this kind of transfer from one water system to another. And it should certainly make it impossible to use EU money for this purpose. Any Spanish government attempt to avoid the directive by starting work before it comes into force raises a second issue. For any agricultural products grown in these new irrigated lands will certainly be massively subsidised and therefore contrary to competition rules. The water will cost 8p per cubic litre to farmers in the south-east; the real cost (dams, reservoirs and pipelines) will be more like 60p per litre. This happens to be about the cost of water from a desalination plant, such as the one opened at the holiday town of Blanes, just up the coast from Barcelona, in 2002. That surely offers one way forward, that and the careful husbanding of the precious water resources that Spain does possess, just as the Muslims demonstrated a thousand years ago. Not dams and pipelines and golf-courses consuming three million litres of water per course per night.

The unique landscape of the delta is unlikely to survive the plans in their present form. One effect of the many new dams required in the Ebro valley water system is that sediments will be held up at the dams rather than being carried down and spread across the delta. If we add to that the probable impact of global warming on sea levels, a scientific study by Carles Ibáñez and his colleagues at the University of Barcelona has shown that the likely sea level rise in the delta will be over 50cm by the end of this century, implying that 45% of the land area of the delta will simply cease to exist. The only way such an eventuality could be avoided would be massive expenditure on sea defences, turning the delta into something much more like the Dutch polders, an artificial fortress against the sea with a far less interesting variety of plants, birds and animals than at present.

So far, we have stressed the external threat to the delta, but there are also issues that need to be sorted locally too. These include the long-term impact of the use of unsustainable agricultural methods, particularly fertilizers, the residues of which are now threatening the delta. There is also too much development taking place within the park, centred both on existing towns and villages, but also the notorious urbanisations that have spoiled so much of the Catalan and Spanish coats. In 1988 only vigorous campaigning succeeded in overturning a plan for an urbanisation to be called Eucalyptus II, for no less than 10,000 people. There has been a general failure in the delta to develop eco-friendly forms of tourism, with the exception of the cheerful, disciplined groups of school-students with their bikes and their teachers. Intrusive power cables and the occasional plastic greenhouse do little to add to the attractions of the landscape. Both visitors and local people seem to manage to produce large quantities of litter. There also seems to be a lack of park wardens to control use of the recreational areas, a complaint made of other Catalan national and natural parks. Four-wheel drive vehicles use the cycle tracks at Punta del Fangar, and the beach as well, despite signs warning of nesting birds (in Spanish and Catalan only, despite the obvious fact that tourist agencies encourage foreign visitors).

The other delta activity that seems strange to many visitors is shooting. The Park authorities have taken the point of view that with up to 4,000 hunters active in the delta, it is better to come to a reasonable agreement with the eleven well organised shooting clubs, covering dates and species and numbers of birds that can be shot, than to attempt to ban hunting completely. Some 40,000 birds, mainly ducks and coots, are killed annually, but as the display at the museum/interpretative centre of the Casa de Fusta points out, hunting has 'deep sociological roots'. And political clout too, no doubt.

National and Natural Parks and the Politics of the Environment

The Ebro delta is by no means the best known of the Catalan parks, and if some space has been devoted to it here, it is because of the wide range of issues it raises for Catalonia, Spain and Europe. Much more typical is the National Park of Aigües Tortes i Sant Maurici, which covers 10,000 hectares of Pyrenean mountain and lake between 1,600 and 3,000 metres high. Access to the valley is not easy. There are no equivalents of the motorway and railway flashing past the Ebro delta. From the Vall de Boí side, and the famous cluster of Romanesque churches, there are four to five kilometres of badly rutted track to reach the park. This is unlikely to be improved, because it is seen as a simple way of persuading people to use the minibus, jeep and guide services of the park authorities rather than their own vehicles. A National Park, designated by the Madrid government — and this is Catalonia's only National Park — has more power than a Natural Park, and in any case there are far less people living here than in the delta to argue about possible conflicts of interest. In summer the lower slopes are awash with juniper, raspberries and rhododendron, and harebells and mountain pinks in the meadow areas. Above the mountains slopes are spruce and pine stretching up to scree and rock beyond the tree-line.

Within the park are a number of little stone refuges such as the one at the Estany Llong (Long Lake) which serves tea, coffee, beer, wine and juices, sandwiches and bacon and eggs to walkers who sit around friendly, long, pine tables. There is sleeping accommodation above, up a ladder and through a hatch. It is homely and adequate, modestly fit for purpose. The Estany Llong itself is one of the most perfect spots in the mountains, accessible to those who don't mind a stiff walk but might think twice about the wilder peaks and ridges of the Pyrenees. Its blue waters dissolve into emerald green, purple, brown, grey and orange. The rest of nature is very simple — a china blue sky, grey rock, light green grass, dark green pine and spruce. The sound of cow- and horse-bells chimes through the pure, clear air as the animals graze leisurely in the lakeside meadows. It is almost surreally beautiful, as long as you do not mind company. The Catalan habit of enjoying nature in crowds is never far way, and you can be sure that if you settle down to enjoy the beauty of the Estany Llong in summer, then others will soon join you.

This balance between wilderness and public access seems to be relatively satisfactory in the distant mountains of Aigües Tortes, but elsewhere the same problems outlined in relation to the Ebro delta recur. The Natural Parks have been established by the Generalitat since 1980 in both mountainous and wetland areas. These include the Cadí-Moixeró Park covering the mountains to the south of the Cerdanya, the volcanic hills of the Garrotxa, the Medes Islands off the Costa Brava at Estartit and the coastal marshes between Empúries and Roses (Aiguamolls de l'Empordà). The Medes islands, despite their proximity to busy coastal resorts, have a certain natural protection afforded by their island status. They are home to important colonies of sea-birds, while coral can be viewed from glass-bottom boats. In the past the islands have been used for various purposes, and a military garrison remained until 1890. The lighthouse is now fully automatic and solar-powered. The last human beings abandoned the islands in 1932, so it is relatively easy for the authorities to control visitors. Even hunting is banned . . .

Much more controversial is the Aiguamolls de l'Empordà Park, lying hard up against the ruins of Empúries to the south and the holiday resort and fishing-port of Roses to the north. The story of this wetland area repeats a tale well known throughout Europe of agricultural interests wanting to drain the marshes and exploit the rich alluvial soil. The landscape that this produces around the village of Sant Pere Pescador (St Peter the Fisherman) is extremely attractive with small fields (*closes*) hugged by drainage ditches on each side, but is of little use to the large colonies of wading-birds (storks, herons, flamingos, kingfishers — very similar to the Ebro delta) that traditionally inhabit the marshes where the rivers Fluvià and Muga struggle to reach the sea. During migration-time in spring, 125 species have been registered here in just one day. Yet the difficulties of the park can be clearly seen from the detailed maps contained in the Generalitat's tourist literature. From Sant Pere, one narrow arm of the park stretches south along the sand dunes towards Empúries, and another thin arm extends two or three miles up the Fluvià River. There are then two larger areas to the north, disconnected from one another. And in the middle the enormous holiday complex of Empuriabrava, with its marinas, its airport, its tower blocks, creating the botched landscape seen looking either south from the pleasant little promenade at Roses, or north from the village of Sant Martí d'Empúries. There is conflict here, but for the moment there is a stand-off between conservation and development. But there is always the possibility of such rivalries being re-opened: the very presence of a multi-storey tourist complex, visually dominating the flat marshlands, will make it that much more difficult to defend the park against further human exploitation.

The Generalitat does an excellent job of promoting their one National Park and numerous Natural Parks. A further important initiative in creating an infrastructure for a more environmentally friendly, greener, version of tourism are the *vias verdes*, an initiative of the central Spanish government to develop long-distance walking and cycling routes through rural areas. In Catalonia, this

involves the two old railway lines that once linked Girona
with the coast at Sant Feliu de Guíxols and with the inland
market town of Olot. The latter is longer and more stren-
uous, including a climb up to 620 metres (2000 feet)
between Amer and Olot. There is a shorter stretch, also
following a disused railway line, from Ripoll to Sant Joan
de les Abadesses, a pleasant afternoon stroll. But the most
exciting aspect of this project is a linking section between
Sant Joan and Olot alongside the route of the old Roman
road through the picturesque and little known Vall be
Bianya. Projects of this sort generate other small rural
businesses — guest houses, bike hire, restaurants and
cafes. In the Vall de Bianya, at the last count, seven of the
old farmhouses were offering holiday accommodation with
varying combinations of environmentally friendly activities such as walking, cycling or swimming. There is a long
way to go, but a start has been made.

Towards a Greener Life-style?
As we saw at the beginning of this chapter, green issues
are not just about what governments do but about how
people live. The basic premise of Agenda 21 of the Rio
Earth Summit, now more than a decade away from us, was
how public agencies could stimulate and support public
interest in green issues. While there have been small-scale
initiatives all over Catalonia, it has taken some time for
Barcelona City Council to pick this up, more concerned as
they are with attracting more and more profitable business to their city. The City's Environment and
Sustainability Council, which includes business associations, trade unions, large companies, neighbourhood
associations, universities and non-government organisations, was only set up in 1998, and took until 2002 to offer
any way forward. It has established ten Agenda 21 objectives for the period 2002–2012. They contain the usual glib
commitments to waste recycling, preserving natural
resources and protecting open spaces. But it is too soon yet

to measure and evaluate progress. Certainly, on a hot summer's day when the smog hangs like a yellow stain across the city, it is hard to see progress. The motorway rings designed for the 1992 Olympic Games have tamed the car but not replaced it. And while public transport is consistently above London standards, it never seems to actually meet the total transportation requirements of the city.

Sustainable development was one of the themes of the Universal Forum of Cultures. Yet, like citizens of most great cities, the average Barcelona resident simply consumes too much energy, too many natural resources, too much water to make the city seem in any way sustainable. Under these circumstances, the city puts the burden back onto the countryside. It is the rural areas which have to provide the food, the water, the energy that the city craves. For example, although it seems clear that the chief winner of the transfer of Ebro waters will be the southeast of Spain (Castelló de la Plana, Valencia, Alicante, Almería) the plan does envisage some transfer of water north to Tarragona and Barcelona. At the moment, Barcelona obtains most of its water from Pyrenean reservoirs. If the Ebro option is abandoned, it is likely that a combination of desalination plants and policies designed to reduce water consumption will be necessary in Catalonia.

In a relatively dry country like Spain, water is always going to be an issue. Rather more surprising is nuclear power, which since 1990 has consistently provided about 30% of all Spain's electrical power. There are four nuclear power plants, in Catalonia, two on the coast at Vandellós, and two up the Ebro valley at Flix and Ascó, roughly equidistant between Tortosa and Lleida. The Vandellós reactors come as a particular surprise as they are less than thirty kilometres south of the international holiday resort of Salou. A search on the Internet for information about these reactors offers the unlikely combination of nuclear power and naturism. Perhaps wisely, the tourist web-site fails to mention nuclear power, and prefers to show pictures of happy naturists than of the giant power installations that dominate the whole zone. It also fails to mention continuing plans to attract further high tech industry into this area, with substantial state subsidies. It is perhaps because it is difficult to market a beach resort next door to a nuclear reactor, that L'Hospitalet de l'Infant, Vandellós's near neighbour, has entered the niche market of an official naturist beach and camp-site. They are no doubt very attractive as long as the naturally modest naturist visitors keep their eyes firmly fixed on the beach and the sea and don't take occasional peeps over their shoulder at the nuclear installations. Those who feel uncomfortable in the presence of both nuclear power and nudity would be advised to keep well away.

Vandellós 1 was one of the first reactors in Spain, working on the gas-cooled system, and started as early as 1968. Its safety record was not good, and following a fire in 1989 it was closed down and never reopened, finally being dismantled in 2002. Modifications demanded by the Spanish nuclear authorities proved too expensive. The situation was extremely complicated since the reactor was privately owned, and it took some time to work out exactly how decommissioning could be achieved and the enormous costs met.

Building started in 1980 at Vandellós 2, and the pressurised water reactor (PWR) has been in use since 1988 and is scheduled to generate electricity until 2028. A well publicised accident on 8 July 1990 raised alarm throughout Catalonia, happening as it did in the middle of the tourist season and with the wind blowing from the southwest. Had there been any escape of radioactive material from the reactor, Tarragona and Barcelona were both in the direct line of fire. As in other countries, nuclear power gets a bad press, and yet it is clear from the figure of 30% nuclear contribution to the electricity grid that without nuclear power, Catalonia would have to either seek other forms of energy or reduce its consumption. Traditional non-renewable sources such as coal and gas are not available, there is little tidal flow in the Mediterranean and winds tend to be light and variable. Substantial hydro-electric power is generated in the Pyrenees but there would be large-scale opposition to the flooding of more Pyrenean valleys to create lakes and dams. This leaves, of course, the sun.

One of the ways in which environmentally friendly architects like David Mackay have worked is to use tradi-tional building designs to try and keep flats and offices cool without excessive use of air-conditioning. It is quite hard to understand why more use is not made of solar power in an attempt to make individual buildings much more self-sufficient in energy. This has certainly happened in the more rural areas, where solar panels attached to rebuilt ancient Catalan farmhouses are a common sight. Many such houses are owned, unsurprisingly, by refugees from city life, as in much of Western Europe. Here it seems particularly important that incomers to rural life should not expect the same level of services they may have enjoyed in the city, or that at least they should be prepared to pay handsomely for them. The valleys inland from Girona are good examples of these processes. Increasingly, houses in the valleys are seen as attractive homes for peo-ple who work in Girona or as weekend retreats and holiday homes for Barcelona folk. Traditionally, the farm-ers of these valleys have depended on water supplies from wells. This is limestone country and there is abundant water in underground water systems. In addition, most farms store water for summer use in enormous cisterns and tanks. Only in extremely dry years does it run out. Gradually piped water is coming to the valleys. Some of the older people are opposed to it, objecting to paying for something that they feel they are unlikely to want to use. The pricing policy is critical here. The standing charge is kept low to encourage everyone to sign up for the new sup-plies. But the water is metered and charges quite high. Thus for farmers, commuters and holiday-makers, there is a strong incentive to continue to draw water from the traditional sources, and to use local water for most purposes. There are low energy as well as high energy versions of how this gradual suburbanisation of the Catalan countryside can be handled. Everything is interconnected. In some parts of Catalonia, the traditional solution of well-digging brings up not pure water but brackish water polluted by chemicals from modern intensive agriculture. It is a European as well as Catalan problem: ways have to be devised to encourage farmers to conserve the countryside and farm it in less intensive ways, rather than exploiting it always to maximise crops and profits. But without a market for organic foods, subsidies to farmers to change their ways have no hope of succeeding. What consumers want, or can be persuaded to want, still matters.

Chapter 15

The Other Catalans

Trying to Understand

> La luz que de la catedral de Córdoba nos alumbra no es
> mortecina ni temblorosa. Es intensa, penetrante. Ilumina
> el camino. Propone el abrazo de las comunidades del
> mundo.
> (The light that shines upon us from the cathedral at
> Cordoba is in no way faint or trembling. It is intense and
> penetrating. It lights up our pathway. It suggests the
> growing together of the world's communities.)
> King Juan Carlos, Cordoba, 28 May 1986

The King of Spain did not get as far as to call Cordoba
cathedral a mosque, but it was a start, and it is certainly
encouraging to find sign-posts directing visitors to the
mosque rather than the cathedral. There is a great deal of
healing to be done. Catalans persecuted Jews and held
Muslim and African slaves. Pirates from North Africa cap-
tured Christians and held them prisoner, ransoming the
wealthy and aristocratic and selling others into slavery.
Cervantes, author of *Don Quixote*, was himself a captive at
one time. It is a grim and gruesome history. But history is
of the essence in understanding the to and fro of relations
between all parts of Spain and North Africa, not least the
human trade across the Straits of Gibraltar at the beginning of this new century. This has built up a large illegal
migrant population in Spain and leaves the bodies of those
who die when their flimsy craft are wrecked in those
treacherous waters, washed up on the shores of Spain and
Africa.

In the introduction to his magisterial book, *Culture and Imperialism*, Edward Said described the 'contrapuntal ensembles' that constitute cultures today. He concluded that

> No identity can ever exist by itself and without an array of opposites, negatives, oppositions: Greeks always require barbarians, and Europeans Africans, Orientals, etcetera. The opposite is certainly true as well.

While in general, this book has attempted to avoid material not available in English and which many readers will be unable to follow up, the important work by Sami Naïr and Juan Goytisolo *El peaje de la vida* will be an exception. There is little material available in English on immigration into Catalonia from outside of Spain. In general this introductory section follows their analysis quite closely, but since their book deals with Spain generally, we shall also stress the specific emphases necessarily involved for Catalonia. Thus while Naïr's historical survey stresses the importance of Muslims in Spain from the eighth century until expulsion, a Catalan dimension must include the extensive medieval trading empire of the Catalans, which took Catalan traders to many of the ports along the North African coast as well as to their more permanent colonies in the Mediterranean islands, Italy and Greece. The expulsion of Jews in 1492 and of Muslims in 1525 appeared to erect a clear boundary between Christian Europe and the Muslim Mediterranean, but there was continuing contact. Piracy continued to trade in human beings as well as in merchandise. While the Catalans were initially excluded from the imperial adventures in America, from about 1750 they became very involved, especially in the Caribbean. In the twentieth century, after the Spanish War, substantial numbers of Catalans emigrated to Latin American, while in recent years, an unknown number of Latin Americans, especially Colombians and Ecuadorians have been absorbed into

Catalan society, both legally and illegally.

Well before globalisation came to be used as a term for the increasing economic and cultural interdependence of the world, Spain was at the centre of vast movements of goods, people and ideas, a process in which Catalonia played its own part. Yet the first large-scale movement of people into Catalonia in modern times came as a result not of migration from other countries but by internal migration from the poverty-stricken south and west of Spain itself. While Catalonia was industrialising, large areas of Spain still consisted of enormous estates owned by absentee landlords, with no improvements carried out that might have ameliorated the life of the landless peasants who comprised the majority of the population. From 1900 this created a focus for tension and unrest in Catalonia. The new arrivals were identified often as political troublemakers, members of Anarchist or Communist cells. In turn, politicians such as Alejandro Lerroux stirred up anti-Catalan feeling by appealing to class solidarity between 'Spanish' and 'Catalan' workers for other, darker purposes. Lerroux received the covert support of the Madrid government, already fearful of the activities of the largely middle-class Catalanist movement. Only in the 1930s did a more working class and revolutionary version of Catalanism begin to appeal to the working class.

The 1950s and 1960s saw a fresh wave of immigration from other parts of Spain into Catalonia. Again the government exploited tension between the Catalans and the new arrivals as a form of divide and rule, fearing that they might make common cause, as they did in the great demonstrations of the transition years (1976 and 1977). One of the constant touch-stones of identity for migrant workers has been football, and the rivalry between the Catalanist Barcelona club and the Espanyol Club (*espanyol* or *español* simply means Spanish). Espanyol represented the pro-Hispanic community in the city. But as Barcelona victories against Espanyol began to become a foregone conclusion, such rivalries transferred to the Real

Madrid team, especially during the Francoist dictatorship. It followed that becoming a Barça fan was the key proof of the ability to integrate for Andalusian, Murcian or Galician immigrants.

Many of the new arrivals were parcelled off to the shanty towns on the hills above the city of Barcelona, living in tumbledown shacks with little in the way of services such as water and sewage, let alone street lighting, pavements and schools for their children. Manuel Vázquez Montalbán has recorded this period in a very evocative way in his *Barcelonas*. It is another writer, Francesc Candel, who provides the title for this chapter. *Els altres catalans* (The Other Catalans) was the title of his 1964 book, ironically the best-selling book in Catalan of the Franco period. Montalbán comments that Candel observed how previous waves of Andalusian immigrants had been Catalanised by contact with the organised working class through trade unions and political parties, whereas these new immigrants from the south tended to live in ghettos and had little contact with Catalans. As for the language, 'they did not resent Catalan but neither did they need it' (Barcelonas, p.161). Just six years later, in 1970, came another important landmark book. *Al sud-oest del riu Besós* (To the South West of the Besós River) recounted the collective efforts of the residents of the shanty towns and new blocks of flats immediately west of the Besós River, now the site of the 2004 Universal Forum of Cultures, to improve their conditions of life. In the process it gave one of the best accounts of the origins of the Catalan citizens' movement, well supported by the clandestine Communist Party. A further five years later, 1975, Victor Alba was to remark how Candel's book had opened people's eyes to the 'other Catalans' but not their political understanding:

> ... there has been very little talk about the social problems caused by their low wages and inadequate housing and education. Few people understand that the best way

to Catalanize the immigrant is by enabling him to find in Catalonia not only a higher standard of living, but possibilities of just treatment and regard for his human dignity that were completely lacking in his past . . . Through their experience they should have the opportunity to discover that they will have a greater chance of being guaranteed their rights if Catalonia obtains a certain measure of political recognition. (Catalonia: a Profile, p. 235)

Yet despite the unity achieved during those emotional displays of the 1970s, nearly thirty years later the political left was still attempting to put together a coalition to dislodge the conservative nationalists from the Generalitat. The shadow of the flamenco star Carmen Amaya's attempts to conceal her origins in the slums between the city and the Besós River still falls across Catalan politics.

Migrants from beyond Spain

Together with Italy, Greece and Portugal, Spain is paying the price for its economic development of recent years, coupled with its declining birth-rate. The opposite has occurred on the southern shores of the Mediterranean, where economic underdevelopment has got worse and has coincided with a population increase that is difficult to control. The countries south of the Mediterranean will continue sending a significant proportion of their population abroad in the coming years. There are two clear alternatives. On the one hand, such population movements will be dictated exclusively by the blind laws of the market, and manipulated by those involved in the illegal traffic of migrant workers, thus aggravating still further the existing conflict in Spain (and other places). On the other hand, population flows can be organised by public bodies, community organisations, the countries from which these migrants come, immigrant organisations, employer and trade union organisations, and thus be controlled to everyone's benefit. (Sami Naïr, El peaje de la vida, p. 147, author's translation)

More recent arrivals to Catalonia have been more diverse

than was the case up until the 1970s. Yet there is that sense in which the South has long represented for many Catalans the alien, threatening 'other' in their lives. Thus if Murcia and Andalusia are a first step removed from the ideal Catalan, North Africa represents a second step away and black Africans from Sub Saharan Africa a third. Language, religion and skin colour all play a part in this. The Colombians and Ecuadorians, most of whom are of mixed ethnic origin, have evidently darker skins than the Catalans, but speak Spanish, which puts them on a par with the Andalusians. Africans usually have to learn Spanish, are usually Muslims, and are recognisably different in the street. Thus what can at one level be seen as a series of historical facts about population movement becomes radicalised as fear, racialised as hostility against the 'other', and politicised as the issue of 'what to do' about the 'problem' of immigration. And as Goytisolo makes clear, there is nothing casual about the arrival of migrant workers, whether legal or illegal. They have come and continue coming because of the dynamism of the Spanish economy, its increasing wealth as a member of the European community, the relatively lax employment laws and the dramatic decline in the birth-rate with its implication of a declining and ageing population. The legal arrivals have some rights, though not the democratic right of the vote. The illegals have no rights at all.

These new workers gather preponderantly in the great industrial cities of Spain, including Barcelona, but also more generally in the coastal areas, so that both Tarragona and Girona provinces have substantial new immigrant populations. Yet even so, migration from the countries of the South (Africa, Latin America) accounts for only half of the immigration into Spain. The other half are people from the advanced industrialised world in search of a better lifestyle or (as retirement pensioners) a permanent holiday in the sun. By the year 2000, of 700,000 foreigners with a residence permit, nearly 400,000 had been born in the countries of the European Union. Of the others, most were from ex-Spanish colonies such as Morocco, Equatorial Guinea, Philippines and Latin America. Yet the situation of these various migrant communities is very different. European Union law allows for free movements of people, and therefore there is no hindrance to UK passport holders who want to settle in Spain. Other groups have to seek either residence permits, valid for five years or work permits of one year, or resort to illegality. Nearly 60% of the Latin American group have a residence permit, and half of those coming from Asia. But 92% of East Europeans have only a one-year work permit, like 85% of the North Africans and 70% of sub-Saharan Africans.

There are some limited opportunities for the 'good' migrant workers with their official papers to improve themselves. At the same time, the economy is desperately in need of cheap, unskilled labour in sectors such as tourism and agriculture. These are the 'bad' migrants, usually illegal, the subject of abuse and violence, exploitation by employers, occasional outbreaks of mob violence such as those at El Ejido in the south, and Terrassa in Catalonia, and arbitrary swoops by the police attempting to show they are doing something about the 'problem' of illegal immigration. The only truth about illegal immigration in Spain and Catalonia is that no-one knows the figures. Yet it is impossible to imagine the dramatic economic growth of Murcia and Almería in particular without this unofficial labour. As Naïr writes of Almería:

> How could the car-driver imagine, travelling along the motorway that crosses the fields of Níjar, that beneath those greenhouses in which winter vegetables are being grown by intensive methods, are workers from North Africa and sub-Saharan Africans who are wearing themselves out for pay packets more appropriate to a colonial regime? (author's translation)

The legal position of migrant workers in Spain can be understood as just another variation on the laws existing in other EU countries, such as Germany. The regulations are restrictive but do conform to European law. The peculiarity of the Spanish and Catalan position is the significance of illegal work in the Spanish economy and the attraction therefore that illegal migration into Spain carries for people from the countries of origin. Spanish unemployment rates have generally been higher than those in other European countries. Although some of this is down to the continuing impact of Spain's adjustment to EU entry and the economic downturn of the 1980s which coincided with it, there is no doubt that the ease and extent of illegal work in Spain has tended to present official statistics that include as unemployed substantial numbers of people who are actually working in the illegal labour market. Thus illegal immigrants doing illegal work are twice cursed, once by their illegal presence in the country, and a second time by their exploitation in an illegal labour market.

In one of the most interesting passages of the Naïr/Goytisolo book, Naïr questions whether the silence, the forgetting of contemporary Spain, does not include a forgetfulness of the years of dictatorship when Spanish people themselves were migrants, forced to flee to other European countries and to Latin American by political oppression, and by the oppression of poverty, the most persistent and debilitating oppression of all. For many years in the mid-twentieth century, the Spanish worked alongside migrant workers from Turkey and from ex-Yugoslavia in the factories of Germany and Switzerland, the hotels of Paris and London. Manuel (*I'm from Barcelona*) in the television comedy series *Fawlty Towers* is perhaps the best known and best loved of all those emigrant Spaniards, more loved in the unreality of television than in the reality of the workplace. In one sense it is pointless to ask about the history of a fictional character, but it would be a reasonable supposition that Manuel had migrated at least twice, first from the south to Barcelona, and later, to that dreadful hotel in Torquay. If the British are European by leisure pursuit, seeing France and Spain as pleasant holiday locations, the Spanish are European by vocation, because so many of them have worked in other European countries at some time in their lives. So at one level there are identities based around strong and mythical entities such as 'Spain' and 'Catalonia'. At another level, the European identity, unlike in the United Kingdom, has a strong appeal. What does not appeal is that more fluid sense of national identity that can include the flows of migrant workers into Spain and Catalonia from outside of Europe.

It is at this point that we reach the key to understanding the very different position of Latin American migrants from others. They speak Spanish, they have little difficulty in acquiring a knowledge of Catalan, they may have darker skins but they share a cultural past, a history, which is officially acknowledged. If they have a religion, they are Christians, and usually Catholics. After the financial and economic collapse in Argentina in the late 1990s, many Argentinians rediscovered their Spanish ancestry and were allowed to enter Spain legally. Like European migrants, they are considered somehow a good thing, part of the way the world should be, part of the new prosperous European Spain. But that other half of Spain's history, of Catalonia's history, which is about contact across the Mediterranean between Europe and Africa, between Christianity and Islam, is much less acknowledged, as we have seen at various points in this book. Thus it is on African migrants that the weight of prejudice, misunderstanding and exploitation falls. They are the victims, the others, who confirm the European identity of both Catalans and Spanish.

Concern over the position of illegal migrant workers in Spain has extended beyond the country. Writing in 2001, Glyn Ford, Member of the European Parliament for South West England, and a tireless campaigner against racism and xenophobia, outlined the background to the riots at El Ejido in Almería. Writing a year on from the point at which El Ejido first became a focus for racist violence, he documented the way in which migrant workers were organising themselves to resist:

> The town's establishment was only stirred into action when the immigrants, who work as agricultural labourers beneath the sea of plastic which coats the countryside, organised a strike in protest. February is peak picking season for the peppers and tomatoes and the protest threatened to hit growers' pockets. The result within days was an agreement backed by central government and the province's autonomous government between the growers, the trade unions and the representatives of migrant workers.

The terms of this agreement, however, have never been implemented. The grants that have been allocated have gone mainly to Spaniards as compensation for loss of earnings or damage to property. Some of the North Africans fled in the face of 'violence, intimidation and blacklisting', while others took advantage of free bus tickets from the Town Council and left for other parts of Spain. Housing conditions are comparable with the South African shanties of the apartheid era or the Barcelona shanties of the Porcioles era:

> Currently groups of eight to ten men live sharing shacks constructed of wood, corrugated iron and plastic sheeting with no electricity and no water. The nearest available water supply is two kilometres away.

Ford concurs with Naïr and Goytisolo that there is an intimate link between the racism, the working conditions and the nature of the local economy, built on the exploitation of cheap labour:

> In the summer months temperatures in the greenhouses can reach 45 degrees centigrade. No Spaniard wants the backbreaking work . . . The large majority of them are illegal. Everyone colludes in it. It's simple. This is the bottom of the pile. The work is so awful that once any of the workers acquire a work permit they immediately leave to find

better jobs elsewhere.

Catalan Connections

Immigrant organisations in Catalonia have not only been active on the political front, campaigning for changes in the laws and for better conditions of work, but also in the cultural field. A significant amount of this work has gone on in the Ciutat Vella (old town) district of Barcelona, especially the old port district once referred to as the Barri Xinés, perhaps better known to British readers as the *Barrio Chino*. In a lengthy article in 2000, a London lecturer, Parvati Nair, looked in detail at an apparently model multicultural project in Ciutat Vella, called *Xenofília*. She concentrated on the photographic work, in an exhibition called 'Crossing Borders', of Núria Andreu, who has been involved in anti-racist work in both Germany and Spain. This is how she described the work:

> Andreu's work focuses on the Moroccan inhabitants of Ciutat Vella . . . in order to portray aspects of their social and communal lives in the Catalan capital. In particular, she attempts to put forward visible expressions of ethnic identity which serve to differentiate the immigrant community from the surrounding cultural and social contexts. The overall professed aim of her work is to inform the local Catalan community about the nature of the Moroccan ethnicity now in their midst, in order to secure a stronger neighbourhood understanding.

This sounds like a good sound liberal multicultural project, with which British readers will have little difficulty in identifying. But Nair's account goes further. While Andreu considers her work anti-racist, in trying to obtain a greater degree of tolerance of and opportunities for minority groups, Nair is concerned that the actual context of inequality — work, lack of political rights, racist hostility — makes the aim of social and cultural equality problematic. Her criticisms appear to rest on what she sees as the contradiction between two working hypotheses: Andreu's aim 'to counter traditional attitudes in

Catalonia and the rest of Spain which view the nation as a closed space'; and 'Andreu's underlying assumption of a clearly delineated borderline between communities.' This lays bare rather neatly the contrast between anti-racist work, which normally attacks underlying political, economic and social inequalities, and multicultural work, which treats cultures as somehow separate and equal.

Nair softens her position towards the end of this article, admitting that 'the photographs shed light upon the cultural fluxes of Catalan identity, as Barcelona is revisited through migrant lives.' Yet her central point remains crucial: cultures interrogate one another but in doing so make explicit positions of rank and importance. The Moroccan identity is a minority one, just as the Andalusian identity in Catalonia has always been a minority identity. Neither can assume an equal position with the Catalan identity, until the cultural assumptions underpinning that identity change. Thus exhibitions like 'Crossing borders', and the 'Africas: artists and the city' at the Contemporary Culture Centre in Barcelona in 2001, do not change the inequalities but do establish the circumstances under which a new cultural identity, more complex, more interesting in many ways, might emerge. Such initiatives also deal with practical questions, and parallel to the 'Africas' exhibition architecture students set up their own displays in the Ciutat Vella, dealing with issues such as the use of urban public space, and the kind of housing requirements which immigrants have — many of them still arrive singly and hope and work for eventual family reunion. A major part of the virtual forum conducted over the Internet in the run-up period to the Universal Forum of Cultures related to the issue of cultural identities and the relationship between these and issues of development. Coinciding with the Forum, the Parliament of the World's Religions met in Barcelona, an important initiative since religion complicates ethnic tensions in many parts of the world. The Cultural Forum slogan of 'Solidarity and Co-operation' returns us to the territory of Sami Naïr's appeal that any attempt to solve the problem of migrant workers in Catalonia and Spain must take account of economic relationships of inequality across the Mediterranean.

Changing Places: a Time for Reflection

Migratory processes are a legacy we have inherited from the twentieth century: decolonisation which appears to set the countries of the south free, and economic globalisation which locks them back into a series of unequal dependency relationships. For small elites in these countries of the South, there is prosperity. For the mass of people the only alternative to misery in their own country is the search for a better way of life in one of the countries of the North. As we have seen above, a major problem is precisely the identification of migration as a problem. It is not migration itself but the inability of governments and communities to handle the underlying causes that gives rise to the present situation of crisis. For example, when the government in Madrid moved in 2000 to regularise the legal status of many migrant workers (but of course leaving those still denied residency or work permits in an even worse position), the application of the new law was extremely uneven. As Stephen Jacobson points out in his review of the Goytisolo/Naïr book, over one third of all applications were turned down. But whereas in Asturias in the far north, where there is low immigration, only 2% of applications were refused, in Barcelona, with its relatively high population of migrant workers, 71% of applications were refused, 'an outcome that led to hunger strikes and the occupation of a number of churches in the Catalan capital.'

We have also seen how the racialised issue of immigration coincides in Catalonia and Spain with the further real problem of lack of control over the labour market and an inability or unwillingness to achieve proper working conditions, with adequate pay, limits on working hours, and proper regard for health and safety issues. Migrants do not

301

leave their country for another country in order to live off charity or social security payments; they migrate to work and earn money. Some of this money will go back to their country of origin, some will be saved in the expectation of being able to reunite their family in the new country. The saddest road-signs in southern Spain in the summer are the detailed information in various languages for migrant workers trying to reach the ferry port of Algeciras, the gateway to Africa. Migration means separation from home, family and culture. Such was the case of the Irish in the USA in the nineteenth century, the Spanish in Germany and Switzerland in the 1950s and 1960s, the North Africans and Latin Americans in Catalonia today. It is the willingness of employers to employ workers on an illegal and exploitative basis that makes the hazardous trip worthwhile, despite the risks of fraud and of drowning in the Straits of Gibraltar. In simple terms, employing illegal workers enables an employer to increase profitability by paying below the minimum wage rates and refusing these illegals the rights granted to other workers.

Further difficulties are created by the way in which public services are administered. To give an example from Girona province, nearly two-thirds of children at one school in Salt, just outside the capital, are from migrant families. Given the experience of the Generalitat in the 1980s and 1990s of moving to Catalan-language schooling in areas with large Spanish-speaking populations (in the industrial belt of Barcelona, we are often talking about majorities rather than minorities) one would have expected that similar methods, particularly language immersion, might have been used with the new arrivals. Yet this does not seem to have happened, and there are difficulties in allocating the necessary additional resources to schools in this position. It seems like a problem about to become a crisis. We know from the English experience in areas such as the old East End of London, East Lancashire and West Yorkshire that such a concentration of non-native English speakers in one school can become a focus for racist activity. But there seems to have been inadequate thought given either to transferring good practice from one field to another, or from one country to another.

The reaction of migrant groups to the circumstances of their lives can equally generate local difficulties. There was a well publicised case in 2002 in Premià de Mar, up the coast from Barcelona, where the local Muslim community wanted to build a mosque. The community leaders had a clear idea of where they wanted the mosque built, the municipal authorities came up with sound, practical reasons why this was not a good site, and there was a stand-off for some time. Needless to say, 'sound practical reasons' included the impact on local property values. The refusal of the town council to allow the building to go ahead on the Muslims' preferred site was perceived as a straightforward case of anti-African, anti-Muslim prejudice. The refusal of the Muslims to compromise was in turn seen as somehow typical of the refusal of migrants to conform to local customs and procedures. The whole issue was complicated by the fact that the mayor was a woman, and the male Muslim leader refused to deal with her, even turning his back on her in public, providing both newspapers and television with excellent pictures. Very little of this media attention was in any way helpful to good community relations.

If incidents like that in Premià de Mar, or the combination of popular racism and institutional neglect which operated at El Ejido in Andalusia, are examples of how not to move forward, a contrary example may be taken from the work of the Islamic Cultural Association in Vilanova i la Geltrú. Their community leader, interviewed by the local paper in 2001, said that he had been surprised and pleased by the amount of interest in Islam shown by local people in the aftermath of the 11 September attacks in New York City. When the North African population had reached just over 1000 (2% of the population) in late 2001, the Town Hall set up a Civil Rights unit to safeguard fundamental human rights of migrant workers and to discourage discrimination. The Islamic Cultural Organisation is committed to dialogue with other groups in the town. Catalonia has been slower to recognise its Muslim past than with its Jewish past. While the expulsion of 1492 and the work of the Inquisition was seen as resolving the issue of the Jews, anti-Muslim feeling continued to be inflamed by several centuries of piracy in the Mediterranean and the often bloody colonial wars fought by the Spanish in North Africa. Even on the political left, there is still simmering antagonism over Franco's use of 'Moorish' (i.e. North African) troops in the military rising of 1936. Such wounds are hard to heal, especially if they are not talked about.

Unlike in Barcelona, with its large Latin American population, migrant workers in Vilanova tend to be either from North Africa, working in construction and fishing or from Eastern Europe and ex-Yugoslavia, working in agriculture. Fishing is a particularly interesting case, with a division emerging between the technical jobs (the use of radar to seek out fish, or of IT applications in the fish market) and the unskilled jobs aboard the fishing-boats. Thus an occupation that has symbolic value in Vilanova, and is part of its image as a fishing port and holiday resort, is being increasingly staffed from outside Catalonia. Sixte Moral, the mayor, in conversation with the author in 2001, was keen to talk about immigration, which he immediately identified as the most obvious difference in the town over a ten year period. Previous migrant workers had come from the south of Spain, as he explained:

> "My father's from Andalusia, although I've never thought of myself as anything but Catalan ... But there was a common factor, that nearly all of us had the same religion, we dressed the same, and we did things in the same way. We all liked *chorizo* is another way of putting it! The present immigration is quite different, people of a different colour skin, who don't eat *chorizo*, often dressed differently, a

different religion. So the challenge is how to integrate them into our society, respecting of course their human rights, their rights as citizens, but also introducing them to the ways of their new country. Respecting women, and the equality of women and men, is obvious for us, but some of the new arrivals have to be told. Things like compulsory education until you're 16 — and that's part of your responsibility as a citizen. Some of the new wave of immigrants have become integrated, particularly the children who take part in the human castles (*castellers*). But it is more difficult with these new arrivals."

More difficult it may be, but at least the town's mayor has thought this through. Equality, he says, is a key aim, and you can never give cultural difference a positive valuation unless you have real equality of opportunity. Otherwise difference is just a euphemism for inequality. He noted the fact that often new arrivals live in poor housing with inadequate sanitation, and the tendency towards ghetto schools. These have to be tackled, he thought, if the new Catalans were to get a fair deal.

There is, of course, another side to all the talk of racism and discrimination. The Catalans have a long history of solidarity with those facing persecution. In recent years, such efforts have ranged from support for the people of Nicaragua, faced by USA-backed guerrilla incursions, to the well documented moral and practical support given to the people of Sarajevo to rebuild their city after years of Serb bombardments. There is also active support for the displaced Saharan people in the long-running dispute with Morocco, including summer holidays in Catalonia for their children. Sometimes it is easier to provide practical help than to deal with underlying tragedy, including the 2,000 bodies washed up every year in the Straits of Gibraltar, as Goytisolo suggests in his final paragraph, with its echoes of the song 'Blowing in the Wind':

How many bodies will be washed up on our shores, how many stowaways dragged from beneath lorries, before the powers-that-be, all of them, not just in Spain but in their countries of origin, decide that enough is enough, and that it's time to respond to this search for a future in a way that doesn't involve the wholesale displacement of peoples and the refusal to offer them a new home. It is an odd and surprising form of barbarism in an age that never misses an opportunity to show off its democracy and its human rights. (author's translation)

The Weight of History

Catalonia has been here before. Once we get away from the weight of that thousand years of history which we challenged in the first part of this book, of an essential unchanging identity of the Catalan nation, Catalonia has many precedents on which to build. This has always been a country of border crossings, situated as it is between Spain and France, between the great heartland of Spain and the Mediterranean and what lies beyond. One of the best places to reflect on these issues is Ulldecona, a small town down beyond the Ebro at the far southern end of Catalonia, a smiling little market town which in June 2002 was celebrating the opening of the new road up to its partially restored castle — a golden stone keep on the top of dry hills, with an enormous view of mountains and coast, sea and irrigated plain. Further south you could make out the ancient castle of Penyíscola, once famous as the home of an exiled and disputed pope, and in more recent years for the filming of the culminating scenes of *El Cid* on its beaches. It has seen a lot, has this coast, the coming and goings of Muslims and Christians, sometimes at war with one another, sometimes in alliance, sometimes in peaceful trade, sometimes bearing off captives into slavery. One of the Catalan students showing visitors around the castle on that day was rather suitably called Mohammed. The red and yellow Catalan flags were fluttering in the keen breeze blowing around the heights of these sheer stone walls. But only part of the history of this site can be claimed for Catalonia: the site began life as an Iberian (pre-Roman) settlement and was for 400 years a Muslim fort. In 1180, control of Ulldecona passed to the Templars, a form, one might say, of medieval globalisation with their international network of property, private armies and trading relationships. They wanted to build a town up here, and although permission was given in 1222, the site was too crowded. In 1272 the town moved down to the plain, closer to the rich irrigated fields and the main route of north-south travel.

Sometimes the past is a great burden to us, but sometimes it can show the way to a different, more plural future. It traces out the lines of that long and difficult road of peace that the poet Espriu foresaw. Except that when Espriu wrote of understanding the languages of all Spain's children, he had a more limited range of languages in mind than the polyglot mixture of contemporary Catalonia. It is a more difficult task, but potentially a more rewarding one. As Sami Naïr writes, a nation is an organised community with its myths, its rituals and its ways of behaving, its common history, imagination and beliefs. It has taken Catalonia a thousand years to become what it is today, but all through its history there has been change. Maybe part of the problem is that we do have too fixed a view of these matters of national identity. And that change, rather than stasis, has been the more common human experience.

Chapter 16

Catalonia, Spain, Europe and the Global Age

'Survival in fact is about the connections between things . . .'
(Edward Said)

Identity and Integration
I have tried to establish throughout this book that there is a clearly defined Catalan identity rooted in a distinct language, history and culture. At the same time, Catalonia exists as part of a dense and interdependent worldwide fabric of connections and interdependencies for which the 'Global Age' is useful shorthand. I want to emphasise that this concept of globalisation is not just a contextual feature of Catalonia in the twenty-first century but impacts on how that identity is experienced by modern-day Catalans. There is a temptation to turn the back on the rapid and often troubling world in which we all now live. Just as in England there are those who opt for a defensive 'little England' identity, so in Catalonia there is a similar psychological urge to pull up the drawbridge and make believe that, despite all the evidence, nothing has changed. There are fortresses of the mind as well as those built by anxious medieval warlords. There are, however, Catalans who have embraced the Global Age. I am thinking of those who have taken part in solidarity work with the peoples of the South, or in the rebuilding of Sarajevo, as much as those who have become involved in the high profile events such as the 1992 Olympics Games or the Universal Forum of Cultures, events symbolic of Catalonia's global presence.

The global boom of 1993–2000, the golden age of globalisation, produced as much poverty as it did wealth in the countries of the North. While one minority in our societies lives in poverty and insecure employment or unemployment, a further minority enjoys unchecked and imaginable wealth, while between them a large middle stratum are comfortably off but insecure enough to be reluctant to see taxes rise in an attempt to eliminate poverty. In the South, it will be quite clear to the reader that the plight of many countries in Africa and Latin America is dire. Furthermore, that their problems spill over into the North. While small elites in Africa and Latin America grow rich, their impoverished people slip quietly away across the border to join the flow of migrant workers, legal and illegal, to Europe, North America and the Gulf states. It is rather worse than that, because so often those who go are the better educated, the more skilled, those whose aspirations have been raised but not satisfied by globalisation. The South, then, is present in the North in the most real way possible. Its people. The Africans and Latin Americans in Catalonia, and in other parts of Spain, are not there by accident. They are there in reaction to the processes of globalisation and because their labour is needed.

Faced by this influx of newcomers, there are three possible reactions. The first is violent, hostile opposition to the immigrant. Globalisation is more likely to produce racism and xenophobia than tolerance and international understanding, as we have seen in Catalonia and Britain. Secondly, the host nation can revise its 'imagined community' to include the newcomers, as suggested by Sami Naïr in the previous chapter. The third reaction confines the problem to the urban areas: yes, there is a problem, but it is Barcelona's problem, or perhaps of Girona and Tarragona too ... An issue, that is, for others, until the new Catalans arrive to fill the vacant berths in the fishing-boats, the vacant seasonal jobs in the market gardens and slaughterhouses, or wherever the work is sufficiently hard, the rewards sufficiently low, to deter the locals.

Is it too idealistic to believe that people can imagine their nation in a different way? The evidence of history is that it can be done. Even if we restrict the historical framework to just the last 200 years, Catalonia has moved progressively (if by no means smoothly) from Spanish to Catalan in its language, from an agricultural economy to an industrial economy, from the horse-and-cart to the motor-car, from Monarchy to Republic and back again a good few times, from centralised autocracy to decentralised democracy — again a good few times. And when there have not been leaders brave enough to expedite the process, the people themselves have learned to adapt, adjust and survive.

Manuel Castells, a Catalan who has reinvented himself as a West Coast USA professor and prophet of the Global Age, was warning in the 1990s that some people were in danger of over-estimating the reach and spread of globalisation. Not all processes, he argued, not all countries, not all parts of all countries were as yet included in the Global Age. That was important at the time, and still is, for those of us who want to argue that individual nations and regional groupings such as the European Union can and do have an element of choice in negotiating their relationship with globalisation. Yet in many ways, the events of recent years have surpassed the warnings of Castells. Few people can now be unaware of the impact of global processes on their locality. They may become aware through the actions of multinational firms, when production is moved from a local factory to a place where wages are lower, or when a call centre moves abruptly from Britain to India. They may read or hear about the dictates of the World Trade Organisation, or the competition rules set down by the European Commission in Brussels. To take a simple example, the privatisation of public utilities: it is no longer a question for governments of the political Left or Right as to whether to privatise. The questions are about how fast the process should go, or the exact nature of the regulatory schemes put in place by national governments, so that at least some of the benefits flow to consumers as well as to over-paid senior managers and shareholders. Even some multinational firms have been surprised at their successes within the World Trade Organisation. At the world water summit in 2003, a number of multinationals (including Thames Water) argued against further privatisation of water in countries of the South on the grounds that it is very difficult to extract profit from poor people's basic requirement of water. As the factory owners of nineteenth century Britain discovered, it helps business if the workers selling their labour in the market place have sufficient money to buy back some of the products.

Looking both ways

Catalonia reflects something of the complexities of globalisation. It is concerned with its relations with the Spanish state and its position in Europe, subject to the rules of the European Union but also able to enjoy some of its benefits. The common currency makes slipping over the border into France easier than it has ever been, and offers the opportunity to live, work and study in other countries. For many Catalans, Europe is still part of the grace of democracy. Yet Catalans enjoy too the benefits of a globalised economy and culture, from McDonald's to the Internet via international pop music, Hollywood films and world travel. Of course they suffer too some of its conveniences, including genetically modified (GM) crops, jobs lost as multinational firms move investment to locations where labour is cheaper and the social dislocation that comes with uncontrolled flows of migrant workers in search of the promised rewards of globalisation that are nowhere apparent in Africa and Latin America. That is the great contradiction of the Global Age — it promises rewards to all, but in practice it rewards the few and not the many.

The project of Catalan nationalism has always been controversial. By the time Catalonia had achieved its state of autonomy, Catalonia was already more Spanish and more Anglo-Saxon than it had been fifty years before, as my friend Xavier Muñoz, writer and businessman, has argued. This was not just a matter of the inroads into the Catalan language and culture made by both Spanish and English. The other complicating factor was the way in which foreign economic interests had bought their way into the Catalan economy. This world of international capitalism uses English as its language of exchange. Thus while the position of Catalan has been shored up in relation to Spanish, it has continued to give way to English. In relation to the economy, Spain's membership of the European Union means that decisions are not only made outside Catalonia but outside Spain. The position at the turn of the century was that because international business recognises nation-states more easily than stateless nations, Madrid has grown economically at the expense of Barcelona, with the majority of foreign firms preferring to make their Spanish headquarters in Madrid than in Barcelona. The relative fortunes of two great football clubs in recent years tells its own story — Real Madrid up, Barcelona down. The decision by David Beckham to move to Real rather than Barça in 2003 was just the latest twist in that story. In 1984, Xavier Muñoz saw little to be gained for Catalans in replacing the all-powerful state by the all-powerful multinational or the naked power of money. Yet that is what has happened, and as we shall see it lies at the root of Catalan demands to renegotiate relations between Catalonia and the rest of Spain. In concluding that only a project based on participatory democracy at all levels of society could shore up Catalan identity, he set an agenda that is still being pursued in Catalonia.

These issues are still unresolved. While globalisation has impacted more and more on Catalonia, the Generalitat has pursued policies that, while startlingly successful in the educational and cultural fields, have become increasingly irrelevant in the economic and social fields. As mayor of Barcelona, Pasqual Maragall was able to establish a firm place for Catalonia within the global economic community. There has been substantial foreign investment in the city, which is also viewed as an attractive venue for international meetings and congresses. It remains to be seen whether, as President of the Generalitat, he can work the same kind of miracle again, especially bearing in mind the complicated electoral situation and the tensions that will no doubt emerge within his coalition. Throughout his time at the Barcelona Town Hall, he emphasised not political ideology but the virtues of good government which the city had for so long lived without — efficient administration, social inclusion, attention to the basics of jobs, housing and transport. He was the model of the social democratic politician, with or without the singular advantage of being the grandson of Catalonia's best-loved poet. The urban improvement schemes in the working class suburbs, even the Olympic Games themselves were in the best traditions of those rational social democratic ideals (remember Sert's TB clinic built in the depths of the Spanish War) that both Catalonia and Spain had rejected so violently in 1936. When the question of national identity was most obviously at stake, in relations between Catalonia and the Spanish state, he preferred to emphasise the practical questions of 'Who pays?', 'Who does what?' and 'Who checks that they have done it?', rather than to become embroiled in ideological debate. The issue of Catalonia and its government at the start of the new century is no longer as straightforward, or as matter-of-fact as such questions would suggest. Catalonia has opted for change, but the nature and outcomes of change remain unpredictable.

For someone born outside of Catalonia, or for Catalans with even a passing acquaintance with a wider world, it is much easier to identify with political Catalanism — the notion that there exists a Catalan dimension to every issue, whether social, economic or cultural — than with nationalism, with all its baggage about the essence of the nation. The late Edward Said (his own identity hovering

314

between the Anglo-Saxon and Arab worlds), wrote of the need to challenge 'the fundamentally static notion of identity' and the 'supposedly unbroken tradition' of nations. (Culture and Imperialism, p. xxviii) Some at least in Catalonia are now wondering whether it is not time to revert to a more ancient tradition of thinking about a political community as a collection of free individuals, each with her or his individual rights. The rights of the nation are then seen to rest on these individual rights, and it stands to reason that the political form that such a nation takes may vary from one generation to the next. There is no ultimate answer to the national question.

Part of the reason for the demise of the CiU nationalist government in Catalonia was that it had become exhausted in the process of achieving some of its objectives, yet had never offered people the satisfaction of reaching a safe harbour. 'So it's natural,' Xavier Muñoz wrote in his introduction to a 2003 book of essays, 'that Catalanism goes on searching for a way to achieve its primary objective, which is nothing more nor less than realising ourselves as free citizens, rather than victims, of this country of ours.' He went on to point out that there had never been a majority in favour of independence. Catalonia has always looked outwards — to Spain, to Europe, to the world — for its fulfilment as a nation. But to achieve a consensus on what Catalonia is and what Catalonia desires is an integral part of establishing its place in the world.

People have come to expect different things from different levels of government, and although that inevitably includes elements of unproductive conflict and uneasy compromise, there are general advantages to be obtained when these different levels of government do engage in fruitful debate about how to achieve the common good. Yet while the attentions of the Catalan political classes were inevitably focused on the Generalitat elections of 2003 and the Spanish General Election of 2004, the relevance of Europe and globalisation could not be ignored. More than

315

a mere context, they are part and parcel of private and public life in Catalonia, just as surely as they are in England. A sophisticated modern society coheres at different levels, from the village square to the European Union and the debates of the World Trade Organisation and the United Nations. What Catalonia brings to those debates must not be a one-dimensional view of an essential Catalan identity, but a broad new Catalan identity that can accommodate the rights of Catalan women as well as men, gays and lesbians as well as heterosexuals, migrant workers and the children of migrant workers as well as those with rather deeper roots in the Catalan soil. It is a matter of individuals, but of individuals who share in the complex and overlapping identities characteristic of the twenty-first century. In political terms, the liveliness of local government and of civil society — the hundred and one organisations that groups of citizens set up to promote their particular cause or interest — is just as important as who runs the Generalitat or the Spanish state.

Catalonia and the Minotaur

The Minotaur plays a key role in history and the news. He is Power. At times disguised, he adopts benevolent and peaceful shapes; from his palace, he pretends to invite people to handle the mechanisms which control the affairs of this world: he awards a medal to a scientist or approves bonus pay for a worker. But such sharing of power is an exception. The Minotaur is normally aloof and commands respect, more so with every day that passes. Power is peace and war, revolution and reform, justice and injustice, the common good, and evil. Abstract in theory, it is a daily reality one needs to know how to handle. Some countries are familiar with it; others do not seem to get the hang of it. The latter is the case in Catalonia.

(Jaume Vicens i Vives, in Sobrer, <u>Catalonia: a Self-Portrait</u>, p. 97)

The historian Jaume Vicens i Vives was one of the towering figures of mid-twentieth century Catalan life. His historical works are written in a dense, academic language, but we are fortunate that such an explicit passage in his thinking about his own country should be available in English. His key point in this essay, written in 1954 at a very low point in his country's fortunes, is the failure of the Catalans ever to deal seriously with power. The essence of pactism, the system developed in the Middle Ages to settle disagreements between rival groups, and which still has a profound psychological influence on the country's leaders, is in essence a system of compromise. What can be a strength in bad times, can also be a weakness in good times. And perhaps now is precisely one of those good times when Catalans should state unambiguously the terms under which they wish to be part of Spain, part of Europe, part of the Global Age. Vicens i Vives takes a broad-brush approach to Catalan history, an approach that could be seen as an essentialist reading of what Catalonia is about. Implicitly throughout this book, and explicitly in this final chapter, I have criticised essentialism, preferring a view of the country that deals in the social and economic facts rather than with abstraction. I have also insisted that there are certain mental habits, certain cultural norms, within which people occupying a particular place and time grow to maturity, and it seems to me that Vicens i Vives has identified and argued cogently for this particular feature of Catalan life.

It is, furthermore, an approach that fits with what is happening in Catalonia today. The political classes are restless. The Spanish Constitution predates the Stature of Autonomy (*Estatut*). So the *Estatut* does not cover central themes which were either not felt to be important in 1978, such as transport, or which were simply not issues at that time, such as information and communication technologies. The notion of returning to Catalonia its historic powers has been an illusion. Catalonia today is not the Catalonia of the Republican period of the 1930s, let alone the Middle Ages. The need to replace the *Estatut* is now a central theme of Catalan politics. It reflects the desire to move Spain as quickly as possible to a confederal system more like that in place in Germany. By and large this has served the Germans well for the last sixty years, including the traumatic period of rebuilding the nation after the Nazi period. One obvious way forward would be to replace the present upper house of the Spanish parliament (the Senate) by a chamber representative of the historic nations (Galicia, the Basque Country and Catalonia) and the Spanish regions (such as Aragon and the Balearic Islands). At the moment, there is no body in which the regions and nations come together to discuss and sort out common issues. The lack of a forum for debate between the regions and nations is particularly ironical given the leading role that Catalonia has taken in the European Committee of the Regions, which is the body of the European Union especially concerned with regional policy

The argument, then, about Catalonia's relations with Spain is again out in the open. It is hard to predict how it will work out over the coming years. What I think we can now say is that there is a general recognition in Europe of the rights of nations to re-invent themselves as states if they so desire. This right was clearly established in the break-up of the Soviet Union, with the Baltic states of Lithuania, Latvia and Estonia leading the way towards independence. More recently there has been the curious and instructive case of ex-Czechoslovakia. It was very difficult for an outsider to understand exactly why the Slovaks wished to leave. Their economy was clearly weaker than that of the Czechs, and while few doubted the viability of the Czech Republic, many doubted whether Slovakia could go it alone for very long. Yet less than a decade later, both countries joined in the major enlargement of the European Union. If ex-Yugoslavia represented the tragic aspect of the break-up of states, ex-Czechoslovakia repeated the process as comedy or even farce. In a similar way, it is hard to see Spain demanding that Catalonia should remain tied to a marriage that no longer suited her. Perhaps then the Catalans might start to take an interest in the Spanish football team — when it no longer claimed to represent them as well.

A Global Role for Catalonia

It is not that nations no longer matter. More that they matter in different ways. The Pujol years at the Generalitat were not in vain. While Catalonia has become more closely integrated into Europe, more exposed to globalisation and the economic and cultural power of the USA, it has also become more Catalan. Its language and culture have become much better known both inside and outside the country. For all that the 1992 Olympic Games were supposed to be about a city (Barcelona) they inevitably became about a nation (Catalonia). It is unsurprising that the politician most closely identified with the Games and the city, its mayor Pasqual Maragall, spent the next decade working to become the President of the Generalitat, the President of Catalonia. That is the natural ambition of any Catalan politician. It was the Olympic Games that gave Catalonia the chance to project itself upon a world stage — its language, its popular culture, its great international artistic figures, its architecture, its extraordinary ability to party.

A decision to move towards independence, any more than a decision to go for, say, confederalism, does not detach Catalonia from its international obligations. One might refer to respect for the human rights of migrant workers, or responsibilities to observe the terms of the various European treaties and international agreements to which Catalonia, through its membership of the Spanish nation-state, has signed up. Catalonia, inside or outside of Spain, would continue to work with other countries to tackle the mounting problems created by inequality: the drift of population from the countries of the South to those of the North, the inequalities created in all countries, the rapid degradation of the environment, the threat of climate change. My own sense is that it is within the European Union that so many of these problems can begin to be resolved. And that such a Europe, committed to democracy and the decentralisation of power (the benevolence, one might say, of the Minotaur) is the kind of power block that might be taken seriously in the world, pinning its blue flag to the old republican virtues of liberty, equality and solidarity.

Catalonia may be a thousand years old as a country, but there is both continuity and change. The country I visit now is no longer the country that I first visited in 1962. The nation that chose (in its great majority) the losing side in the 1936–39 war was a different nation from the nation that kept backing the wrong horse in the wars of the seventeenth and eighteenth centuries. The Generalitat of the Middle Ages is not the Generalitat of the twenty-first century. No doubt Catalonia will continue to reinvent herself. That at least is my wish for her future.

Bibliography

General books about Catalonia

Victor Alba *Catalonia: a profile* (Hurst, 1975)

Alastair Boyd *The essence of Catalonia* (Deutsch, 1988)

J.H. Elliott *The revolt of the Catalans: a study in the decline of Spain* (1598–1640) (Cambridge University Press, 1963)

Salvador Giner The social structure of Catalonia (Anglo-Catalan Society, 1980)

Robert Hughes *Barcelona* (Harvill, 1992)

John Langdon-Davies *Gatherings from Catalonia* (Cassell, 1953)

John Langdon-Davies *Spain* (Batsford, 1971)

Rose Macaulay *Fabled shore: from the Pyrenees to Portugal* (Hamish Hamilton, 1949)

Jan Morris *Spain* (Penguin, 1982)

Jan Read *The Catalans* (Faber, 1987)

Colm Tóibín Homage to Barcelona, (Simon and Schuster, 1990; revised edition, Picador, 2003)

Josep Trueta *The spirit of Catalonia* (Oxford University Press, 1946)

Manuel Vázquez Montalbán *Barcelonas* (Verso, 1992, translated by Andy Robinson with new introduction by author; first published 1990)

Jaume Vicens I Vives *Approaches to the history of Spain*, (University of California Press, 1967, translated by Joan Connelly)

On the twentieth century and the Spanish War

Adrian Bell *Only for three months: the Basque children in exile* (Mousehole Press, 1996)

Gerald Brenan *The Spanish labyrinth: an account of the social and political background of the civil war* (Cambridge University Press, 1943; second edition, 1950)

Tom Buchanan *Britain and the Spanish Civil War* (Cambridge University Press, 1997)

Ronald Fraser *Blood of Spain. The experience of civil war 1936–1939* (Penguin Books, 1981; first published 1979)

Soledad García 'Collective consumption and urban protest in Barcelona during the Franco era', in (ed) Josep Llobera, *Family class and nation in Catalonia, Journal of Anthropology* (special issue) volume X, nos. 2 & 3 (Winter 1990), pp. 197–209

Walter Gregory *The shallow grave: a memoir of the Spanish Civil War* (Five Leaves Press, 1996; first published Victor Gollancz, 1986)

George Orwell (ed Peter Davison) Orwell in Spain (Penguin, 2001; contains complete text of *Homage to Catalonia* plus articles and letters)

Paul Preston *Introduction to exhibition catalogue 'The Spanish civil war'* (Imperial War Museum, 2001)

Paul Preston *Franco* (HarperCollins, 1993)

Hugh Thomas *The Spanish Civil War* (Hamish Hamilton and Penguin, 1977, third edition revised and enlarged; first published 1961)

Colin Williams, Bill Alexander and John Gorman *Memorials of the Spanish Civil War* (Alan Sutton Publishing, 1996)

On nationalism, language, cultural diversity and sport

Benedict Anderson *Imagined communities: reflections on the origins and spread of nationalism* (Verso, 1983)

Albert Balcells *Catalan nationalism, past and present* (Macmillan, 1996, ed G. Walker, translated by J. Walker)

Manuel Castells *The information age: economy, society and culture* (Basil Blackwell, 1996-1998, 3 volumes)

Daniele Conversi *The Basques, the Catalans and Spain: alternative routes to nationalist mobilisation* (Hurst and Company, 1997)

Valentine Cunningham *The Penguin Book of Spanish Civil War Verse* (Penguin Books, 1980)

Helena Drysdale *Mother tongues* (Picador, 2001)

Glyn Ford 'The strain in Spain', in *Making European progress* (European Parliament, 2002, pp. 191–192)

Sir James Frazer *The golden bough: a study in magic and religion* (Wordsworth Editions, 1993; first published 1922)

Generalitat de Catalunya *The Catalan language today* (Generalitat de Catalunya, second edition revised and updated, 1992; first edition, 1990)

Montserrat Guibernau *Nations without states. Political communities in a global age* (Polity, 1999)

John Hargreaves *Freedom for Catalonia: Catalan nationalism, Spanish identity and the Barcelona Olympic Games* (Cambridge University Press, 2000)

Stephen Jacobson 'A darker Spain', review of J. Goytisolo and S. Naïr *El peaje de la vida* (2000), in *Times Literary Supplement* 31 August 2001, p. 27

Michael Keating 'The minority nations of Spain and European integration: a new framework for autonomy?' *Journal of Spanish Cultural Studies* 1.1, March 2000, pp. 29–42

(ed) Elie Kedourie *Spain and the Jews: The Sephardi experience, 1492 and after* (Thames and Hudson, 1992)

Mark D. Meyerson *The Muslims of Valencia in the age of Fernando and Isabel: between co-existence and crusade* (University of California Press, 1991)

Jan Morris *Trieste and the meaning of nowhere* (Faber and Faber, 2001)

Parvati Nair 'Albums of no return: ethnicity, displacement and recognition in photographs of North African immigrants in contemporary Spain' *Journal of Spanish Cultural Studies* 1.1, March 2000, pp. 59–74

Edward Said *Culture and imperialism* (Chatto and Windus, 1993)

Jude Webber and Miquel Strubell *The Catalan language: progress towards normalisation* (Anglo-Catalan Society, 1991)

Kathryn Woolard *Double talk: bilingualism and the politics of ethnicity in Catalonia* (Stanford University Press, 1989)

Art, architecture, urbanism, music and literature

Pablo Casals *Joys and sorrows* (Macdonald, 1970)

Javier Cercas *Soldiers of Salamis* (Bloomsbury, 2003, translated by Anne McLean; first published 2001)

Patrice Chaplin *Having it away* (Virago, 1993; first published 1977)

Patrice Chaplin *Albany Park: an autobiography* (Hodder and Stoughton, 1987)

Kathryn Crameri *Language, the novelist and national identity in post-Franco Catalonia* (Legenda, 2000)

Salvador Espriu *Lord of the shadows: poems* (Dolphin, 1975, translated by Kenneth Lyons, ed J.M. Castellet)

Juan Goytisolo *Marks of identity* (Serpent's Tail, 2003, translated by Gregory Rabassa; first published 1966)

Gijs van Hensbergen *Gaudí: the biography* (HarperCollins, 2001)

Joaquim Homs *Robert Gerhard and his music* (Anglo-Catalan Society, 2000, ed Meirion Bowen)

Daniel-Henry Kahnweiler and others *Picasso 1881–1973* (Paul Elek, 1973)

David Mackay *Modern architecture in Barcelona* (Anglo-Catalan Society, 1985)

Marilyn McCully and others *Homage to Barcelona: the city and its art 1888–1936* (Arts Council of Great Britain, 1985)

Roland Penrose *Picasso: his life and work* (Granada, 1981; first published 1958)

Joan Perucho *Joan Miró and Catalonia* (Alpine Fine Arts Collection, 1988, translated by Kenneth Lyons)

Antoni Pladevall and Montserrat Pagès *This is Catalonia: guide to the architectural heritage* (Generalitat de Catalunya, 1988)

Peter G. Rowe *Civic realism* (MIT Press, 1999)

(ed and translated) Josep Miquel Sobrer *Catalonia: a self-portrait* (Indiana University Press, 1992)

Paul Scott *The corrida at San Feliu* (Martin Secker and Warburg, 1964)

Manuel Vázquez Montalbán *Southern seas* (Serpent's Tail, 1999, translated by Patrick Camiller; first published 1979)

Colm Tóibín *The south* (Serpent's Tail, 1990)

James Woodall *In search of the firedance: Spain through flamenco* (Sinclair-Stevenson, 1992)

Christopher Woodward *The buildings of Europe: Barcelona* (Manchester University Press, 1992)

Ken Worpole *Here comes the sun: architecture and public space in twentieth-century European culture* (Reaktion Books, 2000)